AF708638

The Tacoma Public Utilities Story

THE FIRST 100 YEARS: 1893–1993

The History of
Tacoma City Water
and the
Belt Line Railway
by John S. Ott

The History of
Tacoma City Light
by Dick Malloy

Edited by Dick Malloy

Tacoma Public Utilities
3628 South 35th Street
Tacoma, Washington 98409

© 1993 Copyright Tacoma Public Utilities. All rights reserved.

First Edition.
ISBN 0-9637684-0-9

Library of Congress Catalog #93-60904

Printed in the United States of America on recycled paper.

No portion of this book may be reproduced or transmitted in any form or by any means, electronic or mechanical, including photocopying, without permission in writing from the publisher.

Tacoma Public Utilities Leadership In Our Centennial Year

Management
(As of January 1, 1993)

E. E. Coates
Director of Utilities

Mark Crisson
Superintendent, Tacoma City Light

Kenneth F. Olson
Superintendent, Tacoma City Water

Dennis H. Dean
Superintendent, Belt Line Railway

Public Utility Board

Barbara J. Bichsel
Chair

Bil Moss
Vice-Chair

Dawn Lucien
Secretary

Carl W. Virgil

Daryl Hedman

Tacoma City Council

Karen L. R. Vialle
Mayor

Greg Mykland
Deputy Mayor

William H. Baarsma
Robert W. Evans
Ruth L. McElliott
Paul E. Miller
Harold G. Moss
Hal Nielsen
Dolores I. Silas

The Employees Of Tacoma Public Utilities In Our Centennial Year

Tacoma Public Utilities could not have survived for 100 years without our employees' hard work, dedication and commitment to the people of our serving territory. We dedicate this book to employees of the past and salute the following current employees. We commend this history to future employees as a guide to greatness in the next century.

Mark Aalfs
Red Abicht
John Ackley
Mary Adams
Roy Agnew
James Alewine
Cecile Alward
Cherie Ambrose
Beverly Amburgy
Edward Anderson
Jack Anderson
John Anderson
Steven Anderson
Dennis Angeline
James Antush
Martin Antush
Charles Apgar, II
Gary Armfield
James Armstrong
Terry Armstrong
James Arnold
Thomas Arter, Jr.
Francine Artis
Gary Ashworth
Gregg Aubry
Carlena Aust
Larry Ayers
Virginia Ayler
Ralph Baarslag
Rollin Bach
James Baggarly
Michael Bailey
Gerald Baker
Joann Baker
Michael Baker
Wendell Baker
David Baldwin
Deanna Ball
John Ball
George Balles
David Baranski
Denice Barber
Kenneth Barber
William Barcus
Steven Barkhoff
Jack Barlow
William Barlow
Robyn Barnes
William Barnhart
Dean Barrett
Jack Barrett
Oliver Barry
Marsha Batie-Hopkins
Lynnette Baugh
Raymond Bearden
John Bearson
Robert Beatty
Barbara Beckstead
Gene Beckstead
Carl Beech
David Beech
Lori-Ann Bell
Jim Bellamy
Carol Bellinger
D'Angelo Belton
Thomas Bender
Ronald Benham
Steve Benjamin
James Bennett
Charles Benoit
Brian Berdan
Richard Berdan
Byron Bergman
Jack Bernhardsen
Kathleen Berry
Martin Bertram
William Beslow
Rick Beutler
Nancy Bevis
Joe Biggs
Frank Billington
Paul Binkley
John Bisceglia, Jr
Debra Bjork
Robert Bjork
Donald Bjornstad
Charles Black
Hollis Blackburn
Debbi Blann
Edward Blann
Terrence Blodgett
Raymond Bocott
Bradley Bogue
William Bogue
Jerald Bohnett
David Borrowman
Donna Bosch
James Bosch
Rick Boskovich
Leonard Botley
William Bowen
Dennis Bowie
Karl Bowman
Robert Boyd
William Bratton
Yvonne Braune
Russell Brethower
Gale Bridges
Gary Briske
William Brizius
Fred Brocker
Kristy Brokman
Sally Bronow
Timothy Bronow
Timothy Brooks
Randol Brookshier
Alvin Broussard
Charles Brown
Cliff Brown
Delores Brown
John R. Brown
Jon J. Brown
Jane Brown
Michael Brown
Richard Brown
Korte Brueckmann
Judy Bryant
Mark Bubenik
Mark Buchanan
Lawrence Buck
Larry Buckner
Thu-Tram Bui
Darlene Burke
Robert Burke
Lee Burki
Robert Burleigh
Franz Burnworth
Todd Burnworth
Burnece Burrell
Celeste Burris
Robert Burton, Jr.
Timothy Burtron
Lee Busch
Stanley Bushnell
Frederick Butts, Sr.
Teresa Byard
Marlys Bye
Lucille Byrd
Edward Caballero
Terrence Caillier
Thomas Cain
Candace Callaway
Timothy Cameron
Norman Camp
Douglas Campbell
Herbert Campbell
Linda Campbell
Michael Campbell
Randall Campbell
John Canonica
James Carey
Sandra Carlisle
Michael Carlstrom
Sonja Carlstrom
Linda Carlton
Kit Caron
Lawrence Carpenter
Craig Carrara
Gary Carrara
Randy Carrara
David Carroll
Donald Carroll
John D. Carroll
John M. Carroll
Karen Carroll
Sean Carroll
Thomas Carroll
Linda Carson
Carl Cason, Jr.
Christopher Cassidy
Karen Cassidy
Michael Cassidy
David Castro
Fernando Castro
Gayle Castro
Mark Castro
Janelle Castroni
Gordon Cavanaugh
Max Chabo
Wendy Chafe
Richard Chamberlain
Emmy Chan
Kenneth Chapman
Scott Chase
Ronald Chesley
Jackie Chin
Kenneth Choy
Cheryl Christensen
Diane Christensen
Ken Christopherson
Cynthia Chritton-Meeker
Mary Church
Conrad Cinq-Mars, Jr.
Kenneth Clark
Otis Clark
Richard Clark
Wayne Clark
William Clark
Thomas Clarke
Martin Cleveland
James Click
Shirley Clifton
James Cline
Edward Coates
Milagros Cochran
Arthur Codute
Clarence Coleman
Gordon Coleman
Susan Coley
Christine Collette
James Collins
Jeanette Collins
Richard Collins
Robert Collins
Jacob Colter
William Conrad
Joel Cook
Mary Corak
Linda Corkery
Richard Cornelius
Shirley Coronado
Georgia Correy
Edward Corrigan
John Corrigan
Doyle Cottrell
Gary Cox
Melvin Craig
Stephen Craig
Patricia Crane
Norman Crawford
Rosalyn Crawford
Albert Crayne, Jr.
Zonna Crayne
Mark Crisson
Tedd Crist
James Croan
Walter Croshaw
Vickie Crumbley-Fulmer
Jeri Crumbley
Julius Csonka
Floyd Cummings, Jr.
Philip Cunningham
James Curley
Glen Curnutt
Ross Currah
Todd Currier
Richard Curtice
Linda Curtis
Raymond Curtis
Joel Cusato
Julie Dahlen-Reichel
Lori Daniels
Wendell Daniels
Warren Darnell
George Daulton
Susannah Daulton
Brian Davelaar
Gary Davick
Mark Davies
Oscar Davis
Ronny Davis
Scott Davis
William Davis
Gerald Davy
Dennis Dean
Larry DeForrest
Scott Demarest
Sharon Deptula
Michael DeTracy
Steven Deuel
Timothy Deuel
Patricia DeVaul
Patrick Devere
David DeVito
Claudia deVries
James Dimond
Robert Dimond, III
Robert Dimond, IV
Mariano Dizon, Jr.
Kimberly Dodge
Loren Donahue, Jr.
Philip Dooley, Jr.
John C. Dorfner
John E. Dorfner
Clarence Dorn
Duane Dotlich
Donna Dougherty
William Dries
Brian Drury
Eric Dugan
Paul Dugan
Long Duong
Douglas Durant
Michael Duree
Robert Durkee
Michael Dybdahl
David Dye
Veronica Dykas
Patti Easton
Oliver Edick
Bruce Edwards
Gary Edwards
James Edwards
Lawrence Edwards
Karl Eisen
Martin Ellis
Dennis Ellison
Carl Elseth
Heidi Eltrich
Joseph Eltrich
Steven Eltrich
Seth Ely
Kathryn Emerson
Frederick Emrick
Kam Eng
Jim Eng
Jerry Engh
Veronica England
Raymond Erb
Carolyn Erickson
Eileen Erickson
Roger Erickson
Walter Erickson
Charles Erway, Jr.
Kathleen Erwin
William Erwin
Lorronishae Escalona
Wayne Estes
Andrew Evancho, Jr.
Jane Evancho
Terry Evans
Kathryn Everett
Kenneth Faber
Norman Fahlbeck
Clifford Fairbanks
Robert Faison
Steven Farvour
Paul Federighi
Chris Feely
Kenney Fengler
Mohammad Fesharaki
Kenneth Fewell
Jacob Fey
Norman Fiacchi
Ingrid Fields
Steven Fischer
Kathleen Fitzgerald
Joan Fitzpatrick
Dennis Flanery
Theresa Flannigan
Jerry Fogle
Joseph Folden
Elaine Fordice
John Forgey
James Forrest
Clyde Fortney
Cynthia Foss
Carl Foster
Kenneth Foster
Robert Foster
Russell Foster
Melodie Fox
Richard Frazier
Tommie Frazier
Craig Freeman
James Fry
Joseph Fugle
Sandy Fuller
Daniel Gaffney
Joann Gales
Gilbert Gallegos
Mark Gamble
Gary Gandee
Cathy Gantenbein
Timothy Gappa
Edgardo Gariando
David Garner
Betty Garrison
Jack Gaskins
Donald Gavranich
Barrett Gee, III
Donald George
Glen George
Karen Gerken
Don Gesch, Jr.
Craig Gibson
Dennis Gibson
Fawn Gilbert
Sue Gilbertson-Keliher
Gary Gilhuly
Susan Gill
John Gillespie
Joseph Gillespie
Joseph Gilligan
Stephen Gilstrap
Phyllis Gilven
Sharon Glassy
Thad Glassy
Dara Goble
James Gonce
Steve Gordon
George Gorman
Leonard Goss
Dawn Gossage
Sing Gould
Arthur Gouley
John Grady
Michael Graeber
John Graham
Sharron Graham
Clifton Graves
Clement Gray
Gregory Greenhouse
Charles Gregg, Sr.
Bryan Gregory
Robert Grewing
Tonya Griffith
Marvin Guenther
James Guthrie
Paul Hackett
Richard Hafterson
Marion Hahn
Robert Hahn
Sarah Hahn
William Hahn
Barry Hale
Terry Hale
Rebecca Halkoski
Kelly Hall
Margaret Hall
Martin Hall
Wayne Halvorson
Frederick Haman
Stephen Hamel
Doug Hamer
David Hammond
Rodney Hams
James Haneline
Laurie Hannan
Gregory Hannus
Allen Hansen
Loren Hansen
Melvin Hansen
Richard Hansen
Robert Hansen
Theresa Hansen
C Fred Hanson
Stephen Hanson
Deborah Hardy
Teresa Hargrove
Mark Harkness
David Harlacher
Jodie Harper
Frank Harris
Ronnie Harris
Lois Harrison
Eleanor Hart
Roy Hartford
Deana Harty
Richard Hartzell
Richard Haskins
Melvin Hastings
Jerry Hatch
Dorothy Haugan
Sandra Hawker
Robert Hays
Louis Hayward
Joel Hazelton
Melvin Heacock
Mary Heath
Marcie Hedman
Scott Heffron
Margrethe Heimgartner
Bryan Heller
David Henderson
Ralph Hendrick
Paula Henry
Gary Henwood
Sean Heppe
Rita Hereim
Steven Hermsen
Coral Herrera
Eric Herrmann
Albert Hess
Dennis Hess
Jonathan Hewitt
Paul Hickey
Joseph Hicks
Willi Hickstein
Clarence Higdon
Samuel Hildreth
Sandra Hill
Thomas Hilsendeger
Robert Hinzman
Joseph Hitchins
Rick Hite
Dennis Hitt
Wayne Hoffman
Larry Hoffman
William Hogan
Philip Hogman
John Hoisington
Robert Holden, Sr.
Christi Holovacko
John Holst
Harold Holt
James Hood
Sandra Hooper
Sally Hoover
Melita Hopkins
Thomas Hopkins
Jeremy Horner
Larry Horsman
Donald Horst
Martha Horst
Albert Horton
Sandra Hoult
Charles Houser
Grace Hrvatin
Arthur Huber
Caronda Huddleston
Larry Huddleston
Jared Hunt
Dean Hunter
LaVerne Hunter
Denise Hupp
Roland Huske
James Hymer
Jerald Hymer
O. Okonkwo Imo
Sherri Ingalls
Brad Ingle
Anthony Isaacs
Beverly Ivy
Joseph Jackl
Thomas Jackl
Clark Jackson
Garth Jackson
Arnold Jacobsen
J. Jay Jacobsen
Christina Jacobson
Ronald Jacobson
Cyndy Jacoby
Benjamin James
Paul Jauron
Raymond Jeanson
Betty Jenkins
Jane Jenkins
Joseph Jenks
Cary Jensen
Eric Jensen
Gary Jensen
Kristin Jensen
Cinda Johnson
Clarence Johnson
Dale Johnson
Dennis Johnson
Duane Johnson
Dwight Johnson
Eric Johnson
Gary E. Johnson
Gary L. Johnson
Harold Johnson
Kevin Johnson
Morgan Johnson
Vernon Johnson
Barbara Johnston
Robert A. Johnston
Robert L. Johnston
David Jolliff
Deborah Jonas
Brett Jones
Elizabeth Jones
Lawrence Jones
Ruth Jones
Stanley Jones
William Jones
Woodrow Jones
Holger Jorgensen
Jolene Josey
Darl Judd
Jacqueline Judie
Hardev Juj
Howard Junge
Earl Kahawaii
Einar Kalleberg
Sharon Kalleberg
Paul Kaman
Dale Kamerer, Jr.
Claude Kammerzell
Jean Kampen
Steve Karavitis
Elizabeth Karna
Loni Kasahara
Bradley Kasemeier
John Kasmarsik
James Kaul
Keagan Kauzlaric
Joshua Kay
Earnest Kelley, Jr.
Michael Kelley
York Kempe
Conan Kempf
Anthony Kendall
Patrick Kennedy
Barry Kensrud
Dawn Kester-Cook
Cydney Ketchum
Harden Keys, Jr.
Gary Kiehl
Amy Kildahl
Edmund Kilga
Roger Kilgus
Jimmey Kimmel
Bryan King
Philip King
Terry King
Robert Kirchmeier
John Kirk
John Kirner
Kurt Kirschman
Steven Klein
Stacey Klinzman
Douglas Klippert
Renee Knarreborg
Victor Knarreborg
Allen Knesal
Norman Knesal
Ronald Knoll
Ronald Koecke
Dennis Koehn
Nancy Kohncke
Richelle Krienke
Bruce Kroeger
William Kroll
Carol Kruckeberg
Norman Kruse
Veronica Kulman
Susan Kunkel
Frank Kurowski
Rickey Labouve
David LaCaille
Bruce Ladd
John Lambert
Arthur Lambright
Stephen Land
Thomas Landree
Aron Langberg
Mark Langberg
Rick Lantz
Mark LaRiviere
Darryl LaRoche
Byron Larsen
Sandra Larsen
Brian Larson

Elizabeth Larson
Lynn Larson
Reuben Larson
Timothy Larson
J.J. LaSanta-Perez
Hugh Latimer
Marion Laurendeau
Fred Laurente
Darren Lawrence
John Lawrence
Vance Lawrence
Donald Laybourn
Vivian Leach
Hun Lee
Ronald Lee
Allen Lehtimaki
Alan Lentz
Cecelia Lenzi
Catherine Leone
David Lerman
Michelle Lewis-Hodges
Sharon Lewis
Dan Lidren
Michael Lien
Jerry Liles
Chona Liloc
Edgardo Liloc
Roger Linville
Susan Lisk
Michael Little
Thomas Lizotte
David Llapitan, Jr.
Tresha Locke
Craig Lohrey
Charles Lombardi
Earl Loneia
Harold Long, Jr.
Kenneth Long
Paul Long
James Louthain
Darla Love
David Lovelace
James Lovstrom
Marsha Lovstrom
Robert Lujano
Odon Lukacs
Charles Lundin
Rosalie Lundin
Clarence Lupo
John Tien Luu
Thomas Lyman
Wilfried Maass
James Mack
Michael Magruder
Darleen Majors
Janice Malovich
Ben Manchester
Joan Mann
Kevin Maple
Wilmer Marcil
Sallie Marincin
Robert Marion
Randall Marquis
Edith Marren
John Marshall
Laurence Marshall
Lisa Marshall
Donald Martin
Jerald Martin
Judy Ann Martin
Monique Martin
Ronda Martin
Sherry Martin
Susan Martin
Thomas Maruca
Ivan Mas
Donald Massie
James Mateljak
Patricia Mateljak
Dianne Mattsen
Lauri Mattsen
Richard Mattsen, Jr.
Teresa Mattsen
George May
Vicki May
Richard Mazurek
Scott McCall
Patrick McCarty
Robert McClamma
Rudi McClellan
Harlan McCord
Edward McCoury
Robert McCoy
Sheila McCoy
Linda McCrea
David McCulloch
Gary McDonald
Theodore McDonald
John McDonell
Michael McDonough
Sharon McDuff
Michael McGuire
Merri McHugh
Lawrence McIntosh
Dylan McIntyre
Robert McKenney
Ronald McKonly, Jr.
George McLam
Carol McLean
Judith McLean
Dean McLeod

Marshall McLeod
Terry McMullin
Daniel McNabb
Charles McPherson
Alan Medak
Iris Melm
Patricia Menzies
John Mercer, III
Thomas Meriwether, Jr.
Kenneth Merry
Rustin Messenger
Christy Mettler
Charles Metzenberg
Brian Meyer
Charles Meyer
Jack Meyer
Peter Meyer
William Micenko
Jack Michel
Glenn Miles
Barney Miller
Edwin Miller
Gilbert Miller
John Miller
Martin Miller
Peter Miller, III
Robert Miller, Jr.
Ronald Miller
Brian Milliken
Faye Mills
Evva Minch
Milford Mitchel
Catherine Mitchell
Glenn Mitchell
Guy Mitchell
Dalene Moore
Jack Moore
Kim Moore
Sheryl Moore
Vicky Moore
Dylan Morford
Keith Morisette
J. C. Morrison
Bobbi Moschkau
Richard Mosier
Calvin Mousseau
David Muldrow
Gregory Munford
Gary Munson
Florence Murphy
James Murphy
James Musselman
Steven Myers
Kurt Myking
Charles Myrick
Philip Myton
Jean Naccarato
James Nadeau
Erwin Nadong
Amy Nagy
Josie Najar
Gregory Nanney
Larry Naranjo
Jimmy Nation
Noel Naumann
David Neal
Richard Neal
Dean Nelson
Donald Nelson
John Nelson
Michele Nelson
Robert Nelson, Jr.
Rolf Nelson
Terry Nelson
Marion Nemia
Steven Neslund
Jeanette Neufeld
Terry Nevius
Harry Newman
Sandra Newman
Forest Newsom
Kelly Nichols
Robert Nichols
Arlene Nicholson
Gerald Nicholson
Diana Nihem
David Noble
Glenn Noble
Connie Nolen
Neal Norberg
Donald Norris
Mary Norton
Ralph Norton
Richard Norton
Vincent Noyes
James Nunn
Robert Nye
Ronald O'Brien
Michael O'Farrell
Michael O'Grady
David Ockrassa
David Ogden
Wade Ogg
John Ohlson
Jon Ojen
Emmett Olarte
C.J. Oliver
Christian Oliver
Leif Olsen
Kenneth Olson
Rudolf Omero

Michael Orlando
Joseph Orth
Henry Ortiz
Tadashi Osada
Curt Osborne
Rita Oster
Lin Ostlund
Steven Otis
John Ott
Leonard Otte
Patrick Overbay
Harold Owens
Major Owens
John Pace
Gerald Pagni
Angela Palmer
Cynthia Palmer
David Palmer
Kathy Palmer
Samuel Palmisano
Anthony Pantley
James Pappas
John Paris
Gary Parker
Lance Parker
Nancy Parr
Dean Paschich
Michael Patten
Kenneth Patterson
Michael Patzer
Jon Paxton
Doris Payne
Victoria Pedersen
Kenneth Penton
Dean Percival
Mark Percy
Joey Perea-Hottman
Johanna Perez
Rodney Perez
Jim Perich-Anderson
Terrance Person, Jr.
Michael Pesin
Maris Peters
Richard Peters
Clara Peterson
David Peterson
Gene Peterson
James Peterson
John Peterson
Diana Petry
Kenneth Pettie
Ila Pettus
Terry Phibbs
Alice Phillips
Dona Phillips
Robert Phillips
Thomas Phillips
Arthur Pickens, Jr.
Vida Piera
Thomas Piocos
Janis Pipal
Daniel Pitsch
Terrance Plumb
Robert Pollard
Donald Pontsler
Donald Porter
Harold Porter
Russell Post
Chuck Potter
Keith Preece
David Price
Phillip Price
Sandra Price
Deborah Privett
William Privett
Kenneth Psaris
Andris Pudists
Juris Pudists
Ralph Pulsifer
John Purvis
Kyle Quaranto
D. Chad Quilici
Tony Randall
Lydia Randolph
Hazel Ratliff
Andrew Rausch
Donald Rayburn
Laurel Rayevich
Deborah Read
Douglas Read
William Read
Clyde Rector
Lashell Rector
Theresa Reed
Thomas Reese
Paul Rehse
Jennifer Renken
Viki Reynolds
Nena Rice
Toni Rice
Peter Richardson
Steven Rick
Gerald Rider
Janet Rider
David Riggers
Michael Riggins
Mary Beth Riggs
Daniel Rios
Edward Ritzman
Luis Rivero
John Roberts

Steven Roberts
Warren Roberts
Marc Robertson
R. Carlton Robinson
Richard Robinson
Ronald Robydek
David Rodahl
Leo Rogacki
Barbara Rogers
Diane Rogers
Steven Rogge
Veronica Rollins
Henry Roney
Fred Rose
Dan Ross, Jr.
Jeanne Ross
Lisa Ross
Steven Ross
Timothy Ross
Wayne Ross
John Rourick
William O. Routley
William J. Routley
Gina Rowan
David Rucker
Samuel Rupert
Lyle Russell
Richard Ryan
James Sage
Wayne Sageman
Renee Salmon
Julius Samuels
Jose Sanchez
Willie Sanders
Jesus Santiago
Sharon Sarandos
Rutha Sawyer
John Say
Lannie Scearcy
Susan Schaaf
John Schaefer, Jr.
Robert Schaefer
Larry Schaffner
Donald Schmidt
Harry Schmidt
Mark Schmidt
Steven Schmidt
Carl Schnauer
Rodney Schramm
Brenda Schull
Gene Schulz
Konrad Schuman
Cynthia Schwieger
Robert Scott
Kenneth Scudder
Dwayne Seay
Janet Sego
Charles Seiler
Charles Selfridge
Charles Semakula
Leonard Senzek
Barbara Serr
Kenneth Severe
Merrill Severson
John Sewell
Larry Sharp
Phillip Sharp, Sr.
David Shattuck
David Shaughnessy
Charles Shaw
Sheila Sheehan
Robert Sheldon
Kenneth Shelley
John Sheridan
Charlea Sherman
David Sherman
Judith Sherman
Thomas Shilley
Paul Shoblom
Grey Short
Jonathan Short
James Shown
Hedy Sides
Michelle Sikonia
John Silveira
Neil Simmons
Eric Simon
Dwayne Simons
Lewis Simpson
James Sinding
Franklin Singletary
Jeffrey Singleton
Marcy Sizer
Sharon Skaggs
Judith Skinner
Kristine Slabaugh
Jimmie Slade
Samuel Slater
Michael Sloan
Truine Slotke
Constance Smallwood
Joseph Smart
Arthur Smith
Ben Smith
Bryan Smith
David Smith
Leon Smith
Ethel Smith
Judith Smith
Michael Smith
Richard Smith

Carolyn Solitaire
Lawrence Soos
Benjamin Soper
Donald Sorensen
Michael Sorum
Edward Soto
Randy Spacek
George Spear
Aaron Spillman, Jr.
Suzanne Sprague
Sheryl Stahl
Terry Stamper
Billie Standifer
Larry Stankevitz
Theodore Stanley
David Starr
Gregory Starr
John Steadman
Dennis Stearns
Chris Stecker
Peter Steckler
Kathleen Steed
Dolores Stegeman
Theodore Stegeman
Dennis Steinberg
Lydia Stevenson
Michael Stevenson
Lynn Stewart
Ronald Stewart
Linda Stickney
David Stier
Jo Anne Still
Lloyd Stinson
Paul Stokes
Stan Strand
Dave Stril
Karen Strubi
Patricia Stuart
William Sugiyama
June Summerville
Stanley Sundquist
Paul Svoboda
Ronald Swalling
Willard Swanzy
Marilyn Swartz
Terry Swartz
David Swearingen
Rosanne Sweers
Alice Sweet
Michael Sweet
Janet Sweeten
Carl Sweitzer
Charles Swillie
Lyle Swinney
Stephen Swinney
Joseph Taffe
Kelly Tague
Marilou Tainer
Jerome Takahashi
Hollis Tamura
Hoa Tang
Pauline Tang
Bernerd Taylor
Helen Taylor
Patrice Taylor
Linda Terrill
Junius Thomas
Larry Thomas
Wayne Thomas
Donna Thompson
Larry Thompson
Joan Thornhill
Anna Thurston
Steven Tilley
Ralph Tipton, Jr.
Charles Todd
Romi Torres
William Townsend
Rebecca Trejo
Scott Trent
Linda Tresaugue
Lyle Tribwell
Steven Triplett
Chris Trotter
Robert Trowbridge
Allen Trueblood
Jodie Trueblood
Karen Trummert
Pamela Tucker
Randall Tufte
David Tullis
Deena Turmo
George Turner
Kenneth Turner
Sandra Turner
Chauncey Turney, Jr.
Richard Tweed
Rick VanAllen
Chris Vanderbilt
Carmen Vandevelde
John Vawter
Jodi Venables Coy
Sue Veseth
Toby Vice
Jose Vigil
Hector Villanueva
Margie Villanueva
James Viren
Jaime Vivar
Marie Vivar
Chuan Vu

Gary Wada
Gregory Waggoner
Charles Walker
Raymond Walker
Robert Walker
Terri Walker
LaVonne Waller
David Walsh
Marcella Walsh
William Walsh
Andrew Walston
Douglas Walters
Ann Walton
David Ward
Gene Ward
Steven Ward
Wayne Ward
Gordon Watson
Jerome Watson
Thomas Watters
Thomas Watts
Lisa Webb
John Webber
Richard Webber
Robert Weiler
Frank Weite
Kimberly Weite
Earl Welander
William Welborn
David Welch
Calvin Wells
Duane Wendling
Donna Wendt
George Wendt
Barbara Werelius
Lawrence Wescott
Richard Wessel
Jacqueline West
Edmund West
Raymond West
Ronald Whelan
James White
George Whitener
Lynn Whitesell
Richard Whitesell
Grant Whitley
Leonard Whitney
Dwaine Wier
Billy Wigley, Jr.
Arron Wilkins
Paul Wilkins
Charles Williams, Jr.
David Williams, Jr.
Gus Williams
Pat Williams
Robert Williams
Orson Williamson
Lon Willits
Kenneth Wilson
Mary Wilson
William Wimbles
Steve Winden
William Winne
William Winter
Christine Winters
Sylvester Witkowski
Harold Witzl
Dennis Wixon
Noreen Wolfe
Sam Wong
Robert Wonner
Bruce Wood
Roy Wood
David Woods
William Wooldridge
Wayne Worbs
George Wright
James Wright
Jerry Wright
Richard Wright
Ronald Yaden
Linda Yamashita
Benjamin Yau
Yun Myong Yi
Michael York
Deborah Young
Dennis Young
Dwayne Young
Mary Young
Sedonia Young
Michael Zahl
Shelby Zamberlin
Percy Zamzow
Karl Zapf
William Zawlocki
John Zehnder
Abram Zelitchenko
Anita Zetterstrom
Doris Zetterstrom
Paul Scott Zimmerman

ACKNOWLEDGEMENTS

The authors wish to thank the following for their help in creating *The Tacoma Public Utilities Story: The First 100 Years.* First, we applaud the management of Tacoma Public Utilities for recognizing the importance of preserving their history and for their willingness to let the story tell itself—through good times and bad, the triumphs and the tragedies.

Next, our thanks to June Summerville and Sue Veseth of the Community/Media Services staff for shepherding this project with good humor, a deft touch and lots of encouragement.

We are indebted to retired and current employees who allowed us to comb their memories and bring this history to life, including: Aldo Benedetti, E. E. (Ted) Coates, Paul Nolan, Marie (Billie) Berry, Jim Haneline, Ray Heffelfinger, James Keith, Hoby Longworth, Vern Meyer, Ray Millner, Rolf Nelson and Joe Peterson.

Mrs. A. L. Sienko, granddaughter of the legendary Ira S. Davisson, was another source of valuable historical information and we appreciate her insights.

Many employees provided important services, ranging from guiding us through historical records and photos to typing and copying. Our thanks to: Dennis Dean, Rosalie Lundin, Barbara Werelius, Barbara Rogers, Dawn Gossage, Sandy Fuller, Barbara Johnston, Sue Martin, Bradley Bogue, Steve Hanson and Leonard Whitney. A special thank you to Lorraine Graeber, who went above and beyond the call with word processing and other administrative support services.

The Leonhardt Group, a graphic design firm, played a key role in the design and production of this book. Ron Sasaki, Tim Young and Lisa Aklestad were responsible for putting the pieces together and following the project from conception to conclusion.

We appreciate the efforts of the Tacoma Public Library Northwest Room where Gary Reese, Judith Kipp, Brian Kamens and Jean Gillmer provided invaluable help. We are also grateful to the staff of the Washington State Historical Society Archives.

Finally, our hats are off to the *Morning News Tribune* for its fine work in preserving the history of Tacoma. We drew heavily upon the paper's coverage of Tacoma Public Utilities in creating this book. We are also grateful for its gracious help in supplying historical photos.

John S. Ott
Dick Malloy

Table of Contents

The Tacoma Public Utilities Story

1883 - 1893

HUMBLE BEGINNINGS

1

July 31, 1883, was a big day for Tacoma. As the transcontinental train huffed into the station, the crowd stirred in excitement and the band launched into a snappy march. The town fathers waiting to meet the train from Philadelphia adjusted their ties, shifted nervously and put on their best smiles. Charles B. Wright was coming to town.

Wright's reputation—and his money—had preceded him. As one of the seven men responsible for choosing Tacoma as the western terminus of the Northern Pacific Railroad, he had made Tacoma "The City of Destiny." And he had invested a great deal of time and money in the fledgling city.

The local girls' seminary bore his daughter's name and Wright had helped fund the city's first park and university. So today's red carpet treatment—parades, speeches, buildings draped in bunting—was to be expected for the man many called "The Father of Tacoma."

Though just one generation away from its pioneer beginnings when settlers such as Nicholas DeLin, Silas Galliher, Job Carr, Morton M. McCarver and Lewis Starr had founded two separate communities near the mouth of the Puyallup River—"New Tacoma" and "Old Tacoma"—the area had prospered and grown quickly. In 1883, New Tacoma boasted 4,000 residents—six times as many as the pioneer town of 1878.

It's not surprising. The town was ideally located on a deep water bay teeming with fish. It was blessed with abundant timber, other natural resources and a temperate climate. And with the new railroad, commerce with the rest of the nation seemed to promise a bright future.

(Facing page)
From humble beginnings in 1893, Tacoma Public Utilities has become one of the region's largest and most progressive utilities.

Water everywhere, but not to drink

What it did not have was a dependable supply of water. Edison's invention of the incandescent lamp in 1879 had introduced the nation to the wonders of electricity and its acceptance was immediate, but in 1883 Tacoma was far more interested in water, not light. In those days, the most important use of electricity was to drive the water pumps.

And for good reason. Fire was a constant threat. The town was built of wood—most structures, the sidewalks and even some streets. A cigar butt carelessly discarded could lead to a catastrophic fire such as those nearly destroying Seattle, Spokane, Vancouver and Ellensburg in the 1890s. Tacoma's spring-fed, gravity flow water system—with water supplied by small, competing companies—made the city particularly vulnerable.

Fire was a constant threat. . . When Charles B. Wright formed his new water and light company, an audible sigh of relief swept through Tacoma.

While Wright was basking in the limelight during his 1883 visit, *The Tacoma Daily Ledger* ran a lengthy editorial lamenting the lack of a unified water works in Tacoma, calling it "the greatest impediment to the growth of New Tacoma and the most prolific source of discomfort to her citizens. . . ."

The timing was great, no doubt designed to catch Wright's attention. Two weeks later the City Council passed Ordinance No. 96 "granting to Charles B. Wright and his associates privilege to supply the city of New Tacoma and its inhabitants with pure and fresh water." The ordinance required Wright to spend at least $25,000 on the system and to begin construction within 18 months.

No small thinker, Wright expected to spend at least $65,000, maybe even as much as $100,000. An almost audible sigh of relief swept through Tacoma. "The day of wells is nearly ended in Tacoma," hailed the *Ledger*.

On June 10, 1884, Wright incorporated the Tacoma Light & Water Company, with General John W. Sprague as president, and the company began its search for a dependable supply of water. The company remained the only large supplier of light and water until it was purchased by the city in 1893.

Elaborate plans

Wright's plans for the water works were the most elaborate yet seen in Tacoma. Water was to be conveyed through an open-topped box flume, roughly two feet square, emptying into a large reservoir on a hill south of town. Wright's company built two dams in the gullies on either side of the hill, fed by branches of Galliher's Creek. The reservoir, 260 feet above sea level, was to serve by gravity the low-lying districts of Tacoma. Those in higher areas would be supplied directly from Galliher's Creek by a Holly turbine and wheel pump in the gully.

Work on the new system continued into the summer of 1885. Water mains were distributed throughout Tacoma, now a city of 7,500, with the first service installed in the Tacoma Hotel on December 17, 1884. Later that year, the new Hood Street Reservoir was completed. Considered enormous at the time, it was 320 feet long by 113 feet wide and filled to a depth of 14 feet.

PHOTO COURTESY OF TACOMA PUBLIC LIBRARY

Tacoma in the mid-1880s. With fire and typhoid constant threats, the city of 7,500 desperately needed an improved water system. The large building in the distance is the county courthouse.

Despite these early successes, the fledgling company faced a rocky road. Supplying a rapidly growing and greatly dispersed population proved to be a logistical nightmare. The company simply couldn't lay pipe fast enough. Parts and machinery were hard to come by, causing more delays. Leaks in flumes and water mains caused frequent shutdowns, leaving the city without water.

To make matters worse, the city was hit with a full-fledged typhoid epidemic in 1888, with 18 deaths recorded in October—a "ridiculously low" figure, according to the *Ledger*. Clearly, Tacoma had to do something about its water system—beyond listening to Charles B. Wright promise a better system in the future.

Interest in light is . . . light

The city also was clamoring for a better electrical system. Just four years earlier, the city had shown only a mild interest in electricity. An ordinance introduced in May 1884 that would have illuminated the city with electric lights was postponed indefinitely. A later ordinance calling for the inspection and regulation of chimney flues was much more important, Mayor Jacob R. Weisbach said.

By November 1886, however, the Tacoma Light & Water Company was about ready to launch itself into the streetlighting business. Nearly all poles had been placed, wire was being strung and by December "electric dynamos" were in place and ready for operation as soon as lamps—the Edison Municipal Incandescent Light—and additional wire arrived from St. Louis.

The city was hit with a full-fledged typhoid epidemic in 1888. Clearly, Tacoma had to do something about its water system.

The company generated electricity from a small powerhouse in Galliher's Gulch, near South 26th Street and Pacific Avenue. Electric lamps were placed in service on December 26—a nice Christmas present for Tacoma. Setting out to "encircle the city with light," the company had extended service three-quarters of a mile along Pacific Avenue by January 3, 1887.

The service was inadequate and controversial almost from the start. Rates were high—the charge for streetlights was $10 per lamp until midnight, $14 all night—and generating capacity woefully inadequate.

Could a new development described in the newspaper be the answer to Tacoma's generating problems? A man in San Francisco, the story said, had discovered a way to produce electrical power with a battery composed of mud and water into which bits of zinc and carbon had been placed. No expensive generators needed, no insulation on the wires—just safe, economical power.

Growing demand

Well, Tacoma had plenty of mud, but that wasn't the answer for meeting the growing demand for electricity. By 1889 the need had moved beyond just streetlighting. People wanted electricity in their homes. And industrial applications were calling—power for elevators, machines of all types, printing presses, railways and trolley cars.

By 1889, people wanted electricity in their homes. And industrial applications were calling.

By 1890 the last spike was driven in an electric street trolley system serving Tacoma.

Complaints against the company were mounting, despite the fact that the Tacoma Light & Water Company had one of the largest light and power plants in the entire territory. Even a new powerhouse completed in 1889 and equipped with Tacoma's first Westinghouse alternating current generator capable of lighting 1,500 lamps couldn't stem the tide of criticism.

The lights weren't bright enough, there weren't enough of them, and worse yet—the company was lax about responding to outages and other service complaints. Agitation for a municipally owned system was increasing. Faced with these complaints and persistent

PHOTO COURTESY OF TACOMA PUBLIC LIBRARY

Tacoma in the Gay '90s. Should Tacoma take up Charles B. Wright on his offer to sell his water system? The city was still searching for a supply of safe, pure water.

problems with the water system, Charles B. Wright began to see the handwriting on the wall.

Wright wants to sell

Arriving in Tacoma in May 1890, Wright was upbeat and optimistic when asked by a reporter if he'd thought about selling the company. "No," he replied. "Should I sell and my holdings pass into the hands of men who haven't the interest of the city at heart, people might justly say: 'Why, Wright has left us in a pretty fix.' "

But by March 1892, when the agitation for a municipally owned light and water plant came into the open and became *the* political issue of day, Wright had changed his mind. He was tiring rapidly of his six-year-old investment and the last three years had brought him nothing but trouble and a constant cash outlay. Now, his reputation as "Father of Tacoma" was quickly becoming tarnished—and it was going to get worse before it got better.

1890–1893: To buy or not to buy. . .

Whoever named this era "The Gay '90s" obviously didn't live through it. People worked hard—there were few machines or labor-saving devices—and died young. Typhoid was still a major cause of death; aspirin hadn't even been invented.

As if people didn't have enough troubles, the Panic of 1893 was about to hit. When it did, the Northwest and Tacoma suffered the most, says Herbert Hunt, in his authoritative *History of Tacoma.*

As bank crash followed crash "Rich men sawed wood, picked blueberries and dug clams for a livelihood. Women with diamonds and valuable deeds resorted to kitchen labor. . . . Men who had ridden in carriages walked . . . the laborer who had a steady place at $1.50 a day could pity many of his fellows who a few months before had been spending incomes of several thousands a year."

But, as the Gay '90s opened, Tacoma had a more immediate problem—a dependable supply of safe, pure water. Should the city take up Charles B. Wright on his offer to sell his system, or develop one of its own? The best way to answer the question was to form a committee and do a study—some things never change.

A citizens' water committee searches for a supply of at least 20 million gallons.

In July 1891 the City Council passed an ordinance creating a citizens' water committee of 11 prominent businessmen, with millionaire city father Nelson Bennett as chairman. Getting right down to business, they quickly decided that "at as early a day as practicable the city of Tacoma should own its own water works. . . ." The committee set out to find a water supply of at least 20 million gallons—enough to serve a population of 200,000.

Searching for a source

The committee hired an engineer and examined several sources for the gravity system it had in mind, finally settling on the Mashell

Nelson Bennett. Millionaire, city father and chairman of the citizens' water committee.

PHOTO COURTESY OF WASHINGTON STATE HISTORICAL SOCIETY

River. Meanwhile, the Chamber of Commerce was getting into the act, forming a committee to survey the Tacoma Light & Water Company's flume line, reservoir and mains.

The water was excellent, it reported. The flume was the problem—decayed, rotting in several places and leaking. The reservoir was uncovered and unfenced with impurities seeping into the water. Spanaway Lake was clogged with dead trees and grass. More good reasons for the city to have its own system.

All this attention may have been a burr under the saddle for the Tacoma Light & Water Company. Perhaps wary of future competition from the city, it rushed to completion a pumping station in Galliher's Gulch (at Hood and "O" streets). Dubbed "one of the finest and most complete pumping stations on the Pacific Coast" by the *Ledger*, the station was connected to the Hood Street reservoir, the "J" Street standpipe and nearby distribution mains. And it extended pipes to western Tacoma and Old Town, enlarging and improving the distribution system.

After a break for the holidays, Nelson Bennett's water committee settled back down to business. On February 12, 1892, the committee submitted its second report, outlining the cost of the Mashell River system—$1.5 million to $2.2 million, depending on the materials used, for a 30-million-gallon reservoir.

Voting for water

On March 19, 1892, after four months of investigation, the committee made its recommendation to the Council—Tacoma should have its own water and electric light plant and should tap the Mashell River. The City Council agreed and called for a special election to decide if the city should be bonded to acquire its own water works.

But first, there was a break for politics. The mayoral and Council seats were up for grabs and one of the hot issues, of course, was whether or not Tacoma should own and operate its own water and light works. The press and the public grilled the candidates mercilessly. The Republican nominee for mayor, Herbert S. Huson, stood firm on a plank for city ownership. Alexander Parker, his opponent, was a member of the 11-man water committee—which had also recommended the city obtain its own water plant.

After a fierce battle, in which the city's newspapers chose sides and hurled invectives at one another and the candidates, the Republicans captured nine of the 16 Council seats. Huson defeated Parker and the Council was now aligned staunchly against the Tacoma Light & Water Company.

So it was back to the woods and another trip to the Mashell River for members of the new Council. Much waffling ensued. Though the

Council favored the Mashell site, it wasn't sure the people would vote for it. A month passed. No election. No steps taken toward acquiring a new gravity line and the Mashell River project began to lose momentum.

Meanwhile, Charles B. Wright had let the City Council know he was willing to sell, but the asking price was a little steep—$2.1 million. What if, the Council wondered, Wright could be talked down from his asking price? Stalemate at the Council.

Well, not quite. Determined to make a decision, the Council followed the advice of Nelson Bennett's water committee and hired hydrostatic engineer Rudolph Hering—for $50 a day—to make a thorough study of Tacoma Light & Water Company's holdings.

Sizing it up

Hering took careful measurements of the city's existing sources and recent acquisitions. The water quality, though slightly "earthy," was satisfactory, but flume quality was still a problem. With the present population, he concluded, the city needed six million gallons a day and its sources were good for 37 million gallons—enough to meet the city's needs until 1910.

Hering also quashed the Mashell River project—flow measurements had been overestimated as much as 150 percent—and compared the city's as-yet undeveloped springs with three river sources by cost and quality. Hering's findings:

Best Water Quality	Least Cost to Develop	
1. Spring water	1. Spring water	$1.8 million
2. Green River	2. S. Fork Puyallup	$2.1 million
3. S. Fork Puyallup	3. Mashell River	$2.2 million
4. Mashell River	4. Green River	$2.6 million

Meanwhile, the Council had been busy calculating the value of the Tacoma Light & Water Company. The Council's price tag for the

water system matched Hering's estimate of about $769,000. Add the value of the electric light plant and real estate and the total was about $1.52 million—about $600,000 below Wright's initial price.

This caused furrowed brows on the Council and it sat down to re-evaluate the situation. It was clear that acquiring Wright's company was the most expedient way to own a light and water plant. Hering's report simply underscored their own beliefs. So, on January 1, 1893, the City Council committed itself to purchasing the Tacoma Light & Water Company. All that remained was to haggle for an acceptable price and leave the decision to the voters.

An early line crew. Tacoma citizens were far more interested in water than light in the 1890s, though that attitude would change in a few years.

Easier said than done. Wright eliminated the gas works and some property the city didn't want, bringing the price down to $1.85 million. The two parties were still $350,000 apart.

Wright cuts a deal

To buy or not to buy became the burning issue of the day. Hot words flew back and forth. The Council was dangerously split over the issue. One faction, led by Councilman William H. Grattan, was outraged at the company's ridiculously high offer. Peppery Grattan went so far as to accuse the mayor and other councilmen of accepting bribes to support the sale.

More fat was thrown on the fire when the company refused to show title to its lands until after the Council had accepted Wright's offer. Why, the city wondered. Didn't the company have title to the land it was trying to sell? Confusion swept the city. Soapbox orators were on the street corners, urging the crowd one way or the other. Everyone had an opinion and the argument was far more heated than that of the 1892 election campaign.

To buy or not to buy became the burning issue of the day. Hot words flew back and forth.

Then—out of the blue—Wright lopped $50,000 off his asking price. With the Panic of 1893 knocking on his door and the grumbling in Tacoma, Wright may have become anxious. Whatever the case, the new asking price was $1.8 million. Sniffing a good deal and tired of dealing through middlemen, the Council sent a small committee headed by Harris Correll to deal face-to-face with Wright in Philadelphia.

It was a shrewd move—Wright knocked another $50,000 off his price, bringing the total to $1.75 million. Now, Tacoma was on a roll. On February 25, 1893, after an eight-hour session, the Council decided once and for all to put the vote before the people.

On March 4, the Council passed Ordinance No. 790, "An ordinance to provide for the purchase of the water works and electric light plant, and all such water supplies, riparian rights, rights of way, lands, lots, personal property and franchises as are now owned and operated by the Tacoma Light & Water Company." It was signed by the mayor on March 6, 1893, and the election was scheduled for April 11.

Heated oratory

There were tumultuous days before the election, according to the newspapers. "Hot words and vigorous discussion" were the order of the day. Orators for and against attracted knots of citizens along Pacific Avenue "to the discomfort of foot passengers."

Opposition grew—including a meeting at Germania Hall, presided over by Councilman Grattan, where a resolution was passed protesting the purchase at "the exorbitant price asked." There was even the threat of violence on the eve of the election, but the county commissioners refused to appoint 70 deputies to guard the election as requested.

On the morning of the election—April 11, 1893—Tacoma was poised, the *Ledger* said, to decide whether it was ". . . to take a long step forward, or is it to wait idly for something or somebody to push it forward."

The city had its answer the next day. With 3,195 voting for purchasing the company and 1,956 against—and a three-fifths majority needed—the issue passed by 104 votes.

Tacoma had taken a major first step toward municipal utility ownership—and controlling its own destiny.

1893 - 1909

A Turbulent Beginning

2

There was a heady atmosphere around City Hall those first few days after the election. At last, Tacoma was in charge of its own destiny and could begin providing its citizens the quality water and electricity service they deserved.

The new era began smoothly enough. A Board of Water and Light Commissioners was established. Bonds for the plant's purchase ($1.75 million) and proposed extensions ($400,000) were advertised and sparked nationwide interest among bankers and bond brokers.

The bonds were all but promised to Charles B. Wright and, at a meeting packed with representatives of New York, Chicago, Denver and Cleveland brokerage firms, Wright offered to take the bonds at par and five percent interest in lieu of cash.

It was one of the last cordial dealings with Wright. Ahead were six years of litigation, lawsuits, missed opportunities and political intrigue. Both Tacoma and Wright suffered, the era ending with Wright's estrangement from the city he helped build and the water system not much improved.

There was trouble almost immediately. First, Wright was unable to find a buyer for the $330,000 water extension bonds and proposed to pay the amount over the next three months.

Next, the deed arrived from Wright in Philadelphia, but the City Council withheld $100,000 of the $1.75 million owed him, pending an inventory of the Tacoma Light & Water Company's property. In return, company president Theodore Hosmer refused to release the company's books. Eventually, Wright relented and the books were

(Facing page) Horse power. Tacoma hitches its destiny to a new concept—municipal ownership of utilities.

Wright's man in Tacoma. Theodore Hosmer, president of Charles B. Wright's Tacoma Light & Water Company, predecessor of Tacoma Public Utilities.

PHOTO COURTESY OF WASHINGTON STATE HISTORICAL SOCIETY

turned over to Tacoma. Effective July 1, 1893, the City of Tacoma was the new owner of the Tacoma Light & Water Company.

Meanwhile, the City Council had reversed itself and given control of utilities to the Board of Public Works, not its newly appointed Board of Commissioners. The board's first order of business was to take inventory and begin hiring men. It retained Tacoma Light & Water Superintendent Robert H. Lloyd—at a hefty salary of $1,920 a year—and added a meter man, pipe fitters and inspectors.

Rotten to the core

There was plenty of work to do. The city inherited a water system literally falling apart before its eyes. Four serious leaks erupted in the downtown business district and the flume was said to be so rotten in places you could push your finger through the wood. The city engineer estimated the flume was losing 1.5 million gallons daily.

Worse, Dam No. 3 in Galliher's Gulch had washed away several months earlier in a flash flood, depriving the city of an additional 1.6 million gallons of water a day.

The closer the city looked at its new water system, the more discouraging the news. The root of the problem: lack of a significant, dependable supply. Taking flow measurements of Thomas and Patterson Springs—which the city acquired in its purchase of company property—City Engineer James M. Morrison found far less than the five million gallons a day promised by Wright's company.

As the months passed, other sources were investigated—Maplewood Springs in Puyallup and the headwaters of Clover Creek, an artesian well on the prairies southwest of town, Lake Kapowsin (25 miles southeast of town), the Chenius River and Canada Creek. Though significant time and money were invested in these sources, most failed and were abandoned.

Meanwhile, the citizens of Tacoma suffered along with poor service and poor water. Common complaints were of discolored, lukewarm, earthy-tasting, foul-smelling water. The city did reduce rates for both its water and light customers, though that may have been a move to keep customers in the tough financial times. After all, electric light and running water, even in the 1890s, were not necessities.

Residential customers connected to city mains paid a monthly flat rate for water—a minimum of $1 a month, with extra charges for luxuries such as bathtubs (25 cents a month). Customers with a five-room house with one tub paid $2.25 per month.

Making money

A bright spot amid the gloom was the fact that the water and light plants were making money—receipts for July to October 1893 totalled about $25,000, reducing the City Council's "buyer's remorse."

The relationship with Wright was not doing as well. In fact, it had been going steadily downhill ever since the property had changed hands. First, there were charges that Wright didn't have clear title to some of the company's property, causing an uproar in the City Council.

Next, the Board of Public Works—John Fuller, David L. Demorest and President Arvid Rydstrom—accused the company of withholding some $50,000 worth of property from the city. Wright was suspect because of his involvement with a short-lived rival company—the Commercial Light & Power Company. The board assumed that city customers, tools and equipment were being funneled in that direction.

In one of the strangest incidents in Tacoma history, Mayor Huson and the Board of Public Works led a midnight raid on Wright's gas works, making off with two boilers, a pile of pipe and other fixtures. Theodore Hosmer, president of the company, labeled the mayor's actions "a high-handed midnight outrage" and ordered the offenders arrested. Mayor Huson's commando raid landed him and Demorest in jail, though they were soon released on their own recognizance.

The city sues Wright

Frustration was building. With thousands of dollars and months of effort wasted and the water problem no closer to solution, the City Council had to do something. Soon there were the first whispers of a $1 million lawsuit against the company. And they were true—on September 25, 1894, the city sued the Tacoma Light & Water Company.

City of Tacoma v. Tacoma Light & Water Company opened in December 1895—a hotly contested case followed closely by both the press and the public. The city was most angry about the miserable water flow from Thomas and Patterson Springs, declaring it had paid Wright's exorbitant asking price for the company based on the prospect of a 10-million-gallon gravity line from the springs.

The company countered that the city's own engineer—Rudolph Hering—had certified that the springs could produce 10 million gallons, so it wasn't liable.

Testimony dragged through Christmas. Survey charts were examined, flow measurements scrutinized, correspondence analyzed. Engineers on both sides testified.

On January 1, 1896, nearly 16 months after it had first opened the case, the jury found in favor of Tacoma, awarding the city $787,000 in damages. But this was just the opening salvo in a long legal wrangle. The company appealed the decision twice—first to Superior Court and then to the state Supreme Court, where the case was overturned. But Tacoma had the last word, appealing and winning a reversal from the state Supreme Court.

The city was pondering its next move when the grim reaper claimed Charles B. Wright in 1898. The "Father of Tacoma" died embittered against the city he helped build.

A hollow victory

Tacoma watched with amazement as the $787,000 was granted, taken back and granted again. It turned out to be a hollow victory. When the city finally tried to collect its money, it found that Tacoma Light & Water owned no property.

The city was pondering its next move when the grim reaper intervened—Charles B. Wright died on March 24, 1898. Wright had been in poor health for years when he was finally brought down by the flu—and no doubt weakened by the 30-month court battle.

The "Father of Tacoma" died embittered against the city he helped build. In an interview with the Philadelphia press, Wright railed against Tacoma as "a nest of Populists and Communists."

He felt his efforts were unappreciated and he was probably right. Tacoma's attitude toward Wright changed dramatically in 15 years. A city that had hailed him as "benefactor and father" now called him "thief and profiteer."

Tacoma opted to pursue the Tacoma Gas & Electric Company, also owned by Wright, in order to collect the $787,000. Negotiating with Wright's estate, the talks dragged on for several weeks, but the city clearly had the upper hand and ultimately settled for $100,000 cash and attorneys fees of about $25,000. The City Council was pleased with the settlement, dropped its lawsuit—and closed the door on its involvement with the Tacoma Light & Water Company on January 27, 1899.

At the close of a decade and the 19th century, following years of depression and dashed hopes, Tacomans looked toward a brighter future. Years of a constantly changing cast of characters at City Hall had brought little stability or direction to the city's new water and light utilities. The water problem persisted.

The future had to be an improvement. Ex-councilman William H. Grattan called the city's management of the water works from 1893 to 1899 "a series of the most stupendous and expensive blunders in the annals of water exploitations."

Little did he know, he hadn't seen anything yet.

1899–1909: Tacoma City Water continues the search

The first few years of the new century were an era of discovery. Marconi and the wireless. Gold in Alaska. The Wright Brothers and flight.

But in Tacoma, the city fathers were still struggling to discover—and agree on—dependable sources of water and electricity.

The water problem was still acute so Mayor Johnson Nickeus began the search for a new, permanent water source for Tacoma. Clover Creek could supply no more than three million gallons of water a day, so the search widened. City engineers and surveyors examined Maplewood Springs, the South Fork of the Puyallup, the Chenius River, Voight's Creek and Clear Creek. All had drawbacks of some sort—either cost or unsuitable water.

Meanwhile, city employees were busy expanding and repairing the Clover Creek intake. They widened the channel and patched the flume line, reducing the amount of water leaking.

With a band-aid applied to the existing system, the city was able to make it through a couple of summers without serious problems, taking the steam out of efforts to locate new water sources.

The City Council even voted to reduce water rates in 1902, reducing the flat monthly rate from $1 to 85 cents. But growth was

The City Council reduced water rates in 1902—from $1 a month to 85 cents.

coming to Tacoma, demand for water was escalating dramatically and the hunt for water couldn't be put off.

New Mayor Louis D. Campbell, consulting with City Engineer Norton Taylor, narrowed his choices to four: Maplewood Springs, a gravity line from Clear Creek, a well field in South Tacoma or a gravity line from the Green River. Eventually, the well field and the Green River would be the only serious contenders.

Peering down wells

A special investigating committee decided that the South Tacoma well field offered an affordable, if temporary, solution. Wells previously driven in the area had been quite successful and the well system would only cost $75,000 to install. So engineer Taylor began digging a test well within the city's right-of-way along the Clover Creek flume. The well was to be only 40 feet deep and 30 feet in diameter, but the committee hoped it might furnish as much as three million gallons daily.

Using day laborers, the engineer speeded the work through August 1902. With digging complete, a representative of the Ingersoll-Sargent Company, L. Forrest McConihe, was contracted to submerge a Pohle air-lift compressor working in conjunction with a Gould triplex pump to pump water into the flume.

The technology was a success and water from Well No. 1 flowed into the Hood Street Reservoir. Though the well didn't produce the hoped-for three million gallons, it encouraged the committee to create a comprehensive plan centering on a well field in South Tacoma.

The wells proved to be a hit-or-miss proposition. Some produced water, some didn't. Of the five wells completed by 1906, two were complete failures and the other three produced variable results. Meanwhile, Tacoma's citizens were clamoring for water and the heat was intensifying.

Tacoma in 1900. Still struggling to discover—and agree on—dependable sources of water and electricity.

PHOTO COURTESY OF TACOMA PUBLIC LIBRARY

George P. Wright, a new mayor, favored building a gravity system from either the Green or Greenwater river and in August he sent three men off to lock up the water rights. They obtained rights in two places on the Green River at the towns of Palmer and Hot Springs, located 25 and 41 miles east of Tacoma, respectively. They also secured rights on the Greenwater, though they found themselves vying with a like-minded Olympia group.

Another crossroads

Now, Tacoma was at another crossroads—wells or gravity line. The city chose to pursue both with the special water committee calling for bids on a new test well to determine if the South Tacoma aquifer held enough water to serve the city. They also supported an

1906—wells or gravity system?

ordinance introduced by Thomas Bellingham that called for putting the Green River gravity line proposition before the voters.

Meanwhile, City Hall was becoming a political battlefield. George Wright was re-elected mayor and quickly involved himself in a squabble with the special committee over the choice of an engineer to run the water system. Charges flew back and forth.

Wright took on the City Council, accusing them of stonewalling the gravity system. The Council charged that the mayor was purposely blocking development of the wells, proceeding at a snail's pace.

Ruffled feathers were smoothed somewhat with the compromise appointment of Harnett Fuller to supervise the water system. He was given complete charge of both the well and the gravity line projects. Fuller first inspected the South Tacoma wells—which he described as "a patchwork of everyone's ideas"—and then sent two crews to the Green River.

But that didn't do much to alleviate the current water crisis. In the summer of 1906 many Tacomans were still using Clover Creek and an ever-increasing number of complaints were pouring into City Hall. A *Ledger* reporter examined the creek and found ducks swimming in the creek, children and cows wading through it. The water coming from faucets was black, slimy and "vile-smelling."

Fuller investigated the flume and intake a few days later, saying, "The present water supply of this city is a disgrace to civilization and a standing menace to the community."

He recommended abandoning Clover Creek, but—dirty or not—Tacoma couldn't survive without the water. Neither the wells nor Galliher's Gulch supplied enough. Fuller did the next best thing, applying another band-aid by cleaning the flume then patching, enlarging and covering it.

City Hall—a house divided

In late August 1906 Fuller reported to the Council on the water situation. Though a survey of the Green River was six weeks from completion, he announced that a pipeline would take two years and $2.2 million to complete, $600,000 more than a previous estimate. He recommended sinking six or seven new wells as a temporary solution.

City Hall was again divided into two factions—wells versus the gravity line. And the shenanigans and political foolishness escalated. Believing that Fuller was deliberately delaying the Green River project, Mayor Wright ordered Commissioner Owen Woods and Chief of Police Thomas Malony to raid Fuller's office. Without a warrant, they barged in and began collecting charts and maps of the gravity project. Fuller quickly phoned his attorney, who arrived while the raid was in progress. Tempers flared, but order was restored and Woods and company left, but not before taking several stacks of papers and leaving Fuller's office a shambles.

The well faction was having its own troubles. The wells were not living up to expectations, with Wells No. 4 through 7 supplying very little water. Commissioner Woods called them "duds."

Right on cue, Wright submitted a revised outline and budget for the gravity line. With the help of his new, hand-picked engineer, J. H. Cunningham, he presented a proposal similar to earlier plans, but costing $1.99 million, compared to Fuller's earlier estimate of $2.2 million. Though the plan received a chilly reception from the Council, a public vote on the plan was set for September 10.

Another vote, another failure

With the vote quickly approaching, both factions went on the offensive. The well faction worked hard to turn the duds into producers and scheduled a series of tests for all 10 wells. Held two days

Tacoma voters shot themselves in the foot, voting against the Green River gravity line.

before the election, the tests attracted "hundreds" of voters to South Tacoma to see some 4.5 million gallons flowing from nine of the wells—more than expected. With water from Clover Creek, Galliher's Gulch, Crystal Springs and the wells totalling nearly 10 million gallons a day, the mayor's gravity line was in deep trouble.

With the papers trumpeting the wells' success, Mayor Wright became desperate—and committed a desperate act. In a last-ditch effort to convince the voters of the gravity line's importance, he shut down the wells and pump stations the day before the election. Parts of Tacoma were completely cut off from all water.

"Lives and Homes Endangered, Water Famine. . ." screamed the headlines. Wright's ploy was foolhardy—and it also dashed any hopes of pushing through the gravity line project.

On September 10, 1907, Tacoma's citizens once again went to the polls to cast a vote for their future. This time, they shot themselves in the foot, voting against the Green River proposition 2,723 to 1,663.

Let there be light?

Water wasn't the only burning question of the day. At about the same time, Tacoma was also gearing up for a major fight over the source of its electricity.

When the election of 1893 gave Tacoma control over the light plant, the city inherited a plant that was really little more than a distribution system, with most power being bought from Boston-based Stone & Webster, locally represented by the Seattle–Tacoma Power Company.

Horse power wagon—1887. Streetlights were the first major use of electricity, with crews like this erecting poles and stringing wire.

The company, a predecessor of Puget Power, owned the only large-scale power generation facilities in the area—the Electron Plant on the Puyallup River and the Snoqualmie Plant on the Snoqualmie River. So, it was the only game in town—buy from Seattle–Tacoma Power Company or enjoy the dark.

While Tacoma's electric plant was in disrepair—most of the company's steam boilers were immediately rebuilt—it was profitable from the beginning.

By 1894 light plant revenues had already climbed over $102,000 and it was already twice as profitable as the water system. After just one year of operation it was clear the light plant was the best part of the purchase. With a series of early rate reductions, the city began to fashion its reputation for offering rates among the nation's

1907—agitation for building a municipal power plant began to surface.

lowest. Meanwhile, the recession was over and there was a growing demand for power. Consumption grew from 1.2 million kilowatt-hours per year in 1897 to 2.9 million in 1902 and 6.1 million in 1907. Almost all this power was supplied by the Seattle–Tacoma Power Company.

Stone & Webster had quite a lock on power companies and street railway companies (often one of the key reasons for building a power plant) in the Northwest, with operations in Whatcom County, Everett, Seattle and Tacoma.

Agitating for power

Committed to owning and operating its own utilities, many in Tacoma did not like the idea of depending on another company for power. Agitation for building a municipal power plant began to surface and in 1907 the mayor and City Council authorized the

Fire and Water Committee to investigate the possibility of building a hydroelectric plant and report back to the Council.

Engineers C. E. Cummings, J. H. Cunningham and Willis H. Trenner made their report in September 1907, calling for a hydroelectric plant on the upper Nisqually River at LaGrande. They recommended the city immediately acquire all necessary land, land rights, water and riparian rights.

The Council also decided on financing for the project—$2 million worth of warrants, redeemable by a lien on 40 percent of the power revenue, would be issued to the builder to pay for the construction. Next, $300,000 worth of bonds would be issued to purchase the land, riparian rights and rights-of-way.

The city was in an uproar over its power crisis. Tacoma's three newspapers launched a war of words for and against the proposed Nisqually hydroelectric project.

The arrangement, spelled out in an ordinance passed by the Council, would require a two-step approval by the voters—a simple majority on the $2 million bond issue and a three-fifths majority on the $300,000 issue.

A hot issue

The hydro plan attracted little attention until the end of 1908. Then, suddenly, it was *the* topic of conversation. The fuse setting off the powder keg was a new contract with Stone & Webster at increased rates.

Tacoma was rapidly approaching a power crisis. Normal demand was exceeding the existing contracted supply from the Seattle–Tacoma Power Company. The city would either have to initiate a new contract or build its own plant.

The city and the company were in the midst of a rocky relationship, which sunk to a new low on December 6, 1908—when the company turned off all power to Tacoma's water pumps from 8 a.m. to 6:30 p.m.

Now the city was in an uproar. Tacoma's three newspapers launched a war of words for and against the Nisqually Project. The *Daily News* and the *Ledger* lined up against it, and the *Tribune* supported it. The City Council also had ardent power advocates—Councilmen Adelbert Rankin and Richard W. Jamieson—and power opponents: Councilmen Leslie L. Doud and S. Ritter Wilkeson.

The basic objection of the opposition papers seemed to be that there wasn't enough time before the election—now set for December 29, 1908—to fully inform the electorate. Underscoring their point, neither of the opposition papers attempted to print any objective information about the project.

On December 10, the *Tribune* carried a complete review of the power proposition, reviewing the costs and predicting that the Nisqually Project would produce power for about one-third the cost currently being paid to the Seattle–Tacoma Power Company.

While the newspapers kicked the power question around, the City Council went on record endorsing the power proposition by a vote of 14 to 2—Councilmen Doud and Wilkeson the naysayers. The Council also agreed to move the election back to January 2, 1909, further outraging those opposed to the plan.

A war of words

Wilkeson was a worthy opponent, leveling some new blast at the power proposition every few days. Claiming the Light Department was losing money, he said, "I will never change my opinion or my vote upon the power plant. That report of City Controller Meads showing a deficit of some $18,000 on the city light department during the past year knocks the proposition and kills it deader than a cat. I'll never change my vote on it."

In fact, there was net profit of some $113,000 for the past year. The $18,000 "deficit" resulted from the critics' inability to understand a financial statement.

The *News* also carried a lengthy story about power failures in other cities under the headline "140 Reasons Why Tacoma Should Hesitate."

The power advocates, on the other hand, concentrated on supplying as much information about the project as possible. On December 15, 1908, for example, the *Tribune* reviewed the cost of power from the Nisqually Project, explaining that Tacoma would pay $15,000 less for the 20,000 horsepower from the LaGrande hydro plant than it was paying for 7,000 horsepower of purchased electricity. By building the plant, Tacoma would give itself, free of charge, 13,000 horsepower of electricity.

When the newspapers weren't busy defending their positions, they attacked each other. If the *News* and the *Ledger* were really interested in giving the facts to its readers, said the *Tribune,* ". . . why devote columns of space to distorted statements rather than to give the readers of those newspapers the information they claim the people might acquire between now and the election?"

If the opposition newspapers wouldn't provide information on the Nisqually Project, the City Council would. On the evening of December 19, 1908, 1,000 copies of the engineer's report on the Nisqually Project were printed and ready for anyone who wanted more information on the hydro plant.

Councilman Jamieson became a strong public power advocate, decrying a 50 percent cost increase in the power contract recently negotiated with the Seattle–Tacoma Power Company. It was time, he said, to build the Nisqually development.

Councilman Wilkeson, on the other hand, recommended an all-out fight against the company to force lower rates. It would be better than building a $2 million municipal hydro plant. He did admit that power customers might be inconvenienced a bit while the fight was going on.

The last licks

Charges and counter-charges flew right up to the day of the election. City father Nelson Bennett endorsed the plant, asking: "Can Stone & Webster, back in Boston, run our business better than we who live here?"

The *Tribune* attacked Councilman Jamieson with blaring headlines, claiming he was a stockholder in a rival company that held title to the lands at LaGrande and that he was only trying to push up the value of the lands.

A new paper, *The Tacoma Times*, made its debut on the day before the election—January 1, 1909—and came out swinging for the pro-power group. "Equally important to the people of Tacoma as the carrying of the power plant project tomorrow is the repudiation of the

"Can Stone & Webster, back in Boston, run our business better than we who live here?"

diabolical and treacherous campaign that has been waged against it by the power trust gang."

In the *Ledger*, Harnett Fuller, water system supervisor, called the Nisqually plant a "fool move," saying the city had not proved that it could afford or needed it.

In the same issue of the paper, Councilman Rankin went on record favoring the project. Councilmen Wilkeson and Doud were confident the proposition would be defeated.

The final salvos had been fired, the rest was up to the voters of Tacoma.

When the ballots were counted, the Nisqually Project had passed by a margin of about three to one. After years of indecision and doubt, Tacoma had taken firm control of its destiny.

1 8 8 5 - 1 9 1 2

3

Tacoma's Romance With the Rails

Tacoma has had a long-standing romance with rails since 1873. The Northern Pacific, then owned by Charles Wright, stretched across the Midwest and over the Cascade Mountains to the headwaters of Commencement Bay. Tacoma was barely more than a collection of tents, shacks and a handful of lumber mills when the first trains rolled into town.

But with the railroad came transient laborers and pioneers intent on settling the Pacific Coast. The city grew in population and prestige. And the Northern Pacific, snubbing Seattle and Olympia for its western terminus, assured Tacoma's growth.

During the 1880s and 1890s, Tacoma was home to nearly two dozen streetcar companies.

Tacoma attracted several transcontinental railroads to her bustling docks and industrial tideflats. The city "where rails meet sails" also witnessed the rise and fall of many street railway systems. During the 1880s and 1890s, Tacoma was home to nearly two dozen streetcar companies. Not all operated at the same time—they changed hands and names frequently—and few were successful.

The competition to win franchise rights to city streets was fierce. The Tacoma Railway & Motor Company, the Tacoma Central Street Railway Company and the Point Defiance Railway Company, to name a few, competed for passengers and street space. The city's thoroughfares were literally a maze of tracks.

(Facing page) Belt Line beginnings. Until 1925, the Belt Line was known as the Tacoma Municipal Street Railway and carried workers to and from their jobs on the tideflats.

End of an era

In the late 1930s, however, the last remaining trolleys were replaced by buses. Though far less romantic than the old streetcars, the buses were economical, dependable, easier on streets and flexible in their routes. But not all the rails were removed. On Tacoma's industrial tideflats, an often-overlooked short line railroad operated and continues to this day: the Municipal Belt Line Railway.

The Belt Line, referred to in the past as the City of Tacoma's "orphan" or "stepchild" utility, has changed considerably in its eight decades. Its routes have been altered, equipment modernized and upgraded, clients have come and gone. Though strictly a freight-switching operation today, the Belt Line was initially a streetcar line carrying workers to the mills, foundries and shipbuilding plants on the tideflats before World War I. Belt Line buses hauled their last passengers in 1946, but the freight-switching operation, always the railroad's mainstay, continued.

The switching railroad on the tideflats has a history every bit as colorful as the city it serves. The Belt Line, known until 1925 as the Tacoma Municipal Street Railway, was the last streetcar line built in Tacoma. It remains the city's sole link to its days of electric trolleys and conductors.

The switching railroad on the tideflats has a history every bit as colorful as the city it serves.

Roots and rails

Water, not rails, was the burning issue of the day back in the 1880s. But in 1885, businessman Allen C. Mason dreamed of a street railway in Tacoma—mule or horse-driven trolleys from downtown Pacific Avenue out to Old Tacoma. But when he petitioned the City Council for a 30-year franchise, the Council sat on his request for six months, then turned him down because Tacoma simply "was not ready" for a street railway.

Two years later, in February 1887, a new, more progressive Council concluded that Tacoma was indeed ready for a streetcar system. In spite of Mayor Ira Town's misgivings (and his veto), the Council granted a 50-year street railway franchise to Nelson Bennett, well-known and respected businessman.

Bennett knew railroads—he and his brother had engineered and overseen construction of the Stampede Pass railroad tunnel through the Cascade Mountains, Bennett building himself quite a reputation on the strength of this feat. He incorporated the Tacoma Street Railway Company on January 19, 1887, with a capital stock of $250,000. Allen Mason was elected a trustee of Bennett's company.

Though he hoped to have the streetcar line operating by June, Bennett found his franchise too restrictive. He was barred from operating steam-powered engines—which were less costly than electric motors and faster than horses—because of the smoke and noise. Though railroad ties were distributed along the proposed route and rails ordered from Pennsylvania, work never got underway.

A horse-drawn Tacoma Street Railway car took its first run down Pacific Avenue on May 30, 1888. The bright yellow cars with upholstered seats were an immediate hit.

A man who bores through mountains is not likely to let a little bureaucracy stop him, and Bennett and Mason lobbied the Council for a second, less restrictive franchise. He demanded that the Council relax the company's assessed taxes and street-paving requirements and insisted they be allowed to use steam engines. Tacomans grew impatient. *The Tacoma Daily Ledger* followed the events closely and advocated any streetcar system other than "a bob-tail hoss cart." Mayor Town finally approved Bennett's and Mason's franchise on August 19, 1887.

The first run

After shipping delays and seemingly endless debate about what type of streetcar line the city should have, a horse-drawn Tacoma Street Railway car took its first run down Pacific Avenue on

May 30, 1888. The bright yellow cars with upholstered seats for 14 riders and "patent Slawson fare boxes" were an immediate hit. "The whole system worked like a charm," praised the *Ledger*, "and all day long the cars were kept crowded."

The streetcar line extended from the Northern Pacific Railroad passenger terminal on Pacific Avenue to McCarver Street in Old Town. Horse teams and one steam engine pulled the cars along their routes. The streetcars climbed Tacoma's steep terraces without "a single accident and not the slightest hitch."

Bennett's franchise opened the floodgates for other street railway entrepreneurs. The Council awarded four more franchises before Bennett's line was even built. Among those keen on getting a piece of the action were *Ledger* editor Randolph F. Radebaugh, prominent businessman and landowner George F. Orchard, Eben Pierce and Albert A. Honey. A streetcar franchise typical of those granted between 1888 and 1889 was George Browne's, who pioneered the Tacoma & Fern Hill Street Railway Company.

This line extended south from the city limits to the Oakes land addition, which Browne owned, then southwest towards Fern Hill. By providing streetcar service, he hoped to make settling outside city limits that much more appealing.

Rails for real estate

The routes extended primarily south and west of downtown Tacoma. Lines to Steilacoom, Wapato Park, Lake City and American Lake cropped up almost overnight. The same businessmen often involved themselves in multiple railway projects, though the streetcar lines were not a guaranteed financial success.

While the Council handed out franchises, Bennett decided to upgrade his system from horse-drawn cars and steam engines to electric trolleys. He contracted the Sprague Electric Railway & Motor Company of New York to supply cars, a power plant and other needed equipment. But not long after, Bennett sold the Tacoma Street Railway

Company franchise to a group of eastern businessmen. The investors were headed by none other than railroad tycoon Henry Villard, former president of the Northern Pacific Railroad.

Villard's new street railway, dubbed the Tacoma Railway & Motor Company, had several advantages over its competitors. Its capital base of nearly $500,000 allowed for rapid expansion and purchase of electric equipment and, thanks to Bennett's franchise, the company had exclusive rights to some of Tacoma's busiest streets.

Despite the fear of many Tacomans that their city was "moving too fast" in its quest for a "modern" transit system, Mayor Henry Drum approved the company's final franchise on September 30, 1890. The Tacoma Railway & Motor line was the first electric streetcar system in Tacoma.

The "trolley tycoons"

The Council continued its practice of granting franchise rights to local "trolley tycoons," though the Tacoma Railway & Motor Company grabbed most of the headlines. With the company's investment of $350,000, the newspaper boasted it was building "one of the most substantial and complete systems of street railways in the world."

The company built a trolley barn and electrical powerhouse at the foot of South 13th Street and by September 1889 had laid 13 miles of single and one mile of double track in Tacoma. On February 10, 1890, Car No. 11 of the Tacoma Railway & Motor Company rolled down Pacific Avenue on its inaugural run.

1890—the first electric streetcar system in Tacoma.

"Windows in the buildings along the avenue went up with a bang," said the *Ledger* enthusiastically. "Lunch rooms and restaurants were depopulated in a twinkling. Poker, pedro, and faro games were suspended in the midst of deals, chronic hobos left their favorite nooks . . . and proprietors of saloons were suddenly bereft of patrons."

The first electric trolleys in Tacoma truly captivated her citizens. With 11 electric streetcars serving the city by March 1890 and with so many new street railways under construction, Tacoma merchants and real estate brokers could not help but be optimistic. And why not? Tacoma was growing rapidly and, with rails radiating like spokes from its downtown hub, the city appeared on the verge of becoming a bustling commercial and industrial center.

A banner year

1890 was a banner year for streetcar lines in Tacoma. The Tacoma & Lake City Railroad Company and the Wapato Park Belt Line Railway Company laid rails from Tacoma's city limits to points many miles distant. The Point Defiance Railway Company, owned and financed by Allen Mason, was built in just 60 days. In his moment of triumph on a rainy March afternoon, Mason himself drove the silver spike that marked his line's completion.

The euphoria was short-lived. The Panic of 1893 devastated Tacoma real estate values—and many of the streetcar lines.

The boom-or-bust mentality was infectious. Scarcely three months after the Tacoma Railway & Motor Company began carrying passengers, its directors expanded service and bought 32 new cars. A year later the company added a steam and cable line that climbed the South 13th Street hill.

Streetcar lines followed new land additions. From the edge of town, riders could catch cars to Steilacoom, Puyallup, American Lake or Seattle. "Rapid transit" was the wave of the future, "enabling the people to accomplish in 25 years what could not have been done in a century without it."

The euphoria was short-lived. The nationwide Panic of 1893 devastated Tacoma real estate values—and many of the streetcar lines. The few trolley systems remaining in 1899 were ripe for the picking. In a 1927 report to the Council, City Engineer Kenneth G. Harlan wrote that the history of streetcar lines in Tacoma from 1887 to 1899 "reveals a story of financial vicissitudes augmented with numerous foreclosures and sheriff's sales."

Hard times

Harlan's assessment was especially true of the early 1890s. Even the Tacoma Railway & Motor Company, the largest and most stable of Tacoma's street railways, suffered during and after the Panic.

The line had swallowed up two smaller, less well-established street railways in 1889 and 1892 (the Tacoma Central Street Railway and the Tacoma & Steilacoom Street Railway, respectively), but failed to find any takers for its $1 million bond issue for construction proposed in 1890 and 1891.

In May 1892, T. R. & M. President Paul Schulze reported the bad news to the company's Board of Trustees: The streetcar line was "precariously" close to financial collapse. The company never fully recovered. As its financial fortunes waned, the street railway company changed hands at least four times before its sale to the newly incorporated Tacoma Railway & Power Company in 1899.

While the smaller street railways struggled to stay afloat in the 1890s, two companies took advantage of the turbulent financial conditions. The Pacific Traction Company (based in Maine) and the Tacoma Railway & Power Company (of New Jersey) eventually gained control of all the street railway lines operating in and around Tacoma.

Both companies eventually fell under the control and ownership of the New Jersey–based Puget Sound Electric Railway Company. The Tacoma Railway & Power Company was the direct predecessor of the Tacoma Municipal Belt Line Railway.

Belt Line beginnings

Representatives of the Tacoma Traction Company, the City Park Railway Company and the Tacoma Railways Company—the direct descendants of Tacoma's first trolley lines—signed the Tacoma

Railway & Power Company into existence in December 1898 and it incorporated shortly thereafter with a capital stock of $2 million and a $1.5 million bond issue. The owners of the three smaller street railway companies that combined to form the T. R. & P. line purchased more than two-thirds of the bond issue and with that transaction, the company was assured a virtual monopoly of Tacoma's street railway network.

Operations didn't always run smoothly—a serious derailment on July 4, 1900, claimed the lives of 43 riders.

Unlike its predecessors, the T. R. & P. Company endured, gradually expanding its holdings, applying for additional franchises and buying new rolling stock. The result, eventually, was a unified system of routes. Operations didn't always run smoothly—a serious derailment on July 4, 1900, claimed the lives of 43 riders—but the Tacoma Railway & Power Company provided far more efficient service than its forerunners. The streetcar routes covered most of Tacoma, with one exception: the tideflats.

Tacoma's tideflats, an area of marshy ground, tidal inlets and estuaries near the mouth of the Puyallup River, were virtually inaccessible to streetcar traffic in the early 1900s. Two national railroads, the Northern Pacific and the Union Pacific, maintained service to the handful of industries located on the tideflats. But trolley cars had not yet arrived.

That darned bridge

The biggest obstacle to streetcar companies wishing to serve the tideflats was the 11th Street bridge and a city ordinance requiring any street railway operating over the bridge to pay a 10-cent per car "user's fee" and to contribute to bridge upkeep and maintenance. The costs were prohibitive for most companies.

But the Tacoma Railway & Power Company found another way to extend its service to the tideflats industries, approaching the tideflats from the south, not the 11th Street bridge. Beginning at Tacoma's southeastern limits, the line proceeded from the intersection of Canal Street and St. Paul Avenue northwest along St. Paul to South 11th

Street. The T. R. & P. trolleys stopped short of the bridge, allowing riders to hoof it across the City Waterway to downtown Pacific Avenue, where they could catch other streetcars. This awkward, circuitous system of routes remained for the next 10 years.

By 1912, there was a clear need for a direct streetcar route from the city center to the new industries locating on the tideflats. Tacoma was in the midst of a pre-war population and industrial boom and farmers were settling east of town in greater and greater numbers.

The City Council, realizing it had to support the new industries and provide the workers with transportation, searched for alternatives to the decade-old route across the tideflats traveled by the Tacoma Railway & Power Company.

There had to be a better way.

WHITING

1909 - 1913

Tacoma Gets Its Act Together

4

City Water goes for the Green

With the Green River gravity line turned down by the voters, the Tacoma City Council found itself back at square one. It was still without a permanent source of water and the problem was going to get worse before it got better.

The next best two alternatives were both controversial—continue work on the well field or look to Maplewood Springs. At the urging of the special water committee, Commissioner Owen Woods approved the sinking of a new deep well. Later, six other new wells were authorized.

Meanwhile, the water situation was getting critical. Looking into claims that Galliher's Gulch was polluted, the councilmen were in for a rude shock, according to *The Tacoma Times*:

"All along the gulch the councilmen found a disgusting condition. Chicken yards, cesspools and a vault are contributing their germ-laden filth directly to the stream. . . ."

An unholy smell

The bottom of Hood Street Reservoir was coated with a "generous stratum of ooze, disease-laden and of an unholy smell." Some customers were drinking undiluted sewage. If the Clover Creek flume's condition was "negligence," the state of affairs at Galliher's Gulch was nothing less than criminal. The public was outraged and the *Times* blasted the Council:

(Facing page) The powerhouse at LaGrande on the Nisqually River—Tacoma's first hydro-electric project.

"For any councilman who has been in office for the last three or four years to say he did not know what the conditions are . . . is an acknowledgement that he is utterly unfit for the position and that he ought to resign and make room for somebody not quite so dense."

Stung by criticism, the Council created yet another committee to come up with a solution. In one three-hour meeting the committee—Councilmen Doud and Whitman and Mayor Wright—developed a long-range plan calling for turning off the gulch spigot once and for all, completing the six wells under contract and letting contracts for an 18-million-gallon supply from Maplewood Springs. In one meeting, the committee accomplished in hours what the Council could not do in several years.

More experimentation with wells seemed to pay handsome dividends.

The victory, however, was mostly smoke and mirrors. In the annual April election, the public ushered Mayor Wright out and in his place installed John Linck, a former police court judge—and a foe of the Maplewood Springs plan. Three days later a Tacoman by the name of F. L. Griffin obtained a court injunction halting the work, pending a review of funding "irregularities," and the project never again got off the ground.

Whitney to the rescue

As one of his first acts, Mayor Linck appointed Henry J. McGregor his Commissioner of Public Works, who quickly named Herbert A. Whitney, a local engineer, to the position of special engineer.

Whitney took off at a dead run and quickly developed a fan club. He tested the wells and found a number of irregularities—a performance that earned him full control of the Light and Water departments as the second superintendent in November 1908.

More experimentation with wells seemed to pay handsome dividends. Drilling Well No. 6 to a new depth of 216 feet produced a flow of 1.4 million gallons, compared to just 300,000 before. McGregor was ecstatic. After just a few short days of drilling—at a cost of only $500—he had a winner in Well No. 6. The water pressure tore the well cover off. Whitney and McGregor got similar results with other wells.

With the wells producing splendidly, Tacoma was running out of storage space. The Council approved plans for a second standpipe in the rapidly growing South Tacoma "suburb" of Fletcher Heights. And McGregor also received permission to enlarge the storage capacity at the Hood Street Reservoir and build a second basin for the Alaska Street Reservoir.

Whitney tosses a bomb

Though well development continued through 1909, the city was growing rapidly—by 50,000 in just a decade—and the Council was wise enough to realize that a water source two to three times the size of the well volume was needed.

Then, in May 1909, Superintendent Whitney tossed a bombshell into the Council's lap. Bypassing his boss, Commissioner McGregor, Whitney sent a letter directly to the Council telling them that the city must go to Maplewood Springs for its water and that the wells were slowly going dry.

Development at Maplewood Springs should never have stopped in the first place, said Whitney, leaving Mayor Linck and McGregor red-faced. Sparks flew. Linck, shrewd politician that he was, refused to get involved in the fight, leaving McGregor to explain Whitney's insubordination. Whitney, chastised but unrepentant, repeated his claim a month later.

The matter came to a head some months later when Councilman Dr. Johnson Armstrong, reporting on his independent investigation

McMillin takes shape. Reservoirs held only a few days' supply in the early years and more storage space was urgently needed. McMillin was the city's third reservoir.

of the wells, claimed the people of Tacoma had been "deliberately deceived" about the amount of water they produced.

True or not, the "findings" thoroughly discredited the wells and work there came to a screeching halt. The hunt was again on for another water source. At a December 13 meeting, the Council voted against a return to Maplewood Springs and then voted overwhelmingly to put the Green River gravity line on the ballot.

Back to the Green

This time, Tacoma approved the issue by a two-to-one margin. The people also approved a new commission form of government headed by Angelo V. Fawcett (mayor from 1896 to 1898). Gone were the 16 City Council members and with them much of the favoritism, partisanship and bickering that marked Tacoma's long quest for a permanent water supply.

In their place sat the mayor and four commissioners who controlled the various city departments, including light and water. Nicholas Lawson replaced McGregor as public works commissioner.

Almost as quickly as he fired Whitney, Lawson selected engineer John R. Preble to oversee construction of the gravity line from start to finish. He was aided by Assistant City Engineer James C. Manley and City Engineer Wilbur C. Raleigh.

The first business was to secure a right-of-way running along the Northern Pacific Railroad's tracks from the Green River intake to Buckley. The railroad was amiable, agreeing to let the city work within its right-of-way—at no cost—as long as a railroad inspector could oversee the work.

Getting under way

Bids on the first unit of the Green River gravity line were submitted on September 8, 1910. The first unit consisted of the intake, settling basin, drain and two tunnels at the headworks. The $66,000 contract for this work was let to the International Contract Company of Seattle, managed by Raphael X. Basford.

The pipeline builders fought injunctions, weather—and of course—the bureaucracy.

Seven weeks later, bids were called for the construction of McMillin Reservoir, the proposed 105-million-gallon receiving basin fed by the pipeline. McMillin Reservoir was equipped with a bypass line to convey water around the basins when they were being cleaned and a spillway to carry excess water into the Puyallup River.

George P. Wright, the former mayor now heading a construction company, won the contract for the wood pipeline between the headworks and McMillin Reservoir (Pipeline No. 1). Pipeline No. 2 from McMillin to the "J" Street standpipe was constructed by P. E. McHugh, while work on Pipeline No. 3, connecting the standpipe with the Hood Street and Alaska Street reservoirs, was conducted by the Water Department. Pipeline No. 1, by far the longest, ranged from 60 to 39 inches in diameter and was built of both wood and steel.

Work on the gravity system took two full years with hundreds of men employed by the several contractors. It was backbreaking, grueling work. Simply getting materials—including 60-inch pipe—

43 miles from Tacoma was a Herculean task. Several miles of roadway had to be hacked through timber and brush. When there were no railway or logging tracks, equipment was hauled by brute strength.

The pipeline crossed two rivers, the White and the Puyallup. It hugged the contours of the land, descending from 900 to 100 feet above sea level. McMillin Reservoir was eight times larger than Hood Street Reservoir—its two basins covered 16 acres. It was an enormous project with an immense cost—$2.25 million.

Running battles

Along the way toward completion, the pipeline builders fought injunctions from nearby landowners, the weather and—of course—the bureaucracy.

As the pipeline neared completion, a controversy erupted over whether the city should turn the river water into city mains before a hypochlorite water purification plant was built at the headworks. Mayor William W. Seymour wanted to be doubly safe about the water's purity before serving it to the public. But Commissioner Lawson ignored him, turning Green River water into the "J" Street standpipe on May 29, 1913.

The immense water pressure literally blew to pieces the waste-water pipe in the standpipe, knocking it out of commission and seriously undermining Tacoma's water supply for several days. After a second explosion, the standpipe was again put into service and finally, on July 12, 1913, all the water valves in Tacoma were fully opened and Green River water—42 million gallons a day—flowed into Tacoma.

Tacoma had its permanent water supply at last. A decade of well development marked by political corruption, incompetence, wastefulness and botched schemes was behind the city. At the time, the construction of the Green River gravity line was the single largest municipal project in the city's 40-year history.

Diversion dam for the Nisqually hydroelectric plant at LaGrande, about 36 miles southeast of Tacoma. Alder Dam is 2.5 miles upstream.

The gravity line remains the core of Tacoma's water system. With its completion, the Water Department could breathe a huge sigh of satisfaction and relief.

Light Department harnesses the Nisqually

Meanwhile, the Light Department was working on its own mammoth project—the Nisqually Hydroelectric Project.

The divisive election of 1909 had come and gone. The combatants were licking their wounds and gradually pulling together behind the $2 million project.

The *Times* called the election a victory freeing Tacoma from the grip of special interests, proclaiming that the city, with its own electrical supply, could now begin building toward commercial greatness. Councilmen Wilkeson and Doud said they would now do everything they could to see the city power project to a successful conclusion.

The Light Department wasted no time choosing Frank C. Kelsey to supervise construction. Kelsey went to work immediately, outlining a five-phase plan that included surveying, condemnation procedures,

A 1,300-foot-long settling channel removes glacial grit before water enters 2.5 miles of tunnels feeding the LaGrande powerhouse.

litigation, selection of the construction engineer and development of the plans.

Power from LaGrande

Actual construction began in February 1910 at LaGrande, Washington, about 36 miles southeast of Tacoma where the Nisqually is fed by five Mt. Rainier glaciers—Nisqually, Paradise, North Tahoma, Kautz and Van Trump.

The project was an engineering marvel with hundreds of men battling the elements, a capricious wild river and the limitations imposed by tools primitive by today's standards. The completed project, as described by R. H. Richards, an electrical engineer on the project, included a 225-foot diversion dam rising 35 feet above

Inside the Nisqually powerhouse. Work began on the Nisqually Project in early 1910 and was completed in August 1912, at a cost of $2.4 million.

the river. Water captured by the dam was routed into a 1,300-foot settling channel, which removed silt from the water. It then ran through a tunnel more than two miles long blasted through solid rock.

Emerging from the tunnel, the water was carried by a 540-foot pipe across the river, into a second 1,200-foot tunnel and into the powerhouse reservoir, which held 3.2 million gallons—approximately one day's operating reserve.

Penstocks supplying water to the generators. The new hydro project brought rates as low as one cent per kilowatt-hour.

Power to the people

Next, four large pipes—called penstocks—five feet wide at the entrance carried water to the powerhouse 410 feet below the reservoir. Inside the powerhouse stood four sets of Allis-Chalmers turbines and generators, each generating 8,000 horsepower.

Nisqually power was first "stepped-up" by General Electric transformers to 60,000 volts for transmission to Tacoma's Nisqually Substation at South 25th and "C" streets. The 36-mile transmission system consisted of two parallel aluminum lines 50 feet apart. Each line was supported by cedar poles 175 feet apart.

On November 6, 1912, Tacoma's brand new, state-of-the-art hydroelectric project went on line and began furnishing power to the people of Tacoma.

Cooperation—amazing but true

Perhaps even more amazing than the construction feat was the fact that the project was completed exactly as specified in the original plans, on time and on budget—even though three sets of elected officials and three sets of engineers were in charge of construction.

Tacoma had taken a bold and visionary step and freed itself from the grip of the private power interests. It also assumed an obligation —to anticipate and meet the city's growing demand for power.

The Nisqually hydro project was to be only a short-lived solution. Ahead were years of what became a familiar cycle—promoting the use of electricity for all sorts of modern conveniences, shortages, building more generating capacity, and again promoting load growth.

But in 1913 everything was rosy. The city's demand was 20.4 million kilowatt-hours per year and the Nisqually hydro project was supplying all of it.

State-of-the-art in 1912. The Nisqually transmission system—two parallel aluminum lines carrying 60,000 volts.

(Facing page) The LaGrande powerhouse. Completed on time and on budget, the Nisqually Project freed Tacoma from the grip of private power interests.

STORAGE
HOTE STOTHART
B.H.KENNEDY CO.
PLEASE DO NOT PARK HERE
NO PARKING
34-T.

1912-1923

THE BELT LINE GETS OFF TO A SHAKY START

5

"The city cannot lose any way you look at it," said Commissioner of Public Works Owen Woods on August 12, 1912, of a proposed streetcar system serving Tacoma's tideflats. Woods and City Engineer Wilbur C. Raleigh had announced the idea to the public just two days earlier. His crystal ball may have been a little cloudy that day because the city was about to discover that it was possible to lose a great deal of money running a railroad.

The city was about to discover that it was possible to lose a great deal of money running a railroad.

But it seemed a worthwhile project—a trolley line across the South 11th Street bridge, from downtown Pacific Avenue to the Puyallup River or beyond, was bound to benefit the 3,000 tideflats industrial workers and might even prove a lucrative source of new revenue.

Since receiving its 1904 franchise to serve the tideflats, the Tacoma Railway & Power Company had not tried to expand service in that area. The most direct route to the St. Paul & Tacoma Lumber Company and Chicago, Milwaukee & Puget Sound (later St. Paul) Railroad car shops remained the 11th Street bridge, but no private railway would cross it.

The Tacoma Railway & Power Company, asked by the Council to operate a line over the bridge, balked. It would be an expensive, risky undertaking—estimates for 1.25 miles of single track, four streetcars, transformer and car barn topped $87,000.

The Council increased the heat on the Tacoma Railway & Power Company with City Commissioner Adelbert U. Mills criticizing the company for its lack of "pioneering" spirit. But by December 1912,

(Facing page) 8th and Broadway in the early 1920s. World War I brought a promising freight operation for the Belt Line. But with a floundering passenger service, the line was mired in debt.

even Woods had toned down his optimism about the line's potential. Still, he ordered streetcar rail laid across the bridge. "There is bound to be car service over the bridge some time," Woods noted, "and the city is just preparing for it. . . ."

Perhaps—but when? And who would provide it? Aside from the peak morning and evening rush hours, when the workers trudged to and from the mill and railroad car shops, there simply wasn't enough traffic to the tideflats to support 'round-the-clock streetcar service. Nor could the city afford the estimated $87,000 expense to lay track to the tideflats industries. Tacoma was already carrying a bonded indebtedness of nearly $12 million—much of it from Light Department and Water Department bond issues.

Voters approved a future tideflats streetcar line by a paper-thin margin of 22 votes.

The heat is on

The Council did agree, however, to let the voters decide whether the city should build and operate the streetcar line. And, hedging its bets, it also entered eleventh-hour talks with the Tacoma Railway & Power Company aimed at the company taking over the tideflats service. Both were failures.

The meetings produced no results and in a light turnout, voters rejected the proposed $87,000 bond issue by a healthy majority. But the idea of the city building a line in the future passed by a paper-thin margin of 22 votes.

The Council and Mayor William Seymour headed back to the drawing board. They didn't have long to wait before Tacoma Railway & Power officials came forward with an offer, but the talks bogged down.

Both sides began to take flak from city residents, and tideflats employees were clamoring for improved service. In 1913, the impasse seemed broken—just days before another election called to decide, once and for all, if the city wanted to pay $87,000 for its own street railway system.

But then the City Council reneged, scuttling the deal. The voters were no help, either, with a majority in favor of the city issuing $87,000 in municipal bonds to fund the streetcar line—but not the necessary three-fifths required to approve the measure.

Down a new track

Undaunted, the Council took a different tack. So far, discussions between the Council and company (ongoing for more than a year) had centered on one side or the other building and operating the streetcar line independently. In January 1914, the Council raised the idea of the city building the line and the Tacoma Railway & Power Company running the streetcars over municipal track.

Both sides sat down at the bargaining table again in February with a breakthrough coming, finally, on February 9, 1914. Under the agreement, the city would construct the railway for $35,000 and the company would supply the streetcars and conductors, operating the line as an extension of its regular routes.

Transfers between inter-city and tideflats routes would not cost extra and the Tacoma Railway & Power Company agreed to connect its St. Paul Avenue line with the South 11th Street extension. The company was guaranteed a six percent return on its investment and the city four percent, with additional profits to be split evenly. Finally, the city freed the company of its obligation for upkeep on the 11th Street bridge. The partnership would remain in effect seven and a half years.

Department of Public Works employees broke ground on the streetcar line in August and completion was promised by January 1, 1915. As the first steel rails were being laid, war erupted in Europe.

The inaugural run of the first tideflats streetcar was conducted January 10. An electric trolley filled with the Mayor, City Council members and other dignitaries sailed over the new rails. The single-track line originated at Pacific Avenue and South 11th Street, running east across the 11th Street bridge, crossed the Puyallup River and terminated at the Chicago, Milwaukee & St. Paul Railroad car shops—a distance of 1.25 miles.

The track connected with the Tacoma Railway & Power Company line at St. Paul Avenue and Canal Street, forming a triangular circuit. When the line was opened to the public the next day, 1,000 curious riders boarded the streetcars for a ride around the tideflats.

Dwindling income

But once the initial excitement waned, so did tideflats streetcar line income. Less than three months after the municipal line was launched, it began to lose money. Tacoma Railway & Power Company Manager Louis Bean announced in mid-March that daily receipts were totalling less than $30—not enough to pay salaries, much less operating costs. As the weather improved, many workers opted to resume walking to the mills rather than pay the five-cent trolley fare.

The inaugural run of the first tideflats streetcar line was conducted January 10, 1915.

The financial outlook was decidedly gloomy. In its first year, the tideflats streetcar line recorded a net deficit of more than $4,000. Business picked up a little in 1916, as new industries moved to the tideflats and old ones expanded operations. The municipal line posted a net profit in 1916, finishing the year $1,026.58 in the black. The Tacoma Power & Railway Company as a whole suffered, however, and struggled to stay afloat financially.

The war in Europe was the focus of everyone's attention in late 1916. The nation began gearing up for war and Tacoma soon learned that three large shipbuilding companies would be locating on the tide-flats. The Todd Drydock and Shipbuilding Corporation, the biggest of the three new arrivals, announced it would buy 100 acres of tideflats land in December 1916. Along with the Foundation and Seaborn companies, the Todd Shipyards were expected to bring 4,000 workers to the tideflats. All would need transportation.

Bustling tideflats

During the spring of 1917, with construction of the shipbuilding plants underway, the tideflats bustled with activity. The hundreds of workers running about evoked "a scene . . . such as has not been witnessed on the eastern portion of the tideflats for several years," according to the *Daily Ledger*.

The Todd Drydock Corporation acquired the land for its plant between the Wapato and Hylebos Creek waterways, 1.3 miles beyond the reach of the tideflats streetcar line. The Foundation Company shipyard located just south of its competitor.

Track had to be extended to the new businesses—not an easy matter for a financially strapped fledgling railway. Ultimately, the Tacoma Railway & Power Company opted to leave operation of the entire tideflats circuit (including the proposed Todd plant spur) to the city. Their two-year partnership ended May 17, 1917, six weeks after the United States declared war on Germany. But both parties left the door open for future collaboration.

Now, the Council had track to build. The new extension to the Todd and Foundation shipyards stretched along 11th Street east to Alexander Avenue. The total distance between the 11th Street bridge and shipyards was slightly more than 2.5 miles.

To fund the track extension and purchase ties, rails, trolley wire and 10 additional streetcars, the Council approved a $180,000 utility bond issue. But banking houses refused to touch the utility bonds—the street railway's mediocre financial returns guaranteed that—so the Council directed City Light to purchase the entire issue with money from its general fund.

The financial outlook was decidedly gloomy. In its first year, the streetcar line lost more than $4,000.

The city lays track

Meanwhile, the Council called for bids on the rails, ties and streetcars and work began in late August 1917. The extension was constructed by day laborers under the direction of Commissioner of Public Works Charles D. Atkins, who promised an operational line to the shipyards by October 1. Part of the task involved constructing a wooden trestle over the Chicago, Milwaukee & St. Paul Railroad shops. A force of 200 workers was hired to build the trestle and lay rails.

They worked at breakneck speed to beat the October 1 deadline, according to the *Daily Ledger*: "Commissioner C. D. Atkins has been camping on the job most of the time, being on hand at 7 o'clock in the morning and keeping closely in touch with the work day by day. City Engineer L. South Nicholson and his staff have been working

Banking houses refused to touch the utility bonds—the street railway's mediocre financial returns guaranteed that—so the Council directed City Light to purchase the entire issue.

day and night, and the crew of 110 men have been working 10 hours a day, including Sundays."

Construction of the single-track line was hampered by a scarcity of steel and bridge timbers, though, and Atkins failed to meet the October 1 deadline. But he was successful in securing streetcar cars and trailers for a very low price, traveling to Salt Lake City to purchase four electric streetcars, four trailers and an electric locomotive.

The 240-horsepower locomotive could pull as many as 15 loaded cars. The streetcars, with their equally strong motors, were "geared to make 40 miles an hour."

October 1 arrived. Though the Milwaukee Railroad viaduct was not yet complete, Mayor Angelo V. Fawcett went through with the inaugural run as planned. Loaded with city officials, the first of two cars departed Pacific Avenue at 5 o'clock in the afternoon.

The inaugural ride

"Two cars, with glossy paint of orange and black, made the first official run over the city's new tideflats extension line . . . with the mayor as conductor on one. . . . From the stained glass windows of the new cars to their grand cane seats, they were all dressed up for the occasion," said a report of the event.

"Two cars, with glossy paint of orange and black, made the first official run over the new tideflats extension line. . . with the mayor as conductor on one."

The fare was five cents and payment was on the "honor system." The street railway was hailed as an "honest man's car line," a feature that proved its undoing almost immediately.

Mayor Fawcett's triumph didn't last long. The Council reopened negotiations with the Tacoma Railway & Power Company mere days after the mayor's much-proclaimed ride across the tideflats—though it isn't clear why.

Commissioner Atkins may have felt the Department of Public Works wasn't ready to handle the thousands of expected riders, or didn't have the financial resources to hire additional conductors and pay for future extensions to the line. In any case, after a month of deliberations, a two-year contract made the city and the Tacoma Railway & Power Company partners—the second time in three years.

Under the contract the city promised to "save the Company harmless from all claims of every kind and description," including fire, strikes and lockouts, faulty construction and "Acts of God." The city would provide the streetcars and pay the company twice monthly for all expenses incurred.

The company only had to provide the conductors, barns to house and repair the streetcars and electric current (for which it was reimbursed). The City Council was to turn all monthly earnings over to the company, theoretically insuring it against loss.

A flood of riders

Meanwhile, the U.S. war mobilization effort was gaining speed in the closing weeks of 1917. The call for ships by the United States Shipping Board intensified and thousands of new workers flooded the tideflats. It was simply more than the small municipal street railway could handle.

The Todd Shipyards railway extension was finished in late October, but 1,000 workers still relied on chartered ferries to transport them to and from work. Atkins promised to improve service. An emergency Council session authorized $30,000 from the City Light reserve fund for 10 more streetcars.

Along with the new cars, the city added new trackage on Taylor Way. But the improvements did little to alleviate the daily stampede at the shipyards. With all 18 cars in operation, the street railway could safely handle only about 4,000 riders a day—one-third of the 12,000 workers employed on the tideflats.

With all 18 cars in operation, the street railway could safely handle only about one-third of the 12,000 tideflats workers. The men hopped on any car and literally hung from the roofs and out the windows.

The men hopped any car they could and literally hung from the roofs and out the windows. Injuries were common. In March 1918, a Foundation Shipyard employee fell under the wheels of a municipal streetcar car and lost both legs. Four months later, a Todd worker was killed by a switching engine. The riders dirtied the cars, pushed, shoved and, in at least one instance, kicked out a window—sash and all.

To make matters worse, the workers weren't paying the fare. The "honest man's car line" idea was a financial failure and the tideflats street railway finished the year with a loss of $7,400. Tacoma Railway & Power Company Manager Louis Bean appealed to the city for help, which responded by proposing to buy the entire company for $6.5 million, an idea soundly rejected by Tacomans at the polls in 1918.

Federal help

In desperation the city turned to the federal government. The Emergency Fleet Corporation (EFC), a branch of the United States Shipping Board, offered the best possible chance that Tacoma would finally unravel its tangled web of streetcar problems.

In a nine-page proposal, the Council outlined the history of the tideflats street railway and provided a rough outline of its equipment and financial status. In all, the Council applied for $1 million in federal aid for improvements. The EFC advanced Tacoma only $232,400 to double-track the existing line, purchase new cars and build a "pre-pay" and loading station at South 10th Street.

The money was disbursed by the EFC through an open, rolling account, with the city drawing money only as needed. The EFC signed the contract with the Council for the loan on September 11, 1918. The first installment, $50,000, arrived one month later.

Almost immediately, City Engineer James C. Manley began laying out the track improvements, working under H. Roy Harrison, Charles Atkins' replacement as Commissioner of Public Works.

The tideflats streetcar line suffered a net loss of $13,725 in 1918.

Ten more streetcars, purchased with the loan, arrived in December 1918, making a total of 38 municipal streetcars working the tideflats. Things began looking up for the street railway. The Foundation and Todd shipyards agreed to stagger their work shifts, allowing for less crowded and better trolley service.

But despite this new, rosy glow, the Tacoma Railway & Power Company couldn't afford its partnership with the city and operate its other, more established routes. The tideflats streetcar line had suffered a net loss of $13,725 in 1918—more than the company could stand. So Louis Bean turned operation over to the city and all contracts between the City of Tacoma and the Tacoma Railway & Power Company governing the tideflats route were canceled. Only the system of transfer arrangements was kept intact.

City-owned and operated

Control of the municipal line passed to Commissioner of Public Works H. Roy Harrison on January 1, 1919. The tideflats street railway was officially a city-owned and operated enterprise. The *Daily Ledger* boasted that the city would "endeavor to beat the Railway & Power Company at the game of making a streetcar line pay." Within weeks, the *Ledger's* boast would ring hollow.

Harrison appointed new management and hired 100 new employees to fill positions vacated by Tacoma Railway & Power Company and municipal service began January 2, 1919. The day was marked by a new operating schedule, new conductors and added streetcar crews.

One of the biggest problems was the inability of conductors to collect fares from the riders. Only one-third were paying.

The street railway had a new face, but the same old problems remained. The Department of Public Works had not finished double-tracking the line, nor was the pre-pay and loading station at South 10th Street constructed. Conditions on the cars remained crowded, dirty and noisy. Two days after the city began service, angry shipyard workers stoned the municipal streetcar cars on their way home from work.

One of the biggest problems still was the inability of streetcar conductors to collect fares from the workers. Only one-third were paying. The rest were inaccessible on the roofs and sidings or simply jumped off the car when it slowed.

To make matters worse, the Public Works Department didn't have the capital to repair its streetcars. Old and dilapidated motors in some of the secondhand cars idled one-fourth of the fleet. Commissioner Harrison was forced to petition the EFC for a $36,000 advance in order to purchase 10 new motors. A general shipyards strike in early February cut even deeper into revenues.

A serious condition

The freight-switching arm of the municipal line was the sole bright spot in an otherwise dismal year. Between 1918 and 1919, switching revenues topped $41,000.

Each month brought greater deficits with the situation reaching a critical stage in June 1919. Commissioner of Finance Fred Shoemaker wrote an anxious memorandum to Mayor Crocker M. Riddell on June 10, describing the "serious financial condition" of the municipal street railway. Why was the street railway in such dire straits after just six months of municipal ownership?

Shoemaker attributed the problem to the railway's bloated payroll, which by his calculations gobbled up 87 percent of the gross earnings. The large payroll arose from the city adding 25 cars to the morning and evening rush hours. The 50 additional conductors and operators were paid a full day's wages (stipulated by union contracts) for only a few hours' work.

Generally, Shoemaker was right. But the root cause of the rampant indebtedness was the city's contract with the EFC, drawn up two months before the end of hostilities in Europe. With the war over, there were fewer shipyard workers and strikes on the tideflats increased in both duration and frequency.

In September 1918, double-tracking the line and adding crews to the route were needed adjustments. With a peace-time economy, the demands on the municipal line lessened—but it was still operating in a war-time mode eight months after the war ended.

The freight-switching arm of the municipal line was the sole bright spot in an otherwise dismal year. Between 1918 and 1919, switching revenues topped $41,000.

"A wild bull by the tail"

Meanwhile, the municipal street railway experienced a net loss of $72,234 in 1919, bringing its three-year deficit to more than $108,000. The city failed to meet its first $40,000 loan payment to the EFC and Finance Commissioner Shoemaker asked the agency "if some steps cannot be taken for relieving the city of the burden with which we find ourselves saddled." Almost pleading, he added, "We are like the man who had a wild bull by the tail and didn't know how to let go."

The deficit was so great in 1919 that $74,000 had to be withdrawn from the city's general fund and from other departments just to meet operating costs. Designed to be self-supporting, the street railway was not covered in the budget of any city department.

What started as a supplement to the passenger line had in four short years outstripped the city's expectations.

Clearly it was a burden to the Department of Public Works. Nobody could make the municipal line pay.

City officials spent much of the next four years tightening the street railway's belt and imploring the EFC to cancel its $232,400 loan. The EFC eventually sued Tacoma and while the case languished in federal court, the municipal street railway languished in debt.

The street railway also was weakened by its lack of a contract governing its freight-switching service to the Port of Tacoma, tideflats industries and national carriers. By 1922 the city was switching and spotting cars from all four national carriers (the Northern Pacific, Oregon-Washington, Great Northern, and Chicago, Milwaukee & St. Paul railroads) at $5 per car. Monthly switching revenues fluctuated considerably—much of it from hauling flat cars piled with logs to the Buffelen lumber mill on Taylor Way.

Problems cropped up from time to time. The city clashed with the national carriers on such issues as demurrage (whether or not the street railway should be responsible for cars left idle on the sidings for extended lengths of time), freight priority on tracks used in common by all the lines and franchise rights to streets not yet tracked.

Lincoln Avenue, a major east-west arterial across the tideflats parallel to 11th Street, was one such contested street. In the spring of 1922, the Northern Pacific Railroad won a franchise and contract to lay track along Lincoln Avenue (for common use by all the railroads), completing a rail loop around the tideflats that encompassed Taylor Way, 11th Street, St. Paul Avenue and Lincoln Avenue.

Freight bears fruit

Thanks to the track loop and the joint efforts of Tacoma and Pierce County, the tideflats industrial district was opened for development in the early 1920s. The city's switching service between the Port of Tacoma, tideflats industries and national railroads, however, was disjointed and inefficient.

What started in October 1918 as a supplement to the passenger line had in four short years outstripped the city's expectations. The city applied for and received a franchise from Pierce County to lay track across the Hylebos Waterway to East Side Drive County Road and investigated expanding its switching operation to the eastern edge of the tideflats.

In August 1923 the municipal street railway was at a crossroads. Its suit with the EFC was underway and would have a major impact on its financial stability. While the switching service had unrealized potential, it also risked being outmaneuvered and rendered obsolete by the national trunk railroads.

What would the future hold? Would the four-year-old municipal car line continue its downward spiral? Or would it finally achieve stability—perhaps even growth?

1 9 1 3 - 1 9 2 9

Give Us Water, Give Us Light—Now!

6

City Water: Progress and hard times

The Green River pipeline, rushed to completion, wasn't a cure-all for Tacoma's water problems. Pipeline contractors slapped City Water with suits for extra work and all won their lawsuits, putting City Water in a severe financial crunch. The department was criticized for failing to maintain its auxiliary supply, and the Alaska Street Reservoir needed extensive repairs.

And even with its new state-of-the-art Green River pipeline, water purity continued to be a nagging problem. The primary problem was people living in the watershed—lumber camps, the town of Lester and a mineral springs spa.

City Water's inspectors had the authority to arrest and fine trespassers and did so regularly. But it couldn't arrest those living and doing business in the watershed. City Water bought some of the lumber mills and encouraged others to begin sanitation measures. A handful refused to relocate or to install cement privy vaults and there was even one violent incident—a melee between disgruntled loggers of the Page Lumber Company and City Water employees.

Usually, however, moral persuasion worked—the Northern Pacific Railroad, for example, quickly began a "no dumping" policy while trains crossed the watershed.

But water purity was a problem that wouldn't go away quickly. In 1919 an investigation of the watershed by members of the Tacoma Commercial Club, followed by a City Water survey, found "shocking" conditions at the town of Lester and several logging camps. Toilets,

(Facing page)
Hard work.
The 1920s were lean years for City Water, with the poor condition of its facilities a nagging problem. Here a 1923 crew rebuilds the overflow main from the Alaska Street Reservoir.

The "Father of City Water," Willibald A. Kunigk, superintendent from 1917 to 1940.

hog pens and refuse piles, all on low ground and subject to flooding, were a health threat—bad enough that city bacteriologist Dr. Kenneth J. Staniford thought the gravity line should be abandoned.

Quality improves

Instead, City Water installed two additional chlorination plants to go with the existing plant at the headworks. Despite the purity problems, the quality of Tacoma water improved significantly, with typhoid deaths dropping from 12.5 per 100,000 residents in 1913 to 2.1 in 1919. City Water's ability to protect the watershed also improved as it, not the health department, became the responsible department.

Meanwhile, Commissioner of Light and Water Hamilton F. Gronen, a utility veteran, began improving operations and putting

City Water on a sound business footing. He pared the number of utility employees and imposed a flat five percent gross earnings tax on City Water's yearly income.

As the war in Europe gradually drew the U.S. further and further into the conflict, Gronen also aggressively pushed water main construction and extensions to the booming tideflats war industries. At the height of American mobilization in 1917, City Water extended 16- and 12-inch water mains to Tacoma's easternmost limits to serve the Todd and Foundation shipbuilding companies.

Gronen also came smack up against another thorny problem—the water wastefulness of its citizens. At the time, Tacomans used an average of up to 400 gallons a day, compared to 100 gallons a day in New York, Chicago and Philadelphia. Though the city's

With the luxury of a flat rate for water, many homeowners abused the privilege.

many lumber mills were part of the problem, the real culprits were residential customers.

With the luxury of a flat rate, no matter how much used, many homeowners abused the privilege—watering gardens and lawns incessantly, leaving hoses on 24 hours a day and wasting water with leaky faucets. With the new Green River pipeline, Tacoma apparently thought it had an inexhaustible source.

Installing water meters was the obvious answer—Seattle, Portland and Spokane had already done so—but it was a prickly problem, opposed by the public and sure to be a glaring liability when election time rolled around. As a result, the problem hung around and meters were not installed for three decades.

Towering figures

At about this time, two towering figures stepped forward to guide Tacoma's utilities. The first was a new City Water superintendent—Willibald A. Kunigk. Appointed to replace Henry J. McGregor, Kunigk was a 38-year-old German immigrant who went to work for Tacoma City Water in 1911 as a draftsman on the Green River line and quickly worked his way up through the ranks.

In the entire history of City Water, no man would have greater influence on the growth, expansion and conduct of the department. The second giant was Ira S. Davisson, Public Utilities Commissioner from 1918 to 1940. Stern, straitlaced and somewhat autocratic,

Ira S. Davisson, a towering figure in Tacoma history—Public Utilities Commissioner from 1918 to 1940.

Davisson had both passionate critics and ardent admirers. But he was a man right for the times, a "take charge" commissioner who grabbed the reins and took off at a gallop.

Davisson recalls his start this way: "Early in November 1918, I received a call from Crocker M. Riddell, then mayor of Tacoma, requesting me to report at his office in the city hall the following morning at 9 o'clock. I was there at the stated time and was advised the commissioner of light and water [Gronen] had resigned and I had been appointed to fill the unexpired term. Would I accept the appointment? I inquired under what condition was this appointment made. His reply: 'That you make good.'

"After some thought and advice my answer was 'Yes, under that condition I will give the work the best I have in me.'"

. . . the same vexing problems—impure water, consumer wastefulness and hazards to the gravity line.

Davisson and Kunigk soon found themselves tackling the same vexing problems as their predecessors—impure water, consumer wastefulness and hazards to the gravity line.

Lean years

The early 1920s were lean years for City Water, though Davisson did find enough money to buy 10 new automobiles for City Light and City Water—viewed as extravagant by the City Council—and build a new, $100,000, two-story central shop and warehouse, completed in 1922. It replaced four ramshackle storage buildings in use since 1893.

Meanwhile, Tacoma's Green River gravity line was aging. The untreated wood was already showing signs of wear and by the summer of 1920, roughly 1,800 feet of pipe needed replacing. There were so

Getting modern. The '20s were lean years, but Davisson found $100,000 to build this shop and warehouse in 1922. The automobiles were considered extravagant.

many breaks in the line Kunigk was forced to work repair crews around the clock.

Kunigk not only faced cash shortages, but public opposition to replacing deteriorating wood mains. When City Water tried to dig up a street to replace a 20-year-old, 30-inch wood main in South Tacoma, it met stubborn public opposition. The public attitude seemed to be that if they couldn't see a problem, there was no problem.

City Water was also concerned about the condition of its Green River pipeline, which was suffering an increasing number of breaks. Following an extensive survey of the 43-mile line, Kunigk laid out a $1.9 million, 12-year reconstruction plan. Funding was not available until 1923, when City Water began the arduous task of replacing the untreated wood in the line with steel, concrete and creosoted wood pipe reinforced with iron bands.

Replacing the pipe was a slow and delicate process, with the new section of pipe laid parallel to the old and then connected to the main line. It was carried out with an air of urgency, as the reservoirs held only enough water to last a few days without resupply from the pipeline. Using day labor, the City Water contractor laid about 2.5 miles of the new 39- and 46-inch pipe in 1924.

Strategic planning

Davisson and Kunigk also tackled the water storage problem that year. Following his successful re-election as Commissioner of Light and Water, Davisson oversaw the purchase of a 27-acre site for a third storage basin near McMillin Reservoir.

The two were just getting warmed up. In 1925 they mapped a strategy for supplying Tacoma with enough water to meet two decades of growth—a $3 million plan calling for increased reservoir storage and extended service to the tideflats, now booming with growth and requiring millions of gallons of pure water every day.

First, however, Tacoma needed to eliminate its competing water companies—notably the Tacoma Water Supply Company. Dating back to 1890, the company still relied on the copious springs in Mason's Gulch (bounded by North 39th and North 40th streets, Mason Avenue and Proctor Street) and served some 2,300 customers in Tacoma and Ruston.

After three separate appraisals to establish a price, Davisson began negotiations. Tacoma Water Supply, represented by Coler Campbell, asked $195,000—which Davisson rejected as "entirely too high." The deadlock continued through January 1926 when Davisson threatened to pursue condemnation proceedings.

With the expiration of his franchise, Campbell saw the handwriting on the wall and sold to City Water for $150,000. Later, City Water also acquired a small, independent water system in Old Tacoma for $2,500.

Oops!

Poor weather—and mishaps—delayed completion of the new North End Reservoir until 1927.

The master plan

Even while the wheels were in motion for this consolidation, Kunigk and Davisson launched the preliminary stages of their "master plan" for City Water's future expansion. It hinged on the issuance of $1 million of utility bonds to build a new 25-million-gallon North End Reservoir, a 1.3-million-gallon standpipe and 10-million-gallon capacity pump adjacent to the reservoir, a spillway pipe from the reservoir to Puget Sound and a steel water line connecting the "J" Street standpipe and the new reservoir.

It was an ambitious plan and the new reservoir got the top priority. Work started in 1926 on a 15-acre site near North 32nd

The 25-million-gallon North End Reservoir under construction in 1926, part of Davisson's and Kunigk's master plan.

and Shirley streets, but poor weather slowed construction and delayed completion until 1927. Meanwhile, work continued on other fronts, fueled by the $1 million bond issue, with quick progress on the new standpipe, trunk main extensions and extensive Local Improvement District (LID) work.

By now, Davisson and Kunigk had the bit in their teeth. Barely a year after springing their $1 million scheme on the City Council, they unveiled the second half of their "master plan"—a new, plentiful supply of water to serve the booming industries of the tideflats.

The area was short of water and it was hampering Tacoma's growth. Industries seeking to locate there had long clamored for cheaper, more adequate water service. City Water responded by creating new, lower industrial rates, but that was only part of the

To lure new business to Tacoma, the utility needed millions of gallons of water it didn't have.

answer—the utility needed to supply millions of gallons of water it didn't have to lure new business to Tacoma.

Wood products companies, especially, needed cheap, plentiful water. The problems were mounting. In 1926, the San Juan Pulp Manufacturing Company was looking at the tideflats as a home for a new mill, but hesitated to commit itself because of the water rates.

Another businessman looking for a paper mill site wrote to Mayor Melvin Tennent saying: "My first choice . . . was Tacoma, however upon closer investigation I found that there is not a sufficient quantity of pure, fresh water available. . . ."

Hunting for a new source

Pushed by the Chamber of Commerce, City Water explored nearby alternate sources—Maplewood Springs, Hylebos and Clear creeks and the Puyallup River. All were either too expensive or would take too long to develop.

The only remedy was another well, and the N. C. Jannsen Company of Seattle was hired to drill one capable of supplying at least one million gallons a day. Though a disappointment, the 776-foot, $28,000 well did eventually produce an average of one million gallons a day, but it was clearly a stopgap to keep from losing the pulp mill.

Meanwhile, a survey party under Chief Utilities Engineer Jay Stannard was scouting Pierce County for other water sources. It came back with a litany of now-familiar names—Maplewood Springs and Clear Creek, Clark's Creek (a tributary of Maplewood Springs), the Mashell River, Kapowsin Creek and Kapowsin Lake and several sites on the Puyallup River.

Davisson, Kunigk and Stannard decided on the Puyallup River and Lake Kapowsin as Tacoma's "second source"—a supply capable of delivering four times the water of the Green River.

An enormous project

The project would be enormous, a gravity pipeline costing a minimum of $2 million. But it took the City Council just 15 minutes at its January 26, 1927, meeting to approve the Kapowsin pipeline.

Searching for an additional water supply, City Water drilled another well—a temporary solution.

It was all downhill from there, however. Though the state supervisor of hydraulics approved the pipeline, Kapowsin residents and businesses—which would be submerged—bitterly fought condemnation proceedings. Hearings and negotiations dragged on for months. City expenses mounted, climbing to tens of thousands of dollars. The purchase of privately owned lands reached $250,000.

By October 1929, nearly all the small landowners had relinquished their property. Unfortunately, two weeks later the stock market crashed—and with it the hopes of ever completing the Kapowsin pipeline.

City Water not only couldn't afford to spend up to $3 million on the pipeline, but with the Depression forcing closure of many tideflats industries, the demand for water disappeared.

A sad closing to this chapter of City Water's history, the Lake Kapowsin project was never developed. The utility was left with $250,000 worth of lakefront property—which had to be maintained and patrolled—water rights claims and a bundle of survey maps for its three-year effort.

City Light roars off into the 1920s

By the time Johnny—and a million other American troops—came marching home from World War I, Tacoma was already a head-over-heels fan of electricity.

Lamps and fixtures were given to businesses free to build up the commercial lighting business—"giving our stores a prosperous appearance," according to City Light Superintendent Llewellyn Evans. And by 1918 the city boasted 408 streetlights.

Residential customers, encouraged by "the cheapest domestic power" offered anywhere, were adding electrical conveniences, too. "The electric range is beginning to come into its own. . . . A little more consistent education among our people will make the electric range the rule rather than the exception in all new homes," said the 1918 annual report. Some 600 electric ranges—many sold by City Light—were in use at the time.

In fact, electricity was becoming so popular, the city was about to exhaust the capacity of the Nisqually plant and new sources of power were urgently needed. Ahead were years of shortage, as the Roaring '20s turned out to be a period of economic boom and increasing demand.

Stannard to the rescue

Tacoma City Light needed a leader and found one in Ira Davisson. His first years in office were difficult—the Nisqually plant was running at capacity and still not meeting demand, a shortage aggravated by dry summers and freezing mountain winters.

Davisson turned to rival private power companies with little luck. By now the Seattle–Tacoma Power Company had been bought by

With increasing demand, a power shortage loomed—aggravated by dry summers and freezing winters.

the Puget Sound Traction & Light Company. The Tacoma Railway & Power Company was also franchised to provide power to the city. Both refused to sell power unless the city stopped building hydroelectric plants.

With no new sources available, Davisson turned to conservation and found help from several of Tacoma's mills and manufacturing plants. "They agreed to adjust their work schedules to help us meet our peak loads," Davisson recalled.

Let the good times roll

The 1920s ushered in a long period of boom times. Along with flappers, speakeasies and "The Charleston," it was an era of easy credit

and prosperity. People had money to buy the wonderful new products appearing on the market—automobiles, telephones and radios.

But it only underscored Tacoma's power shortage, which Davisson planned to end with a three-pronged program—construction of a steam plant, an intertie with Seattle and Cushman Dam on the Skokomish River. The people of Tacoma had already approved a $300,000 bond issue in 1919 to buy the necessary land and water rights.

Cushman Reservoir. Harnessing the power of the Skokomish River with Cushman Dam was the key to meeting the booming demand of the 1920s.

Getting under way. By May 1924 "Team Cushman" was tackling the Skokomish with 200 men, headed by Jay L. Stannard. The contractor, A. Guthrie & Co., lost no time getting under way.

By 1922, the City Light "Information Book" was describing Tacoma as a city of "conservative modesty" with a population of almost 97,000—and 25,000 homes, 375 manufacturing plants and more than 20,000 automobiles. "All in all, Tacoma is a mighty good city—a city without booms, boosters, or bombast; a city of solidity, saneness and substantiality . . . the city reminds one more of an eastern manufacturing city than a city of the wild and woolly West."

Meanwhile, City Light was ready to begin building Cushman Dam, following almost two years of rancorous condemnation proceedings to acquire the necessary land along the river.

The city paid the lower river ranchers, Skokomish Valley ranchers and local Indians for "fear and apprehension regarding the safety of the storage dam and for interfering with their sub-irrigation and silt-fertilization."

The issue exploded into a white-hot, name-calling controversy.

The great fish flap

It must have tried Davisson's patience; he claimed that land prices "skyrocketed out of all reason. Land once used by the state fisheries as an 'eyeing station' was inflated over 400 percent in an effort to prevent development."

Ah, but that wasn't the way fisheries officials saw the issue, which exploded into a white-hot, name-calling controversy with both sides vilifying each other in the press.

The Fisheries Department claimed that taking water out of the river would endanger the fisheries. But the real source of the conflict may have been an early meeting between City Light and fisheries board chairman Ed Sims. According to the *Daily Ledger*, Sims had his back arched from the beginning: "From the first word there was an attitude of animosity on the part of Chairman Sims. There was no spirit of compromise, or desiring to reach an agreement. . . ." When

City Light officials described the difficulty of locating the dam site elsewhere, Sims apparently said, "I don't care a damn about that."

Sims' side of the story, according to the *Seattle Post Intelligencer*, is that "Tacoma city officials tried to ride roughshod over the board and that they did not proceed in an orderly and respectful manner."

The press loved the fight. The *Tacoma Journal* ranted against the "purile, invalid, pifflous trumped-up eyeing station." It was not an era of journalistic restraint. But the *Tribune* correctly noted that a little diplomacy might have avoided the entire controversy. The land was eventually acquired—but after a year's delay.

Ace in the hole. The Dock Street Steam Plant with a capacity of 9,000 kilowatts, completed in 1922, was designed for emergency standby use.

Gathering steam at Dock Street

Meanwhile, a steam plant at 1145 Dock Street was rushed to completion between May and September 1922. With a total capacity of 9,000 kilowatts, the plant was designed primarily as an emergency standby unit and to maintain service to the business district.

The steam plant did little to take the sting out of an acute power shortage as 1922 came to a close, and the city was forced to buy power wherever it could—including manufacturing plants with their own power generators. The Tacoma Railway & Power Company had nothing to sell and defaulted on its contract.

Cushman was needed urgently and Davisson needed an engineer to get the project rolling. He found just the man in Jay L. Stannard of San Francisco. In Davisson's words, Stannard "proved himself an excellent, capable and competent master of his profession, a gentleman of high standing, well-qualified, faithful, easy to work with and in full sympathy with our requirements."

Davisson not only got a fine engineer, he got a bargain—Jay Stannnard at $7,500 a year.

Davisson not only got a fine engineer, he got a bargain. After interviewing 24 engineers at salaries ranging up to $35,000 he settled on Stannard, who wanted only $7,500 a year. "It's just what I wanted to do," said Stannard. "I made a thorough investigation of the Cushman project in 1917 with the idea of building it for Seattle and I have always wanted to develop that project."

J. D. Ross, Seattle City Light superintendent, gave Stannard a ringing endorsement, saying, "I do not know a man on earth I would recommend so strongly for your work."

Stannard spent his first day "getting acquainted with the boys" and said he did not plan to visit the site immediately. "The ground

State-of-the-art. Electrical gadgets sprouted everywhere—including the bathroom of this "Electric Ease" model home.

is covered with snow . . . we have no time for just junketing, but want to make all our movements count."

Team Cushman takes shape

Stannard's first job was to build a team. He chose B. E. Torpen as superintendent of hydraulic design and construction, Alvin Darland as superintendent of electric design and J. V. Gongwer as assistant engineer of design.

In May 1924, according to the *Ledger*, "The canyon of the Skokomish River is reverberating every day now with the sounds of heavy artillery and the din of 200 men busily engaged in many forms of activity. The construction of the great Cushman power project of the City of Tacoma is well under way.

"The artillery that booms out at intervals during the day is the blasting of the tough andesite rock which forms the canyon walls and through which is being driven a tunnel.

"Carpenters, machinists, plumbers, laborers of many trades and kinds fill up the intervals between the blasts with the hum of their united labors.

"The contractors, A. Guthrie & Co. have lost no time in getting the big project under way. . . ."

Growing sophistication

In August 1923 City Light completed part three of its power plan—a Tacoma to Seattle power intertie—a $175,000 year-long project that allowed the cities to share surplus power back and forth.

Meanwhile, Tacoma's electric system was growing in size and sophistication with four main substations, a new 55,000-volt network connecting them and a distribution system that covered 25 square

Tacoma's electric system was growing in size and sophistication.

miles with 15,000 poles and 1,255 miles of wire. More than 80 percent of the poles were placed in alleys—thanks to the wisdom and foresight of some pioneering engineer—keeping the streets free from "unsightly obstruction."

Up in Skokomish Canyon, the engineers were battling the river and the elements. Unprecedented rains and floods halted work in 1924, but with dry weather in 1925 progress picked up. Work on the diversion and power tunnels had been going forward through the winter and after they were completed, the river was diverted through them and construction on the dam continued.

City Light records describe the construction scene: "All day and all night, and all summer long, steam engines were puffing, trucks speeding, carpenters building forms, riggers manning the concrete tower and chutes at dizzying heights—and always the grinding of the mixer and the steady flow of concrete. Five hundred men toiled ceaselessly but would not be denied."

(Facing page) Almost done. The Cushman Dam and powerhouse in February 1925. On March 23, 1926, the first Cushman power arrived in Tacoma.

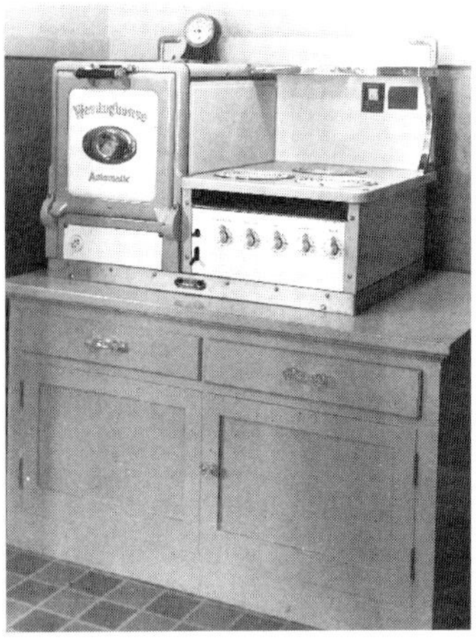

Popular.
In 1925, City Light sold 70 percent of all the electric ranges sold in the city. Some 4,000 of its 31,000 customers were cooking with electricity.

(Facing page)
Hooray for Cushman.
The formal dedication of the Cushman hydro project in May 1926. President Calvin Coolidge touched a key to "set the huge turbines whirring."

By Thanksgiving Day 1925, the last concrete for the dam was poured. On October 20, 1925, the gates at the intake were closed and the impounding of the waters began. The reservoir formed would be 10 miles long, one to three miles wide and 170 feet deep.

A daunting task

As water began filling the valley, work continued on the powerhouse and generating equipment. But before power could reach Tacoma, a daunting task remained—crossing the Tacoma Narrows.

To do it, City Light built an engineering marvel, the Narrows Crossing cable transmission line. With a span of 6,244 feet, it was the world's longest when built. Its 315-foot towers were strong enough to carry the cables when heavily loaded with snow and ice—and with a hurricane blowing at the same time. The cables, first sunk to the bottom of the Narrows and then raised up, were three times as strong as any projected stress.

On March 23, 1926, the first unit of the new plant went on line and at 2:50 p.m. the first Cushman power arrived in Tacoma. In May, a formal dedication and celebration took place, described by Ira Davisson: "Tense was the waiting and joyous were the shouts as the electrical energy freed by President Coolidge as he touched the key which sent current pulsing from Washington, D.C. into the Olympic Mountains and set the huge turbines whirring."

Cushman's two generators were capable of carrying the city's entire load of 32,000 kilowatts. At last, Tacoma's power problems were over—but only temporarily. Writing in the 1927 City Light annual report, Davisson said demand was growing so rapidly a second Cushman hydro plant would be necessary.

Sell, sell, sell

An immediate rate reduction followed the completion of the Cushman plant, giving Tacoma the nation's lowest rates. Tacoma responded by embracing electrical conveniences. And, although

CITY OF
LIGHT

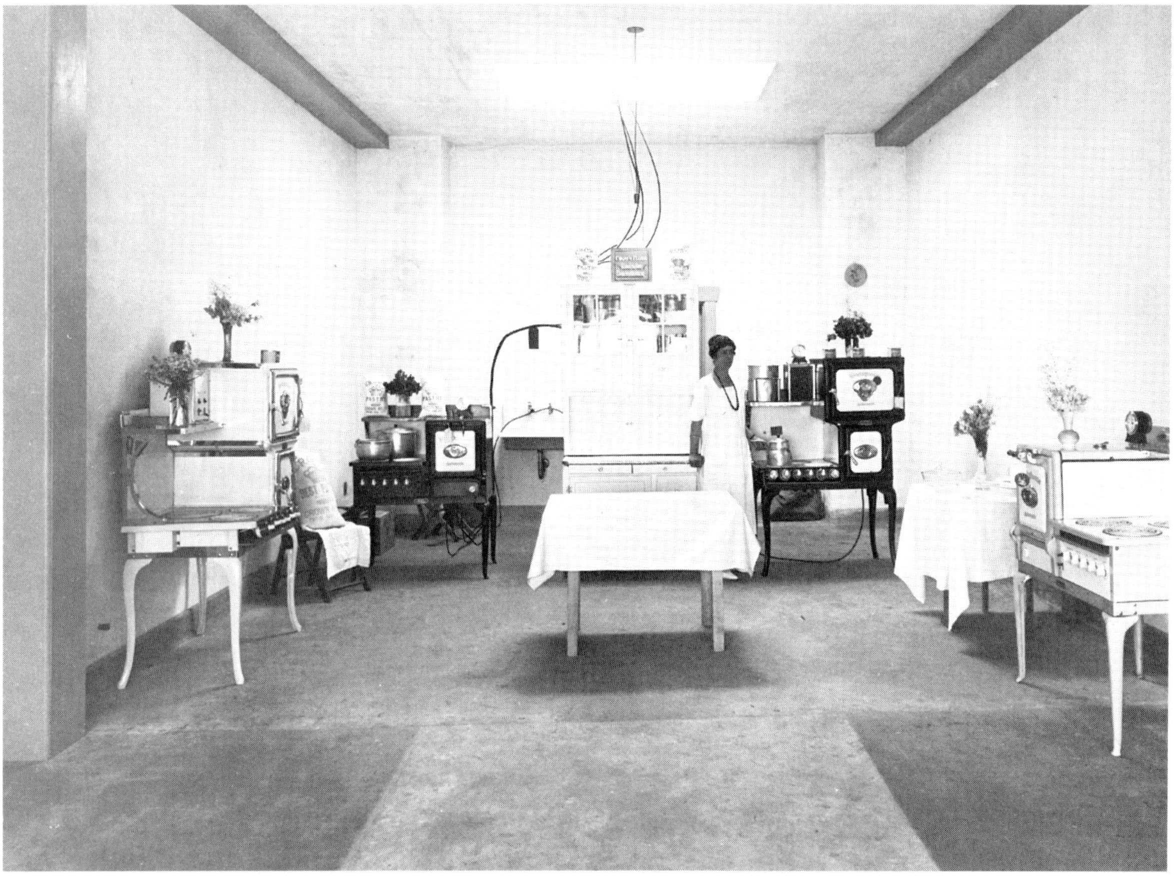

Home on the range. City Light sales of electric stoves surged after the completion of Cushman Dam brought an immediate rate reduction.

women's rights were receiving increasing attention, for City Light's commercial department, the woman's place was still in the kitchen.

"Much of the housewife's labor and drudgery has either been eliminated or eased through the use of electricity for lighting, cleaning, cooking, water-heating, refrigeration and many conveniences . . . of small electrical appliances," said the 1927 annual report. That year, the number of electric kitchen ranges in the city jumped to 5,400.

With increasing demand came the specter of another shortage. So Tacoma City Light went back to Skokomish Canyon and began work in the spring of 1929 on a second power plant and 240-foot dam two miles downstream from the first dam.

Tacoma was in for tough times in late 1929. The stock market crashed, bankers jumped out of windows on Wall Street, the entire

West Coast was hit with a severe drought—and Tacoma with another critical power shortage.

Ah, the pranks of nature

It was enough to make strong men cry, Ira Davisson must have thought. Here was City Light with a state-of-the-art hydroelectric facility, but no water to power it. "Who can foresee the pranks of nature?" he lamented. "All hydro plants were down. . . . It was unthinkable to follow the steps of other cities and relieve their crisis by dumping load, throwing citizens out of work, a step to be taken only as a last resort."

Tacoma needed help fast. If nature wouldn't provide it, the city had to look elsewhere. The solution turned out to be one of the most innovative—and strangest—in utility history. For about 30 days near the end of 1929, the aircraft carrier *USS Lexington*, one of the Navy's largest ships, supplied the city with about 25 percent of its power.

The incident had the drama of a B movie. A telegram to President Hoover implored his help before plants were forced to close down and men thrown out of work. Hoover referred the matter to Secretary of

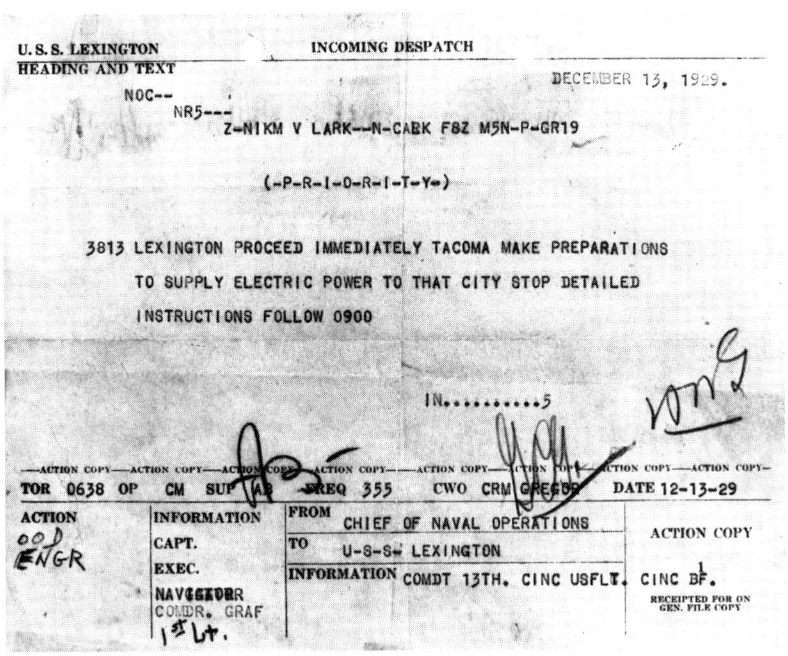

U. S. S. LEXINGTON — INCOMING DESPATCH

HEADING AND TEXT

DECEMBER 13, 1929.

NOC--
NR5---
Z-NIKM V LARK--N-CABK F8Z M5N-P-GR19

(-P-R-I-O-R-I-T-Y-)

3813 LEXINGTON PROCEED IMMEDIATELY TACOMA MAKE PREPARATIONS TO SUPPLY ELECTRIC POWER TO THAT CITY STOP DETAILED INSTRUCTIONS FOLLOW 0900

IN..........5

—ACTION COPY—ACTION COPY—ACTION COPY—ACTION COPY—ACTION COPY—ACTION COPY—ACTION COPY—ACTION COPY—

TOR 0638 OP CM SUP FREQ 355 CWO CRM DATE 12-13-29

ACTION	INFORMATION	FROM	CHIEF OF NAVAL OPERATIONS	ACTION COPY
OOD ENGR	CAPT.	TO	U-S-S- LEXINGTON	
	EXEC.	INFORMATION	COMDT 13TH. CINC USFLT. CINC BF.	RECEIPTED FOR ON GEN. FILE COPY
	NAVIGATOR COMDR. GRAF 1st Lt.			

Help on the way. When a drought rendered the new second Cushman unit useless, a power shortage loomed. Tacoma appealed to the U.S. Navy—and the *USS Lexington*—for help.

Lady Lex.
The aircraft carrier supplied the city with about 25 percent of its power for a month near the end of 1929.

the Navy Charles Francis Adams, who first turned down the request and ordered the carrier to San Francisco for drydock.

Matters looked grim—and dark—in Tacoma. Ira Davisson had no choice but to cut the power to the Cascade Paper Company, throwing 300 people out of work. Streetlights dimmed. Store owners turned off display lighting. The Army at nearby Fort Lewis turned off lights in its barracks at 4 p.m.

The drama built as the *Lexington* got underway on November 20, but—at the last minute—it reversed course and anchored off Blake Island, raising Tacoma's hopes. After days of negotiations between the Navy and the city, the *Lexington* finally steamed up to Tacoma's Baker Dock in a driving rain to be welcomed by thousands of rain-soaked citizens and a soggy brass band.

"Lady Lex" ushers out the decade

At the time, the huge ship was one of the world's two largest mobile power plants, its four giant turbines capable of producing 140,800 kilowatts. When the *Lexington*'s power began surging into the city's system, all the streetlights came back on along with store lighting and displays. The wheels of industry began to turn again. Tacoma was back on its feet.

Shortly after the first of the year, the rain began to fall again and the crisis was over—ending one of the most unusual incidents of the entire decade.

The *Lexington* steamed out of Tacoma on January 17, 1930, heading for a World War II rendezvous with fate. When the gallant ship was sunk in the Battle of the Coral Sea, Mayor Harry Cain paid tribute to the carrier in a 30-minute ceremony and once more said thank you and goodbye to an old friend.

7

City Water: Federal Help for the Lean Years

Licking its wounds over the Lake Kapowsin debacle, Tacoma City Water still was hunting for an auxiliary water supply as the 1930s opened. Wells again beckoned. The tideflats test well proved water existed beneath South Tacoma, flowing deeper than the wells drilled in the early 1900s. For financially strapped City Water, drilling one or two wells at a time was an appealing—and safer—alternative than the multi-million-dollar Kapowsin pipeline.

"The development program can be laid out to keep in step with the growing demand for more water," said Kunigk. "No large amount of capital need be invested in a plant not employed or necessary." The proposed field of wells, dubbed the "A" series, would prove to be both reliable and inexpensive. And—important for an elected official—drilling the wells wouldn't require Ira Davisson to raise water rates.

The N. C. Jannsen Drilling Company, driller of the tideflats industrial well, won the contract for Well 1-A. Sinking the drill bit into the ground near Pump Station C on South 63rd Street and Clement Avenue during the fall of 1929, the company penetrated more than 100 feet of hardpan rock and drilled to 260 feet. Jannsen's persistence paid off when almost 3,100 gallons of water per minute (about 4.4 million gallons a day) bubbled to the surface.

Well 1-A was an unqualified success, with production dwarfing that of any previous well. It was so prolific, in fact, that the City Council passed an ordinance in December setting aside $100,000 for four more "A" series wells.

Pipe for the "A" series well field. Wells were a political expedient—no rate increase was required.

(Facing page) Still searching. For financially strapped Tacoma, drilling one or two wells at a time was safer than another pipeline. Here a rig drills Well 1-A near Pump Station C.

Eureka!
Well 1-A gushes with 3,100 gallons a minute—4.4 million gallons a day.

On April 5, 1930, after a heavily contested bidding war, the City Board of Contracts and Awards offered the Jannsen Company a contract to drill the additional wells in South Tacoma. The company calculated it could extract 12 million gallons a day from the four wells, at a cost of only $40,000. The drilling of Wells 2-A, 3-A, 4-A and 5-A proceeded into October 1930 and produced over 19 million gallons daily.

More pumping and distribution

With the "A" series wells gushing close to a combined 24 million gallons a day, City Water shut down the first-generation wells in South Tacoma and built an expanded pumping system and distribution network. The well water not pumped by station C into the distribution mains was conveyed through a concrete pipeline from South Tacoma to the Hood Street Reservoir. There it blended with Green River water, creating a surplus that the 13-million-gallon reservoir could not handle. A proposed new pump station at Hood Street Reservoir was included in the budget presented by Ira Davisson to the City Council in February 1931.

Despite the economic gloom sweeping the country, Davisson offered an ambitious budget for City Water. A proposed $460,000 bond issue would pay for the new pump station at Hood Street Reservoir, improvements to the Green River intake and pipeline and miscellaneous construction at the headworks.

Davisson also sprinkled his package with several long-range land acquisition programs—none at Kapowsin—including the right-of-way for a duplicate gravity pipeline from McMillin Reservoir to the "J" Street Standpipe. Davisson wanted the land, knowing it would eventually be settled, requiring an additional pipeline. And the bickering with Lake Kapowsin property owners may have been still fresh in his mind.

Hood Street Reservoir. Water from Pump Station C not routed into distribution mains was stored here. Holy Rosary Church in the background.

Hard times were on the way, and for most of the 1930s City Water rode violent waves of financial ups and downs. Revenues rose and fell and only federal grants kept the utility afloat.

Still, construction continued. Under the direction of Chief Engineer Lothrop Crosby and his assistant, Julius Kuehl, City Water replaced the gravity line at a steady pace, cutting in more than five miles of new pipe in 1930–1931 at a cost of more than $400,000.

Grinding to a halt

Reality—and the Depression—hit hard in 1931. With no room in the budget for pipeline replacement, work ground to a halt. No gravity pipe was laid for two full years and the slumping economy began to take its toll.

Depression gripped the utility. Work was limited to routine maintenance.

In 1932 development and extension programs were placed on hold. The only major construction centered around improving the "A" series wells' distribution system and building the new Hood Street Pump Station adjacent to the old reservoir.

Depression gripped the utility. Work was limited to routine maintenance handled by skeleton crews. Construction work and equipment maintenance were deferred. Revenue fell off, as water-using industries and businesses folded. There was little encouraging news.

But with Roosevelt's New Deal came new hope in the form of a variety of public assistance programs. And City Water, guided by Kunigk and Ira Davisson, took full advantage of them. From 1933 to 1938, City Water successfully applied for and received more than $1.8 million in federal loans and grants.

Davisson's uncanny ability to "play the political system," honed by 15 years of local politicking and steering federal funds to Tacoma,

is a highlight of his municipal career. And it helped keep City Water afloat during these troubled years.

Taking a breather. Workers funded by government programs played a key role in upgrading and maintaining the city's water system during the Depression and World War II.

PWA to the rescue

Davisson and Kunigk first applied for and won a $1 million loan from the Federal Emergency Administration of Public Works (PWA) in 1933 to fund two projects: the Green River gravity line reconstruction and the laying of a second transmission line from McMillin Reservoir to Tacoma.

The new line, Pipeline No. 4, was needed to "provide a means of continuous gravity supply to the City at all times until the untreated wood stave sections of Pipeline No. 2 are replaced."

Pipeline No. 4 and a proposed lateral extension joining it to Pipeline No. 2 (along South 64th Street) were needed to provide flexible, improved water service from McMillin Reservoir. Davisson and Kunigk were delighted to hear of the loan's approval by the PWA on November 21, 1933. Of course, the federal money was slow in arriving, delaying construction until October 1934.

Davisson recognized a good thing when he saw it and quickly applied for more federal money—this time a $317,000 loan to fund continued gravity line replacement and construction of Pipeline No. 4.

Of the $1.3 million in federal assistance received by City Water, more than one-fourth of the money was set aside for gravity line reconstruction in 1934 and 1935. The majority of the construction work was aimed at building Pipeline No. 4 and the South 64th Street lateral main.

Construction costs alone were expected to reach $776,000 on the second pipeline, which traversed a course from 128th Street and Meridian Avenue in Puyallup northwest through the communities of

Blowout at Section A. Federal money helped rebuild the Green River gravity line and saw City Water through three very difficult years.

Woodland and Summit. Pipeline No. 4 intersected Pipeline No. 2 at South 64th Street and Park Avenue in Tacoma.

Federal money saw City Water through three very difficult years. Thanks to the PWA loans—a third loan worth $230,000 came through in 1936—the utility was not forced to delay its construction programs for long. Pipeline No. 4 was built and cut in to service, the Green River gravity line continually upgraded and many other projects completed, thanks to Davisson's adroit and ambitious handling of the federal loan applications.

The meter problem—again

Those three tight years also galvanized Kunigk and Davisson into taking action on Tacoma's poor record of water conservation. And that meant installing water meters.

Water meters would have to be installed sooner or later, Davisson warned. Why not sooner?

The "meter question" was still prickly. Tacomans were using way too much water—nearly double that of Seattle and three times that of San Francisco. In late 1936, once safely re-elected, Davisson again tried for meters, arguing that federal money could be used to install 21,000 meters.

The City Council gave its stamp of approval, but the tough part lay ahead—convincing the public. On November 3, 1936, *The Tacoma Times* published a four-column article by Davisson, Kunigk and Mayor George Smitley, with Smitley appealing to Tacoma's civic spirit. "Our approach to working out the solution of this problem [metering] requires a broader vision and a sympathetic attitude on the part of our whole citizenry," he wrote.

Kunigk and Davisson appealed to the public's pocketbook. If Tacoma switched to water meters immediately, said Davisson, it might save ratepayers and the city $250,000. Water meters would have to be installed sooner or later, he warned. Why not sooner? It would be far cheaper to install meters immediately than in five or 10 years.

The appeal fell on deaf ears and city residents found their voice of protest in the boisterous, anti-meter rhetoric of Robert D. O'Neil.

O'Neil and Ira Davisson first clashed in the 1920 city primary elections when they were competing for Davisson's position of Commissioner of Light and Water. Less than one month after beating O'Neil—a City Light foreman—Davisson fired him on charges ranging from insubordination to campaigning on city time.

A civil service inquiry board exonerated O'Neil of all but one of the charges—"conduct detrimental to the morale and efficiency of the department."

O'Neil took on opposition to metering as a holy mission.

A rival for life

Davisson had made a permanent enemy. Bob O'Neil doggedly pursued Davisson at every general election, was a vocal critic of the commissioner and was a perennial fixture at City Council meetings. He vociferously protested City Water's metering and Local Improvement District (LID) programs—anything he perceived as "disadvantageous" to Tacoma.

O'Neil took on opposition to metering as a holy mission—and a great chance to be a burr under Davisson's saddle. He wrote a series of newspaper articles opposing Davisson's plan.

He spoke to the Lincoln Citizens' Club about water rates in November and it voted unanimously against Davisson's metering plan. So did the Proctor Street Businessman's Association. The Tacoma Federation of Improvement Clubs threatened a court injunction.

Undaunted, Davisson plowed ahead with his scheme, applying for another federal grant for the meters. But then the federal government drove a stake into the heart of his plan, drastically changing the loan repayment ground rules so that the plan was no longer practical. Metering was scuttled again.

Regrouping in the latter half of 1937, Davisson and Kunigk focused on two new, high-priority projects. First on their "wish list" was a second tideflats trunk main. The route along Lincoln Avenue had been surveyed in April 1937, but City Water needed $260,000 to begin construction. The Council approved the tideflats trunk main ordinance on September 27.

Davisson fights for a shop

Davisson and Kunigk also wanted a new shop and warehouse for City Water, but they would have to fight the City Council for it. The new stores building, to be erected at the corner of South 35th Street and Union Avenue, was expected to cost City Water $131,000. Though the proposed new building had several advantages over the old shop, the City Controller's office wasn't sure that City Water, despite Davisson's claims, could afford it.

City Water was facing some rather unforgiving debt figures in the near future and its net earnings had been dangerously low. Would

New home for City Water at South 35th Street and Union Avenue. Much needed, but Davisson had to fight the City Council to get it.

the commissioner raise water rates to fund his new stores building, the City Council wanted to know. Would he delay work on the new tide-flats trunk main? Davisson replied that he had not raised water rates once in his 19-year tenure and did not intend to start. He lobbied the Council for five months before winning approval for the stores building. It was completed in October 1939.

The new building contained two meter repair and testing shops, a pipe shop, car wash and service room, a concrete casting room, offices for storekeepers and foremen, a gasoline service station, labs and a locker room.

New main for the tideflats, a $260,000 project in 1938, to supply the growing industrial area.

With the tideflats trunk main under construction and the stores building erected, Davisson could again concentrate on applying for another federal loan. But the public utilities commissioner was 78 years old in 1938, and by that time had lost much of the effectiveness and zeal of his first 20 years in public office.

Two last hurrahs for Davisson, the modern pumping plant and covered reservoir at Pump Station C (above) and the pipeline connecting it with the South Tacoma well field (below).

Davisson's last hurrah

Ira Davisson's last hurrah turned out to be City Water's 1938 federal loan application, which he escorted through the obligatory political hoops by August. The loan, the biggest yet approved by the PWA for City Water, consisted of roughly equal shares of federal and city money.

More than $705,000 in government funds and $760,000 worth of City Water revenue were contained in the loan application, which covered improvements such as the laying of 75,000 feet of cast iron and transit pipe, the replacement of 5.5 miles of gravity main, the construction of a modern pumping plant and covered reservoir at Pump Station C, the drilling of two more deep wells and extensions to trunk main No. 2 on the tideflats. Notably absent from the PWA loan application—any mention of water meters.

At about this time, Ira Davisson was the instigator of a foolish three-year feud with the Tacoma Metropolitan Park Board. The Park Board and Davisson had a history of squabbling over land rights, water privileges and rates. The Park Board had requested reduced water rates, but Davisson adamantly refused, saying the City Charter prevented him from giving the parks a special rate.

The disagreement erupted into a full-blown fight, with the Park Board denying City Water access to its property and refusing to pay

Davisson's longevity and political skills helped see City Water through two difficult decades of growth and expansion.

its $7,000 water bill. In return, Davisson shut off water to the parks, turning them a parched brown.

The bickering echoed back and forth until, finally, Davisson agreed to reduce the Park District's water rates by 25 percent. Water was turned on in Tacoma parks four days before Ira Davisson left office.

End of a brilliant career

Davisson's fight with the Park Board was an ignominious end to an otherwise brilliant career. Davisson was 80 years old when he was voted out of office in favor of Robert O'Neil, who—no surprise—had supported the Park Board.

Davisson's leadership of City Water was inspired and distinguished, though not without its share of controversy and failure. The Lake Kapowsin debacle was perhaps the single most expensive municipal

blunder in Tacoma's history before 1930—and a great campaign issue for O'Neil during the 1940 election.

But Davisson's longevity and political skills at City Hall helped see City Water through two difficult decades of growth and expansion. Tacoma City Water literally rebuilt and redefined itself under Ira Davisson—a significant accomplishment.

Meanwhile, the last big municipal water works projects funded by federal money, the rebuilding of the South Tacoma pump station and drilling of Wells 6-A, 7-A and 8-A, were carried out during the last half of 1939 and completed in July 1940. The projects were nearly finished when Robert O'Neil took office on June 3, 1940.

Thanks, Uncle Sam. The South Tacoma Pump Station, one of the last big municipal water works projects funded by federal money.

A record in stone and steel

The utilities and the city had lost a leader and a legend. Davisson, retiring to his wife and family in their comfortable home at 923 South

Miles of substandard wood mains like these were replaced during World War II.

8th Street, left behind an amazing record, one rarely duplicated in any American city, according to *The Tacoma Times*: "It is written in stone and steel, in dollars spent and dollars saved, in vastly increased resources and vastly reduced rates. . . ."

One of Davisson's last acts was to turn over to the city four large volumes containing typewritten inventories of every last nut, bolt and other asset of City Light and City Water.

O'Neil decided to retain Kunigk as Superintendent of Water, believing the 23-year veteran was his best choice to keep City Water running smoothly. And the new commissioner announced his water policy only two days after he took office. Basing his candidacy on a pledge of "no new meters," O'Neil explained that anyone wishing to change from metered service to flat rate had only to submit a written request to City Water.

Just two weeks later, O'Neil publicly asked Tacomans to conserve water during the summer months, which must have seemed quite ironic to longtime meter advocate Kunigk.

It took Commissioner O'Neil about six months to find his footing and formulate his own long-range plans. Operating in the shadow of Davisson's successes, O'Neil's first challenge was to replace and repair roughly 85 miles of wooden water pipe in Tacoma, most of it laid between 1905 and 1925.

On June 4, 1941, almost one year exactly after taking office, O'Neil unveiled his comprehensive plan for completing the gravity line reconstruction program and upgrading Tacoma's water distribution system. The improvements included drilling two or more of the "A" series wells, installing a bypass pipeline at Hood Street Reservoir to redirect water into the distribution mains when the reservoir was being cleaned, replacing 19,000 feet of gravity pipe and other miscellaneous repairs.

O'Neil asked the City Council to pass a $500,000 bond issue, which it did on June 15. The "water fund" of 1941 was created to pay interest and meet principal bond payments. O'Neil also applied for and received a $100,000 federal loan to supplement the gravity line replacement.

War times, boom times

Work progressed through the summer and into the winter of 1942, an exciting and anxious time. With the Pearl Harbor attack and the United States' involvement in World War II, Tacoma's industries boomed for the second time in three decades. The influx of workers and the growth of Fort Lewis and McChord Air Force Base placed heavy demands on Tacoma's already suspect water mains.

Just as the number of services increased, steel pipe and other necessary materials grew scarce. But war-time shortages didn't affect O'Neil's 1941 construction plan. Most of the gravity main

Most of the gravity line replacement work was finished by April 1942.

replacement work—primarily near Enumclaw and Rhodes Lake, and between South 64th and 94th streets in South Tacoma—was finished by April 1942. But construction of the new "A" wells, proposed in the $500,000 bond issue, was temporarily shelved.

Springing a leak. Blowouts on the old wooden Green River gravity line were common, but work carried on.

New and old, side by side. Replacing the old wood mains with a new 43-mile steel line was a tricky operation. Work began in 1924 and continued to 1952.

(Facing page) Fear builder. Kunigk lived in constant fear that a blowout in the aging wooden line would give way and cut off the city's 55 million gallons a day from the Green River.

City Water had two primary concerns during the war. First, it had to find funds to complete the gravity line reconstruction and restore rotten wood mains in the distribution system. Then it had to figure out how to supply Tacoma's burgeoning population with adequate water when most of the services remained on the flat rate charge.

Meters—O'Neil misses the boat

The commissioner shot himself in the foot on the water meter issue. In April 1942, O'Neil reported that City Water had hooked up more than 1,500 new flat rate customers in 1940 and 1941 and he expected double that number in 1942. And when he had the opportunity to install meters in a new federal housing project in southeast Tacoma or raise rates, he refused to renege on his campaign promises. In fact, O'Neil even lowered metered service rates to residences using more than $1.50 worth of water per month. Yet O'Neil expected City Water to supply a city of nearly 120,000 inhabitants through decaying, 30-year-old mains. The flat monthly water rate for a five-room house

Proud.

Despite the grim grip of the Depression, City Water significantly improved its system during the 1930s. Advertising boasted of low rates and pure water.

with one toilet and bath was still $1.25, a lower rate than that paid by customers in 1893!

O'Neil had far greater success—and demonstrated far more common sense—in engineering an extensive, $3 million improvement program for City Water's post-war growth. The program called for building a new, 25-million-gallon reservoir and replacing more than two miles of gravity line. The federal government approved the first phase of the $3 million project in May 1944. Federal aid for the project amounted to $201,000, with the city providing $400,000 of its own money—enough to support gravity line repairs. O'Neil was not in office long enough to see the improvement program completed.

The few remaining miles of untreated wood pipe in the gravity line posed a constant threat. Kunigk feared losing entire sections of wood pipe in a break, which almost happened in July 1943 when a mighty 6.5-million-gallon leak erupted in the gravity pipeline near the town of Veazie. Writing about Kunigk's plight, the *News Tribune* said: "Just as a dish dryer grimaces and waits for the fateful crash when he drops a saucer, so is W. A. Kunigk . . . tensed against the day when eight aging miles of wooden gravity line give way and cut off the city's 55,000,000 gallon daily inflow from Green River."

If the newspaper story was accurate, then Kunigk could look forward to another nine years of tense moments.

FIVE YEARS OF ACTIVITY

During the Idle Depression Years

FIFTEEN MILLION DOLLARS have been expended for labor and materials in maintaining and extending the Water and Light Plant facilities

SIXTEEN MILLION, THREE HUNDRED THOUSAND DOLLARS have been saved to Light and Power consumers because of Tacoma's Low Rates, as compared with the National Average Rates of the Edison Electric Institute

ONE MILLION, FIVE HUNDRED THOUSAND DOLLARS have been contributed in Taxes and Services, thus reducing your tax burden

CITY OF TACOMA DEPARTMENT OF PUBLIC UTILITIES

THESE ARE SOME OF THE CONTRIBUTIONS OF THE LIGHT AND WATER DIVISIONS OF YOUR DEPARTMENT OF PUBLIC UTILITIES IN KEEPING THE WHEELS OF INDUSTRY TURNING

Municipally Owned and Operated

CITY OF TACOMA DEPARTMENT OF PUBLIC UTILITIES

1930 - 1944

City Light: Hard Times, Good Times and Increasing Demand

8

Not long after the *Lexington* steamed out of Commencement Bay, Mother Nature tired of her pranks and dumped a record snowfall on the Olympics—14 inches in one 24-hour period. "City's Power Problem Looks Rosier Now," said *The Tacoma Times*, with enough water stored behind Cushman Dam to see the city through the winter "without further embarrassment."

But having learned just how capricious rainfall patterns could be, City Light hurried construction of a second steam plant for emergency use. The large, modern plant on the tideflats at Hylebos Waterway and East 11th Street had two coal-fired steam turbines capable of generating 25,000 kilowatts and was ready for service in 1931. Though a standby power source, the steam plant could carry the city's entire load after 9:30 p.m. Touring the new $2 million plant, Mayor Melvin G. Tennent smiled at Ira Davisson and said, "It looks mighty fine, Ira."

"The Electric City"

By now, the city was locked in the iron-tight grip of the Great Depression, but even hard times couldn't stop load growth. Tacoma's low rates encouraged the use of all the new conveniences—electric ranges, water heaters and home heating systems. With its low rates and consumption well above the national average, Tacoma was billing itself as "The Electric City."

That meant Tacoma City Light had no time to waste in rushing completion of its third giant hydroelectric project—the second

Free delivery.

By the 1930s, City Light was not only selling and servicing ranges and refrigerators, but making "demonstration calls to private homes, thereby assisting the homemaker in obtaining greater service from her electrical appliances."

(Facing page)

Proud of its progress, Tacoma Public Utilities ran this message in a 1935 issue of the *Labor Advocate*.

Men and machines—back to Skokomish Canyon in the race to keep up with Tacoma's demand for more electrical power.

Cushman unit. The *Tacoma Daily Tribune* described the "small army" at work on the project:

"Down where the wooded slopes of the Skokomish march to the shores of Hood Canal, the City of Tacoma is carving out a gigantic hydroelectric project. A concrete dam is diverting a mountain stream from the course it has followed for centuries. Two and one-half miles of tunnel carry the potential power to singing turbines at the water's edge. Giant transmission lines guide it into Tacoma."

Taking shape. Cushman powerhouse No. 2 near the mouth of the Skokomish River on Hood Canal. With an installed capacity of 75,000 horsepower, the unit went on line December 31, 1930.

Cushman Dam No. 2. 1.75 miles downstream from the first dam, 240 feet high, eight feet thick at the top and 50 feet thick at the bottom.

Cushman No. 2 went on line in December 1930—just in time to help the city through a cold snap and another power crunch. The hum of the new generators must have been music to Tacoma's ears. "Another dream dissolved into reality," wrote the *Daily Ledger.* "The giant turbine-generator, which is destined to send a magic flow of pulsing power over glistening wires into Tacoma for indefinite ages to come, began to spin sweetly, noiselessly on its massive bearings."

All was not sweetness and light on the political front. In those days the job of Commissioner of Public Utilities was an elected office and in the election of 1932, with Ira Davisson up for reelection to his third term, things got downright hot.

Trouble for Davisson

Davisson had made some powerful enemies in the private power contingent by opposing the extension of Puget Sound Power & Light's franchise to sell power in the city. Puget Power saw City Light's low rates as "punitive" and a move to force the company out—which happened in 1930 when, without a franchise, the company was forced to sell. It was the end of dual electric companies in Tacoma.

As a result, Davisson was a target in the 1932 election. No doubt hoping that a new utility commissioner might give them a new foothold in the city, the private power folks resorted to a devious trick—running alternate candidates with similar names.

Clifford Davis was an accountant with some previous city service. Charles S. Davidson was a contractor. The city's newspapers saw clearly what was happening—"a cheap political trick to bewilder the voters," thundered *Ryan's Weekly*. "The people of Tacoma face a bitter fight on their valuable power system."

The Tacoma Times was particularly vocal in its support of Davisson and its opposition to what it called the "power trust lackeys" and

Homer T. Bone was a powerful writer and a masterful orator and when he spoke, Tacoma listened.

their attempt to "put into office a nobody who will do their bidding and who will undermine the successful foundation of Tacoma's splendid light and power system."

Homer T. Bone—state legislator, U.S. Senator and public power crusader.

A powerhouse named Bone

Another powerhouse in the Davisson corner was Homer T. Bone, self-taught attorney, state legislator and soon-to-be U.S. Senator—a powerful and popular politician who had made his reputation as a public power advocate.

As state legislator, Bone hammered away at legislation that would put the control of power into the hands of the people through the formation of public utility districts. Fighting a powerful private power lobby in Olympia, Bone had little success.

Then in 1929 Bone teamed with the Washington State Grange to introduce similar legislation and stumped the state in support of it. Though the legislature failed to act, the bill was referred to voters where it passed handily.

Riding into the U.S. Senate on Franklin D. Roosevelt's coattails, Bone continued to push for public power, introducing the legislation that created the Bonneville Power Administration, the agency that markets power from the series of Columbia River dams—including Grand Coulee—which are a major source of power for City Light.

Bone was a powerful writer and a masterful orator and when he spoke, Tacoma listened.

"If the people of this city are wise," he wrote, "they will march to the ballot box on February 23 and administer to this crew of wreckers the same stinging rebuke they did in the spring of 1930 . . . when they told Stone-Webster to stay out of this city."

The people did just that, sweeping Davisson back into office for another four-year term with a vote almost three times that of all other candidates combined.

A Depression project replaced poles like these with underground facilities.

Dark days

For many in Tacoma in those Depression days, the vote was all they had. Bread lines and soup kitchens were common, hard cash was

Working it off. Unemployed men dug trenches to pay their utility bills. With their help, Tacoma created one of the nation's most modern downtown distribution systems.

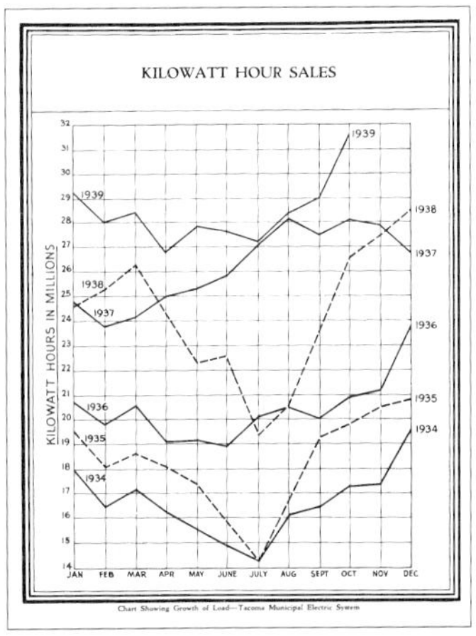

Taking off. Even during the Depression, Tacoma's load grew dramatically, prompting the construction of still more generating capacity.

scarce—prompting one customer to bring potatoes to City Hall, selling them to City Light employees for 75 cents a sack to pay his bill.

During the darkest days of the Depression, Ira Davisson had a brainstorm—putting unemployed men to work digging trenches for underground utilities to pay off their utility bills. Working a few days at a time until their bills were paid off, the part-time workers helped install an underground, three-phase, four-wire secondary network. It gave the city one of the nation's most modern downtown electrical distribution systems.

Despite the crippling grip of the Depression and the difficulty customers had with their bills, load continued to grow steadily and the utility remained in sound financial health. In 1932 it began a multi-year program to expand and improve its distribution system, extending lines to suburbs, perfecting voltage regulation and doubling the number of substations.

Ira Davisson was proud of his utilities and of his employees, writing in the 1939 annual report that "it would be hard to find a staff of employees anywhere more loyal and faithful . . . and who so thoroughly believe in the principle of municipal ownership."

Vern Kent, Davisson's light superintendent, announced that 1939 was the most successful in the utility's history, a good news–bad news story. The utility was financially healthy, with load growing at 10 percent per year.

Too close for comfort

The bad news: The load had doubled in five years and generating capacity to meet it was "much too close for comfort." Tacoma needed new hydro capacity immediately. Though Bonneville power was on the way, Kent recommended relying on the federal agency for emergency relief only while continuing to build municipal plants.

By now, the Depression was clearly over. City Light's Commercial Department was humming. Sales of electric ranges were brisk, doubling every year. City Light opened its Electric Center at 932 Pacific

Center stage. The electric range was the focal point of cooking schools hosted by City Light in the 1930s to teach "electric cookery"—and sell stoves.

Avenue, offering the homeowner a wide range of electrical appliances. A staff of City Light home economists demonstrated how electricity could free homemakers from "the withering heat of cooking by flame."

The utility also was beginning to understand the need for effective communication with the public and began publicizing City Light through advertising and participation in community festivals and parades.

The good times were beginning to roll again, but there were storm clouds on the horizon—in Europe, where Hitler was preparing to march into Poland and touch off World War II. And, in local politics, trouble was brewing for Ira Davisson—upset by O'Neil in the 1940 election.

O'Neil had little time to enjoy his election victory. The city's generating capacity would take it through 1943—if weather and rainfall were right. If not, Tacoma would not be able to meet the demand for power.

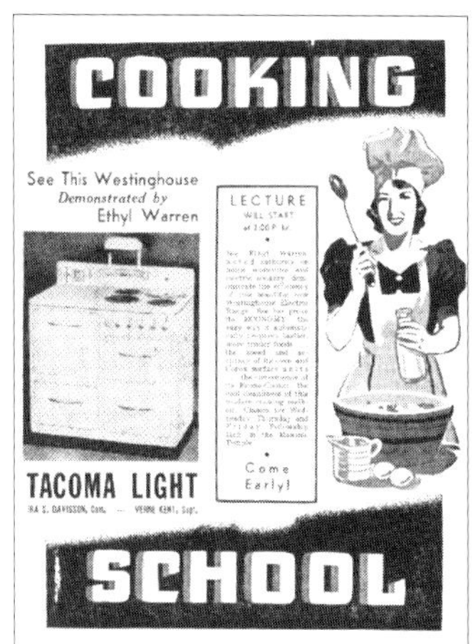

City Light goes to war. This ad seemed to say that electric cooking was patriotic. Selling war bonds at City Hall was a much better idea.

Bonneville power was imminent, marching north from the Columbia on 100-foot steel poles. J. D. Ross, Bonneville administrator and former Seattle City Light superintendent, hailed it as "the forerunner of a new electrical era for the Northwest."

But Bonneville also was viewed with suspicion. City Light officials feared the power would come with strings attached—a federal takeover of Tacoma's system to create a huge Pacific Northwest power combine. "Home rule" became the rallying cry for those wanting to protect municipal ownership.

In the early 1940s Tacoma was learning to live with World War II. Downtown was blacked out, window displays and signs turned off when shoppers left. In 1942, Washington, Oregon and Bonneville mobilized power resources to help the region's aluminum plants produce 460 million pounds of the metal needed for the war effort. Fearing sabotage, the U.S. Attorney General barred German, Japanese and Italian nationals from the region's hydroelectric sites.

In Washington, D.C., Congress was holding hearings on the evacuation of aliens. Washington Governor Arthur B. Langlie testified that an overwhelming majority of Washington citizens thought evacuation of all enemy aliens "immediately necessary." Tacoma Mayor Harry Cain urged selective evacuation of the city's 1,480 aliens.

Busy as woodpeckers

Meanwhile, Tacoma's booming industrial war effort was attracting a flood of new workers, said the *Tacoma Daily Tribune.* "Families are flooding into Tacoma, moving about from cramped to more desirable quarters like proverbial bees in a hive. In turn, utility department employees are being kept busy as woodpeckers on city light poles, making service changes at the rate of 50 per day."

War time, busy time for City Light—supporting the war effort with bond sales and connecting new services for the flood of new workers moving into the area.

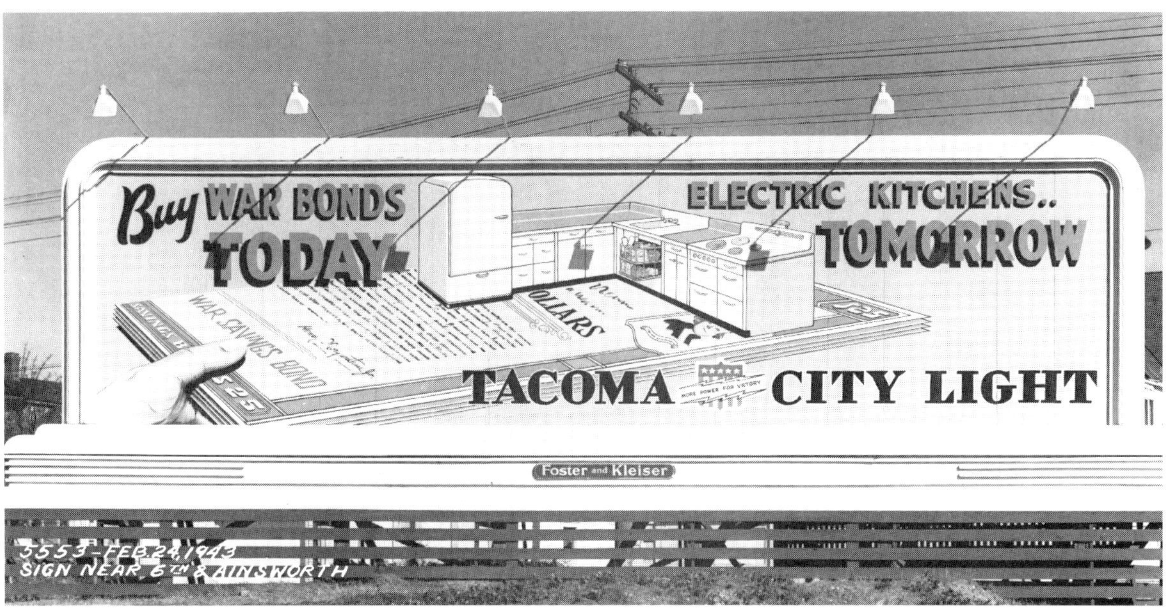

Nisqually central. The Jones Building, headquarters for the City Light team planning the second Nisqually hydro project.

Another busy spot was the seventh floor of the Jones Building at South 9th Street and Broadway where a dozen City Light engineers were working long hours, planning the two tall dams that were the heart of the proposed $11 million second Nisqually hydro project.

Visiting reporters saw "charts of the elevations of the river, the dams and powerhouses. Maps show roughly the area to be flooded by the upper storage dam, the lake which will cover the site of the town of Alder . . . and test cores drilled from the canyon walls and floor at both dam sites."

Tacoma was actually getting two dams for its $11 million price tag. The new 330-foot concrete arch Alder Dam was to be built almost two miles above the LaGrande plant with a powerhouse that would generate 50,000 kilowatts. Water released by the Alder Dam would be impounded again behind a new LaGrande Dam and sent through a new tunnel to generate another 64,000 kilowatts at an enlarged LaGrande powerhouse. When completed, the new 114,000-kilowatt facility would increase City Light's generating capacity by 80 percent.

Gadget growth

The new dam was needed urgently. Pleading his cause before the City Council in 1941, Commissioner O'Neil pointed to an annual load growth of 10 percent that had jumped to nearly 22 percent in the last year.

Why? The increase in home electrical gadgets was a major reason, O'Neil said—Tacoma had one of the nation's heaviest domestic loads. And the area's industrial plants were increasingly relying on City Light for power, rather than their own power plants.

The plant was approved by the Council, though Secretary of Interior Harold Ickes warned work could stop if the project's materials were needed for the war effort. The investment community loved the project, practically jumping at the chance to buy the first $4 million bond issue, driving interest rates to an all-time low of less than two percent.

And no wonder. City Light was in great shape financially—its facilities were valued at more than $25 million with only about $3 million worth of debt that was rapidly being amortized.

A reach?

Ad copy claiming an electric range was as important as the Narrows Bridge may have been overly enthusiastic. Electricity to power the range, however, was becoming a critical need—again.

Cheerful optimism

On September 13, 1944, Commissioner of Public Utilities Clif Erdahl pulled a rope, spilling the last bucket of concrete for Alder Dam. "Another gigantic Tacoma Light department dream emerged from the formative stage into the realm of realization," said the *Tacoma Daily Tribune,* describing "an air of cheerful optimism among city fathers and engineers alike. . . ."

It was a time to indulge in some optimism. Allied forces had landed at Normandy and the end of the war in Europe was in sight. The Nisqually hydroelectric facility was a major achievement and a cause for celebration.

There was no time for City Light to rest on its laurels, however. Even with the Nisqually Project on line, Tacoma's growing demand for power would exceed City Light's generating capacity.

Halfway through its first century, Tacoma City Light was once again at a crossroads.

TAYLOR WAY
Now! DAMP WASH
3c PER LB.
Minimum Bundle 45c
OLYMPIC LAUNDRY MAIN 8181
TACOMA UTILITIES 8 BELT LINE
3020

1923 - 1940

Birth of the Belt Line

9

It was a year of uncertainty for the Tacoma Municipal Street Railway—1923. It was in debt, battling the Emergency Fleet Corporation (EFC) in federal court over its wartime loan—and its freight-switching operation wasn't gaining much respect from city officials, tideflats industrialists or the national railroads.

Then, along came two champions of an improved, expanded tideflats freight-switching service: Ernest Dolge and Jay W. McCune. Energetic Ernest Dolge owned one of the tideflats' largest lumber mills and was chairman of the Chamber of Commerce Traffic and Transportation Bureau from 1922 to 1925. McCune was secretary of the bureau.

The city's switching engine served Dolge's lumber mill and he had publicly complained about the halfhearted freight-switching service to his mill and other tideflats industries. Dolge was frustrated with the scant attention paid by the City Council to the municipal switching operation and resolved to do something about it.

Gathering local support and traveling to other cities to examine their local switching systems, Dolge declared the lack of a belt line a major Tacoma disadvantage: "A public belt line railroad is an artery that carries the city's industrial and commercial life blood. . . . The Port of Tacoma must either absorb exorbitant switching charges or lose business under the present arrangement. This is intolerable . . ."

(Facing page) Born in 1923. The Belt Line would have been better off if its passenger service—a perpetual money loser—never left the barn.

Belt Line cable cars in 1930 at 11th Street and Pacific Avenue.

Tackling the railroads

Dolge's first step—meetings and conferences with the executives of the four national railroads serving Tacoma and the tideflats. Over the next four months, Dolge and McCune met with the Northern Pacific, Union Pacific, Great Northern, and Chicago, Milwaukee & St. Paul railroads.

Getting a mixed reception initially, Dolge argued that their support of a belt line railway would boost industrial development on the tideflats—and business for the major railroads. But the discussions dragged on unresolved through September.

The breakthrough came when Northern Pacific President Charles Donnelly paid Dolge and the Chamber of Commerce a visit in October 1923. The fanfare for his visit, a true public relations coup for the Northern Pacific, couldn't have been better staged. Donnelly was wined and dined by Dolge and Chamber of Commerce officials. A precisely timed editorial by *The Tacoma Daily Ledger*, published the day of Donnelly's arrival, sang the praises of a municipal belt line railroad and beseeched the cooperation of the national railroads.

With all the hoopla surrounding his visit, what could Donnelly do but commit to the belt line—which he did in his dinner speech:

"The Northern Pacific unconditionally accepts the proposal to use the Tacoma municipal line for switching purposes . . ." he said. "The Northern Pacific is ready to relieve the industries of the Tacoma tideflats of switching charges and to add to the income of the municipal car line through switching business. . . . We are willing to rely upon the service of the Northern Pacific, confident of its superiority, to obtain for us the business of concerns which we will open up to other roads who accept the same proposal."

"Divide and conquer" wins

Donnelly's "magnanimous" gesture opened the door for Dolge to rope in the other railroads. Northern Pacific received a tremendous response from tideflats industries and shippers, and Great Northern,

Chicago, Milwaukee & St. Paul, and Union Pacific soon followed suit. Dolge's strategy of "divide and conquer" had worked.

In its contracts with the railroads, the city granted all four railroads common access to municipal tracks—and therefore to the tideflats industries—and promised uniform switching service. The municipal railway would perform all switching duties for a flat $3 per car switching fee. The national railroads charged a two-step rate, in addition to the belt line's fare, based on the cargo destination.

The railroads settled on the following schedule: Shipments from one tideflats industry to another ("intra-terminal") would cost $5.55 per car, with an $8.50 per car fee for hauls outside the tideflats. Lumber companies paid $2.50 per car for log hauls.

Birth of the Belt Line. The city and the major railroads ink a contract giving them access to municipal track in return for uniform switching service from the Belt Line.

At an October 29 meeting attended by Ernest Dolge, Jay McCune, representatives of the four railroads and other city officials, Mayor Fawcett signed the contracts. The belt line had arrived. The *Ledger* boasted: "Tacoma takes rank as one of the few industrial centers of the United States and the only one in the Pacific Northwest to have a large industrial district served by a belt line railroad."

Wiggling out of debt

Meanwhile, the City Council was hard at work trying to nullify its debt to the EFC, eventually settling out of court for $115,000 cash. The Council paid the money out of the General Fund and, soon after, canceled the municipal street railway's own financial obligation to the General Fund and its unpaid share of constructing the Milwaukee viaduct in 1918. The Council also eliminated the railway's annual gross earnings tax.

In one fell swoop, the municipal street railway was relieved of its $112,000 debt . . .

In one fell swoop, the municipal street railway was relieved of its $112,000 debt to the city, though it still owed City Light $348,000—its one remaining financial obligation.

And, with contracts in hand, the freight-switching service began to make money—switching revenues nearly doubling in one year to $54,373 in 1925, the first full year of belt line service. And the street railway posted its very first net profit under municipal ownership in 1925—$9,619.67, a modest beginning.

The municipal street railway, it appeared, had finally achieved some measure of stability. Credit must go to Ernest Dolge and Jay McCune, who also suggested the name of the street railway be changed to "Tacoma Municipal Belt Line Railway" and that the city extend rails around the southern end of the Hylebos Waterway to open

Classy, but unprofitable. The Belt Line's freight business picked up immediately, but the passenger business was troublesome.

the area to industrial development. Dolge was indeed the "father of the Municipal Belt Line."

Disaster strikes

But the luster of his achievement tarnished quickly with a string of disasters plaguing the Belt Line between 1925 and 1929.

At 7:45 in the evening of December 30, 1925, something went terribly wrong with Municipal Belt Line Car No. 9, driven by motorman Clyde Staley. Approaching the 11th Street bridge with the bridge up, Staley's streetcar smashed into the back of another car, broke through both warning gates and plunged off the bridge into the City Waterway. Staley jumped from the car seconds before it plummeted 50 feet to the water below, carrying five people to their deaths.

Prosecuting attorney James Selden couldn't prove Staley guilty of any wrongdoing, though he believed the case had "elements of manslaughter." The jury found Staley guilty only of failing "to exercise reasonable precaution in the handling of the car."

The accident didn't help the Belt Line's financial picture, with damages and personal injury suits totaling more than $40,000—increasing the 10-year deficit to $25,200 in 1926. The crash and loss of life were the darkest incident in Belt Line history and it recovered slowly.

Luckily, strong leadership was on the way. First came Charles H. McEachron, the Belt Line's fifth superintendent, late in the spring of 1926. McEachron, like the municipal railway's past superintendents, knew little of railroading, but made up for it in shrewdness.

Young—just 33 years old at the start of his tenure—handsome and lanky, McEachron brought the Belt Line stability during his 14-year stint as superintendent. The most effective of all pre–World War II Belt Line superintendents, McEachron guided the Belt Line through its transition from electric streetcars to buses, bought its first and only steam engine and expanded the Belt Line's passenger service to the eastern tideflats.

That darned bridge. The 11th Street bridge, scene of a major Belt Line disaster. On December 30, 1925, a streetcar broke through warning gates and plunged 50 feet to the water, carrying five people to their deaths.

Charles H. McEachron, the Belt Line's fifth superintendent—he brought the line stability during his 14-year administration.

Next, a new City Charter amendment shifted control of the Belt Line to Public Utilities Commissioner Ira S. Davisson, a utilities powerhouse. Now, there were two firm hands on the throttle.

Disaster number two

Meanwhile, disaster struck again. On Sunday afternoon, June 24, 1928, a fire in the Belt Line trolley barns quickly spread to the wooden car barn, engulfing nearly all of the trolleys and maintenance equipment. The three-alarm blaze, according to the *Tacoma News Tribune*, "was a spectacular one and thousands of persons, most of them in motor cars, crowded the vicinity."

The fire cost the Belt Line dearly. All but two of the streetcars were destroyed—22 in all—and the new car barn was gutted. More than $276,000 worth of equipment was lost, not a penny of it insured.

The Tacoma Railway & Power Company temporarily loaned the Belt Line enough cars to operate its morning and evening routes. Ira Davisson set out to purchase new rolling stock and searched for a new site for the car barn. He ultimately bought seven secondhand streetcars from the Perry-Baxter-Doane Company of Boston for $30,100. When the new streetcars arrived in Tacoma in February 1929, Davisson found them "in poor shape" and needing substantial repairs.

Later that year work began on a new roundhouse, with the $7,000 timber and frame structure erected over the ashes of its predecessor at Taylor Way and East 11th Street. It housed three tracks, enough to handle the Belt Line's greatly reduced operating force.

Disaster number three

More bad news was on the way. In July 1929 a serious fire, perhaps caused by short-circuiting wires, took the Milwaukee viaduct on 11th Street out of commission. Employees of the Milwaukee Railroad car

Calm before the storm. The Belt Line car barn in 1928, scene of a disastrous fire which destroyed all but two of the Belt Line's streetcars. Nothing was insured.

shops and other industries along 11th Street protested the lack of streetcar service over the viaduct, demanding alternate transportation. The answer—bus service until the trestle could be rebuilt.

McEachron weakly protested that it would take eight buses and a considerable expense to handle peak rush-hour traffic, but the bus service began on February 10. The viaduct, fire and necessity had brought the city its first bus operation to the tideflats—limited as it was—and marked the beginning of the Belt Line's transition from electric streetcars to buses.

All this bad luck, of course, was pounding the Belt Line's bottom line, with revenues yo-yoing up and down from a deficit of $124,412 in 1928 to a surplus of $252,691 in 1937. One piece of good news was the Council's cancellation of the $214,000 in Belt Line debts to

The Belt Line's primary function was not to earn revenue, but to lure industry to Tacoma.

other city departments. But hanging over the Belt Line's head was its $348,000 debt to City Light, which it had been unable to shake since 1918. Interest alone was $1,500 a month, which the Belt Line couldn't begin to meet.

Ira Davisson wanted the Belt Line rid of this debt, but it would have to be approved by the voters—which they refused to do in a 1930 election. Two other Belt Line measures dealing with the extension of service to the eastern side of the Hylebos Waterway also failed.

To serve, not to earn

The Belt Line ended 1930 exactly where it had begun: heavily in debt and losing money. Although a commission of local businessmen looked into the matter and recommended a rate increase, the Council and Mayor Tennent ultimately kept the Belt Line primarily as an inducement and municipal "service" to prospective tideflats

Rails to rubber. The passenger service began to switch from streetcars to buses, but remained a money loser.

industries. The Belt Line's primary function was not to earn revenue, but to lure industry to Tacoma.

Ironically, the Belt Line's fortunes improved during the Depression—revenues increased and the freight-switching operation became the railway breadwinner.

Belt Line annual net income, mired in deficits since 1928, began a slow climb in 1933. From losses of $9,984.87 in 1930, income improved until—in 1935—the Belt Line posted its first net gain under Superintendent McEachron, a profit of $2,668. The cumulative 18-year deficit, however, hovered close to $150,000 during this five-year period.

The Council prodded the Belt Line along its slow, uphill path to financial solvency. An emergency ordinance passed in December 1932 wiped clean more than $79,000 in Belt Line interest owed City Light on the $348,000 loan. Though Utilities Commissioner Davisson didn't pressure the Belt Line to pay its debt, the railway did manage to pay off the first $5,000 in 1934.

The money loser

Part of the problem was that the Belt Line's passenger service consistently lost money. Profits made from freight switching were quickly lost by streetcars. Street railway income had declined steadily since 1920—from a high of $180,000 to $40,700 in 1930. Annual deficits between 1933 and 1936 ranged from $2,700 to $9,600.

The drop in passenger traffic is reflected in the amount of rolling stock operated by the Belt Line during the early 1930s. The entire fleet included nine streetcars and two 18-passenger buses. Ten years earlier 38 streetcars had been required.

The freight-switching operation, meanwhile, grew steadily. The two Belt Line electric switching locomotives hauled 13,500 loaded cars in 1931. Seven years later, the number had increased to 19,300.

In spite of—or perhaps because of—the poor showing of the passenger service, Davisson and McEachron set out to upgrade the system in 1936, buying three new 21-passenger buses. McEachron

The streetcars had become a nuisance on the crowded tideflats.

wanted to convert the entire streetcar fleet to buses and the first three were a "trial." The streetcars had become a nuisance on the crowded tideflats. They interfered with switching locomotives—which shared

On trial.

Buses began operating in 1937 for a one-year trial, leading to conversion of the entire Belt Line trolley fleet.

the same tracks—and couldn't adapt readily to new routes. If an industry wanted streetcar service, the Belt Line was forced to lay track to the site. And much of the city's old track was rapidly wearing out and required costly reconditioning. So the buses began operating in the spring of 1937 for a one-year trial.

From streetcars to buses

At about the same time, the city was negotiating a new franchise with the Tacoma Railway & Power Company. The settlements between Council and company proved to be a major turning point in the city's transportation history, foreshadowing the end of electric streetcars in favor of buses.

The Council and Tacoma Railway & Power Company representatives also discussed the future of the Belt Line passenger service and its possible sale to the company. It was a great opportunity for the city to be rid of the streetcar service. Discussions led to a company offer and the Council voted on the sale January 11, but rejected it on Davisson's advice.

Davisson's decision was probably influenced by the Belt Line's plans to buy six new buses. The White Company, a Tacoma firm, won the contract for the modern, air-conditioned buses on its low bid of $36,271. Davisson and McEachron, pleased with the results of their one-year trial with the buses, decided to convert the entire Belt Line trolley fleet. The city's contract for the buses was unique in that all of

First steam engine. With the freight business growing, the Belt Line bought its first steam locomotive—secondhand for $1,000.

the participating firms were Tacoma-based, a decision hailed by local labor advocates and businessmen.

Meanwhile, with World War II looming, the Belt Line freight-switching service picked up speed in the late 1930s. Shipping and manufacturing on the tideflats increased to the point where the Belt Line was handling an average of 150 cars daily, prompting McEachron to buy a steam-powered switching locomotive—Number 912—from the Northern Pacific Railroad in April 1939.

The Belt Line's electric locomotives needed servicing and the $1,000 steam locomotive was a steal. Though secondhand like much Belt Line stock, Engine No. 912 enjoyed a fairly long life on the tide-flats. It immediately went to work switching cars on Lincoln Avenue.

New Utilities Commissioner Bob O'Neil replaced McEachron with his own hand-picked appointee, Amos Booth.

The era of streetcars on the tideflats came to an end in May 1938 with the arrival of the White Company buses. The streetcar rails, with the exception of those used by the switching engines, were torn out and sold for scrap. Sections of electric trolley wire came down. Motorized buses traveled the routes of the old trolleys, taking workers from their homes to their jobs and back again.

Changing faces

The faces in the Belt Line offices changed not long after the streetcars went out. Ira Davisson lost his bid for re-election as Commissioner of Public Utilities to Robert D. O'Neil in 1940. Charles McEachron, who worked nearly all his 14 years with the Belt Line under Davisson, was also out. New Utilities Commissioner Bob O'Neil replaced McEachron with his own hand-picked appointee, Amos Booth.

Much to his credit, McEachron saw the Belt Line through 14 very tough years. In spite of the string of setbacks suffered by the Belt Line in the late 1920s, he managed the municipal railway out of its habitual yearly deficits. Though still under a cloud of debt, the freight-switching service had proven its value to tideflats industries.

The bus line remained controversial and proved to be a huge headache for Amos Booth and his successor, Neil Kime. Over the next five years, the Belt Line would be put to the test. Guns were booming once again in Europe, signalling the beginning of the most hectic period in the small railway's brief history.

(Facing page) The tideflats in 1927. By this time, the Belt Line had a formal agreement to serve the national railroads—and was in the middle of a string of disasters.

RICHARDSON
WELL DRILLING CO.
R.3 BOX 845 TACOMA
GR.7332
FIXED LOAD
SPEED
71
8084-SEP. 26, '47- DRILLING TEST WELL- SO. TACOMA WAY-NEAR 45th

1945 - 1957

THE "GOLDEN AGE" OF TACOMA CITY WATER

10

In the mid-1940s Tacoma City Water faced a stormy future. Despite its success in bringing water to the city, it now had to face the troubling fact that its supply system was in terrible shape. Its wells, reservoirs and gravity line were being built upon a crumbling foundation.

Ignored for three decades, Tacoma's distribution mains, those carrying water from trunk mains to homes and businesses, were decaying badly. New leaks sprung every day. The problems could have been avoided and the system repaired if Ira Davisson had the conviction, or Bob O'Neil the common sense, to begin a universal metering program and raise Tacoma's outdated water rates.

When Clifton (Clif) A. Erdahl, Tacoma's 16th Commissioner of Public Utilities, took office in June 1944, he faced the results of Davisson's and O'Neil's neglect and had his work cut out for him. An imposing, dignified man with snow-white hair, Erdahl was a consummate politician. A smooth talker and slick negotiator, Erdahl moved easily in political circles.

(Facing page) Well-drilling in 1947. After years of tests and surveys, City Water drilled a third batch of "A" wells—this one near South Tacoma Way and South 45th Street—which produced handsomely.

Erdahl and Kunigk launched their assault on wooden distribution mains during the summer of 1945, work that continued on and off for the next 30 years. The Local Improvement District (LID) was the driving force to fund the improvements—either initiated by citizens or City Water.

Although objection by 51 percent or more of an area's residents could kill an LID, the property owners generally consented. That meant they paid 90 to 95 percent of the costs involved in digging the trenches, removing the wood pipe (some of it 40 years old) and installing new cast iron. City Water paid the remaining cost of installing any main more than six inches in diameter. Disrupted traffic and upturned lawns were the price paid for better water service and fire protection.

LIDs varied considerably—covering as little as one city block and costing only a few thousand dollars to larger projects of more than $200,000 and one square mile of city streets. City Water might be working on one, two or 10 LIDs at any given time. No timetable or grand scheme was followed, but Erdahl and Kunigk used the LID technique to successfully retire dozens of miles of old wood water mains.

A 9-A gusher, one of four new South Tacoma wells producing 28.5 million gallons a day. One well produced 11 milllion gallons daily. Total well output—62 million gallons a day.

More wells drilled

Meanwhile City Water's secondary supply, the South Tacoma well field, was also receiving more attention. The eight "A" series wells, sunk along the old flume line between South 35th and South 78th streets, continued to flourish, leading Kunigk and Erdahl to believe others would fare equally well.

In 1948, after a year of tests and surveys, City Water began drilling a third batch of "A" wells. An unqualified success, the four new wells gushed 28.5 million gallons a day, pushing total well output to 62 million gallons daily. The most prolific of the new wells, 11-A, spouted 11 million gallons daily—promptly dubbed the best well "west of the Cascades." The four wells and housings cost City Water more than $285,000 and can be clearly seen today, sprinkled throughout South Tacoma.

Meanwhile, Northeast Tacoma, across Commencement Bay from downtown Tacoma and annexed by the city in 1927, was now demanding more water. City Water first brought water to Northeast Tacoma in 1929, when crews were in the process of laying the first tideflats trunk main. By late 1946, City Water was again hearing appeals from Northeast Tacoma residents for more water.

Indian Hill Reservoir, under construction in 1950. Local residents formed a mutual water company to help fund the improvements.

346

Marine View pump station under construction in 1950, cornerstone of City Water's Northeast Tacoma improvement program.

With the help of a small Works Progress Administration grant, City Water expanded the Northeast Tacoma water system, laying 1,800 feet of six-inch pipe and installing a chlorination system. But it took local residents until 1949 to form a mutual water company and find the funding for the necessary construction—additional pumping equipment, a pumping station, a 500,000-gallon reservoir and almost three miles of 12-inch pipeline.

The service area covered the entire territory between East 11th Street and Dash Point, about 2,000 potential customers. The system was turned on in May 1951. Development in Northeast Tacoma continued with City Water extensions on the tideflats from 1949 to 1953.

(Facing page) From wood to steel. Water employees wrap a joint in a steel water line in 1946. Eliminating wood distribution lines was a top priority during this period.

More water for the tideflats

World War II brought a manufacturing boom to the tideflats, followed by a period of sustained growth, calling for another large trunk main along Lincoln Avenue—a 36-inch steel and cast iron trunk main, with five lateral extensions. City Water created one huge

LID for the area and helped fund the $360,000 project.

City Water finished two other projects on the tideflats at about the same time: laying a 16-inch steel pipe beneath the Hylebos Waterway in April–May 1950, and building a 32-inch pipeline under and across the Wapato (Port Industrial) Waterway in winter 1952–1953.

Both submarine crossings were impressive. After dredging the channels, the pipe was connected on land and gently lowered into the water. Divers then checked connections and pipe locations. The total cost neared $200,000.

City Water reached another milestone in the early 1950s—completion of the $5.5 million, 43-mile-long Green River pipeline replacement. Superintendent Kunigk, 70 years old in 1950, began the project in 1924 and insisted on staying until it was finished. The last 1.25 miles of steel pipe were cut into operation in September 1952.

The expanded, reinforced pipeline could now convey 72 million gallons of water to McMillin Reservoir, an improvement of 30 million gallons over the original, untreated wood gravity line. Tacoma needed the water—average daily consumption in the city of 153,000 inhabitants had risen to 55 million gallons a day.

City Water's Green River headworks—a vital source of water for Tacoma. Ahead lay a major battle to protect the watershed and the purity of its water.

With the "new" gravity line no longer at risk of imminent collapse, Kunigk could breathe easy at last. City Water had built Tacoma a new lifeline.

Growing sophistication

In the early 1950s, City Water also was growing in sophistication, implementing advancements in radio communications, water purification and chlorination and customer billing. It also had to face a painful reality. Those customer bills weren't bringing in enough cash. Financially, it was in trouble.

After a swing upward in the late 1930s and 1940s, net revenue dropped from $355,265 in 1946 to $46,300 in 1952—embarrassingly low. One of the key problems—City Water's heavy bond redemption schedule created by extensive bond issues of the late 1920s and early 1930s. They nearly broke City Water's back.

To make matters worse, City Water suffered its worst year in 1953—a net loss of almost $60,000. Part of the problem was the "skyrocketing" costs of steel, bronze, cast iron and labor—driven even higher by the Korean War.

The solution to City Water's financial woes was obvious and had been for quite some time. City Water needed to raise rates and install water meters—immediately. City Water needed to start looking toward, and planning for, the future.

Five frenetic years

The next five years, 1953 to 1957, proved to be some of the most important, turbulent and frenetic of City Water's history. A 30 percent rate hike, whispered about since 1951, came to pass. Universal metering was introduced. Two huge reservoirs were constructed, Portland Avenue and McMillin No. 2, doubling Tacoma's water storage capacity.

Coming up for air. A welder working on the Green River gravity replacement line catches his breath. The last 1.25 miles of steel pipe were cut into service in September 1952.

A program to protect and preserve the Green River watershed was announced. The administrative offices of City Light and City Water moved from the fourth floor of City Hall to a brand new, $5 million Public Utilities headquarters building on South 35th Street and Union Avenue, across the street from the City Water stores building.

Willibald A. Kunigk retired after his 39th year as superintendent. The city switched from a Mayor-Commissioner to City Manager form of government in 1953. Commissioner Clif Erdahl was fired and replaced with J. Dean Barline, the new Director of Public Utilities. It was a busy time.

Two events stand out above the rest. First, Tacoma finally bit the bullet and became a fully metered water system, shaking off 60 years of outmoded flat rate service.

And, launching its watershed management program in 1951, City Water took the all-important first step toward establishing control of the 231-square-mile Green River watershed, only two percent of which it owned in 1952.

New government, new policies

A rate increase and meters came with a new form of government. On March 11, 1952, Tacoma voted to change from the old Mayor-Commissioner system to a City Manager format. Under the new system, the four commissioners were replaced by a nine-member City Council and a City Manager (appointed by the Council).

The position held by Clif Erdahl since 1944, Commissioner of Public Utilities, was abolished. The public utilities—City Light, City Water and Belt Line Railway—were grouped into autonomous divisions under a five-person Public Utility Board. The five Board members served terms of one to five years and were headed by a chairman (Gerrit VanderEnde, initially). The Public Utility Board in turn appointed the Director of Public Utilities, who selected the three superintendents.

Tacoma finally bit the bullet and became a fully metered water system.

The switch to a City Manager government helped "de-politicize" the utilities. With more than $94 million in assets, they had long risked manipulation for purely political ends. Clif Erdahl was retained as acting director until the first director was named.

Within six months, the Public Utility Board recommended City Water boost its rates by 30 percent and begin universal metering. The Board's suggestion followed closely on the heels of two reports, conducted by the State auditor and a consulting firm hired by the city, describing City Water's financial situation as "precarious" and calling the flat water rate schedule "unscientific, outmoded and discriminatory."

The proposed rate increase was just the first phase of a long-range Public Utility Board plan for City Water that included metering, elimination of wood mains and improvements to the physical plant. The Board and City Water then launched a vigorous information campaign to alert Tacomans of the impending changes, with a series of "open forum" meetings held in locations throughout the city during December 1953.

The hearings attracted small crowds, maybe 150 people in all. Erdahl, Kunigk and Board members were on hand to answer questions. But those in attendance voiced little opposition to the proposed rate hike.

Eruptions over metering

City Water's $900,000 metering program was a different story. The December 15 meeting at Lincoln High School erupted several times. The majority of the people, Kunigk wrote in 1955, "felt all services should either be metered or all remain on a flat rate . . . thereby eliminating discrimination." Others, including a state senator who attended the hearings, objected to having to pay for meters in order to "benefit people 20 years from now."

Erdahl, Kunigk and the Public Utility Board listened to the objections, but interpreted the small turnout as a sign of public approval of or disinterest in the proposed rate hike and metering program. On March 1, 1954, the City Council approved both the rate increase and metering, effective March 15, 1954.

A four-year timetable was established for the metering program, so that by January 1, 1958, no flat rate services would exist in Tacoma. The 30 percent rate increase was the first since 1893 and was at least 35 years overdue.

City Water had 26,600 flat rate services to switch over and it wasted no time. Bids for the first batch of 10,000 meters were called in April and by May, meters were being installed—following a public information campaign telling customers what to expect.

City Water crews did most of the work, moving from block to block. During the installation, meter inspectors discovered that an astonishing one-third of Tacoma's flat rate services had leaky plumbing. And they discovered other flat rate abuses—residents using water-operated basement pumps, single meters serving multiple residences and continuous water flows for fish ponds and pools.

The meter installation program cost City Water $1.27 million and was funded by the August 1954 sale of $2 million worth of water bonds. By April 1955, one year after the project began, the job was three-fourths complete and six months ahead of schedule. It was finished three months later, in June.

Reaching a cherished goal

At last, Superintendent Kunigk had realized a cherished goal held since 1917—metering of Tacoma's water system. The results were swift and dramatic. Water consumption dropped from 54.7

Installing meters—at last. A $1.27 million installation program began in April 1954 and was completed 13 months later.

million gallons per day in 1953 to 48.2 million in 1959, despite sustained consumption from the pulp mills.

Equally grand plans were afoot in the Green River watershed. The watershed, a 231-square-mile area of heavily forested hills and mountains, had long posed a unique set of problems for City Water. Sanitation, of course, was a primary concern.

Since 1913, logging operations, the Northern Pacific Railroad and the fluctuating populations of such towns as Lester, Baldi, Hot Springs and Nagrom had all presented sanitation hazards. The number of people living in the watershed declined steadily, from some 2,000 inhabitants in 1913 to 250 in 1950, however.

City Water relied on its 1914 agreement with the U.S. Department of Agriculture to protect the watershed from trespassers and

"We called it 'our' watershed, but we didn't own any real estate."

sportsmen. In addition, the city encouraged watershed dwellers to build and maintain proper septic tanks or vaults. And City Water employed a sanitary inspector who lived at the headworks and made weekly inspections of the watershed.

But City Water had neither jurisdiction nor authority over the people. In fact, as late as 1954, City Water owned only 2,653 acres of land in the watershed, much of it near the headworks. As Aldo J. Benedetti, City Water superintendent from 1958 to 1972, said: "We called it 'our' watershed, but we didn't own any real estate. It was just a remote area without a lot of access."

Clear-cut problems

A major problem was clear-cutting by logging companies, causing increased water turbidity from run-off that could render the water unfit to drink for days at a time. In a 1945 article written for the American Water Works Association, Kunigk summarized Tacoma's

needs: "Without a question, the solution for the preservation and protection of Tacoma's water supply can only be found through a long-range plan administered by a centralized authority looking toward a sustained-yield forest management operation."

The second McMillin Reservoir, constructed in record time, was one of two major reservoirs built in 1956.

And the age-old system of "cordial agreements" and cooperation among landowners in the watershed was no longer good enough to insure the Green River's purity. So in 1951, City Water launched its watershed management plan. It was informal and only $150,000 was set aside to pay for land acquisition and studies between 1952 and 1957.

Generally, the plan called for studies to assess the impact of logging in the area. City Water also began harvesting its own timber stands to fund additional land acquisition. The logged acreage was small—one of the largest sales in 1955, 1.5 million board feet, netted $56,000. The money was reinvested in acquiring watershed land—

acre by acre, tree by tree. Modest initially, the land acquisition program picked up speed in the 1960s.

What may have finally snapped City Water out of its lethargic watershed protection was the Army Corps of Engineers' plan to build an $18 million dam at Eagle Gorge, 3.5 miles above the utility's headworks on the Green River.

Eagle Gorge Dam, a flood control dam, had been on the drawing board for a long time. King County residents in the Green River's flood plain had long clamored for it and in March 1949 a bill authorizing the dam was introduced to Congress.

Utility officials, especially Erdahl and Kunigk, were greatly concerned. Not only would the sheer number of men—600 or more during summer construction—and equipment at work on the dam pose sanitation problems, but the churned up mud and sediment would render Green River water completely undrinkable. Commissioner Erdahl appealed to Congress.

Luckily for Tacoma, the Eagle Gorge Dam project was slow to develop. City Water took advantage of the lag and proposed several plans to protect Tacoma's water source. Kunigk, Utilities Attorney Frank Bannon and Sanitary Engineer John Roller spent considerable time conferring with Corps of Engineers officers and King County officials about the dam.

Corps cooperation

Tacoma's appeals did not go unheard. Recognizing City Water's concerns, the Corps agreed to curtail all construction expected to cause river turbidity until City Water could build a second storage reservoir at McMillin. The Corps earmarked $256,000 to help pay for McMillin Reservoir No. 2, a 110-million-gallon basin estimated to cost $1.3 million. The city also obtained 208 acres of land between Eagle Gorge Dam and the headworks.

Construction of McMillin No. 2 was hurried along. The first contract, for pipe and pipe fittings, was accepted December 14, 1955.

Paving and construction contracts were awarded in February and May 1956, respectively. Unimpeded by delays or glitches, the huge basin (1,100 feet by 732 feet by 21 feet) was formally dedicated November 2, 1956, when the first water was let in.

McMillin Reservoir No. 2 was one of two reservoirs built by City Water in 1956. In April 1954, the Board asked the Council to condemn a large tract of land (about 150 city lots) near East 38th and M streets for a 50-million-gallon reservoir. The reservoir was needed to assist Hood Street in supplying the tideflats and heavy industrial areas of the city.

The Portland Avenue Reservoir, as it was subsequently named, was connected to Pipeline No. 4 with a 30-inch trunk main. The principal contractors, Ostruske-Murphy, began work in October 1955, but bad weather delayed construction and the first concrete wasn't poured until August 1956. The $870,000 reservoir was put in service six months later.

Tacoma City Water's "grand old man," Willibald A. Kunigk, finally retired in April 1956. He was 76 years old. During his 39

Plagued with problems, the Portland Avenue Reservoir took twice as long to finish although half the size of McMillin No. 2. The $870,000 reservoir was placed in service in 1956.

years as superintendent, Kunigk shaped the utility in his own image. His name appeared on all newspaper and journal articles and on the door of his official automobile. He was quoted on all matters pertaining to City Water—the sole spokesman.

Kunigk's legacy

He left quite a legacy—the gravity line reconstruction, drilling of the "A" wells, the tideflats trunk mains, Pipeline No. 4, the North End and Indian Hill reservoirs, South Tacoma and Hood Street pump stations, the complete metering of the city—the list goes on and on.

Kunigk brought City Water into the modern era. By and large, he surrounded himself with a competent and able staff and in his later years, Kunigk became something of a figurehead—"The Father of City Water." He also became increasingly set in his ways, difficult to approach with suggestions or new ideas.

Kunigk left a legacy and brought City Water into a modern era.

But Willibald Kunigk brought City Water stability. Taking office in 1917, he calmed the 25 years of turbulence preceding him and brought dignity to an office long serving as a springboard to higher stations and dumping ground for political favorites.

Kunigk's replacement, Julius A. Kuehl, had been the old superintendent's right-hand man, serving City Water since 1919. A surveyor by trade, Kuehl was the logical choice to succeed Kunigk. He began July 1, 1956. To ease Kunigk's sudden transition to "civilian" life, the Public Utility Board hired him as a consultant with the McMillin Reservoir project for a few months after his retirement.

Feted in grand style by city officials and co-workers, Kunigk left his post to travel, but kept in touch with the utility to which he devoted over 40 years of his life. He died in 1976.

The golden era

The construction of Eagle Gorge Dam, McMillin and Portland Avenue reservoirs, the watershed acquisition and metering programs are the highlights of Tacoma City Water during the 1950s. The utility's future was established with these projects. Though it included some dark moments, this five-year period was "the golden age" of Tacoma City Water.

Dedication of McMillin No. 2. The 50-million-gallon reservoir helped the Hood Street Reservoir supply the tideflats and the city's heavy industry.

TACOMA
MUNICIPAL
CITY OF TACOMA UTILITIES BELT LINE
BELT LINE
RAILWAY
902

1940 - 1953

11

The Belt Line: Long Haul for a Short Line

The Municipal Belt Line labored with a split personality from 1924 to 1953. On the one hand, the freight-switching operation was growing and prospering, its role secure—at least temporarily—in the city utility.

On the other hand, the passenger service posed all sorts of problems. Still, the new bus service began on a note of cheery optimism, the *Sunday Ledger* crowing that the Belt Line was "providing its patrons the latest word in transportation."

Bus revenues even picked up a bit in the late 1930s, with gains of $22,500 in 1937 and $6,140 in 1938. It appeared the bus line was finally living up to its potential. Or was it?

The rosy glow faded all too quickly during World War II—ironically, a time when the bus service was the busiest. The tideflats bus service began to lose money steadily and hung like a millstone around the Belt Line's neck from 1940 to 1947, when the city finally discontinued it. What went wrong? It's a story of considerable hardship and woe, whose "happy ending" comes much later in the Belt Line's history.

In 1940 the bus problem fell squarely in the lap of new Belt Line Superintendent Amos Booth. With tideflats industrial expansion and the flood of shipyard workers, the Belt Line's nine buses were simply overwhelmed. So, one of his first acts was to approach the City Council for $30,000 to buy three 40-passenger buses—eventually supplied by Wentworth & Irwin of Portland.

Bright spot. As the freight business picked up, diesel locomotives replaced electric switch engines.

(Facing page) Tough times. Belt Line Superintendent Amos Booth had a tough time of it during the World War II years. The tideflats bus service hung like a millstone around his neck.

Good news/bad news. War-time attracted more riders onto the buses, forcing the Belt Line to find secondhand buses where it could. In poor repair, they plagued the line with expense.

That only solved one problem—downtown congestion was another, with people, buses and switching locomotives creating severe bottlenecks. Meanwhile, war-time rationing of gasoline and rubber was forcing more people onto the buses. By the time the three new coaches arrived in August 1941, more were needed.

New buses simply weren't available, so Booth picked up used buses wherever he could—some from the New York World's Fair, some from the Bremerton Naval Shipyard. They were both a blessing and a curse: they solved an immediate problem, but—with constant breakdowns and costly repairs—they plagued the line with suffocating expense.

Losses mount

Though the line hauled more than 17 million people from 1941 to 1945, it still lost money. Repairs and labor costs were the big reasons. Losses crept up to almost $90,000 in 1946 and the worst was yet to come—a study indicated the entire bus fleet would need to be replaced within the year—to the tune of $162,000.

It was the beginning of the end for city-operated bus service on the tideflats. After a series of meetings with the Chamber of Commerce and the City Council, Commissioner of Public Utilities Clif Erdahl recommended the city turn the bus operation over to the Tacoma Transit Company (now Pierce Transit). The City Council voted its approval and on January 1, 1947, the Belt Line was out of the bus business.

Now, the Belt Line could concentrate on needed improvements to the freight-switching operation, which had picked up considerably during the outbreak of World War II. By mid-1942, Belt Line locomotives were serving 27 industries over 13 miles of track.

Ore, grain, wood products and raw logs were the bulk of the loads, with logs about 40 percent of all freight. With the added business, switching delays along Lincoln Avenue and at the log dumps were bad and getting worse. The Belt Line desperately needed a modern freight-switching yard.

The answer—federal help. Under Amos Booth, the Belt Line applied for and received a hefty $128,000 Federal Works Agency grant. With a $50,000 federal loan and $101,000 of the Belt Line's "own" money—much of it borrowed from City Light—the federal grant funded construction of a new classification yard on 15 acres of land at the end of the Sitcum Waterway near 11th Street and Sitcum Avenue.

Improvements for a new era

Completed in April 1945, the yard was long overdue, remembers former yardmaster James Keith:

New switch yard. Built with federal help, the Belt Line's new 15-acre classification yard was a crowning achievement for Amos Booth.

"It was getting so [that] on the tracks on Lincoln Avenue there was so much freight coming in, you couldn't handle it . . . you just wondered where you were going to go next [with the excess cars]. You'd even think of little holes out on the tideflats where there was a little stub track. . . .Wherever you could find room you had to put [the extra cars]."

Building the Milwaukee Way interchange yard was one of Amos Booth's most significant achievements. With a nod from Erdahl, he also upgraded the line's rolling stock, replacing engines No. 1626 and 1627 in January 1944 with two modern, 50-ton, 300-horsepower diesel-electric switching locomotives. It was the end of electrically powered cars on the tideflats.

It was a new era. On March 23, 1942, the Belt Line became a real railroad when the Interstate Commerce Commission (ICC) officially declared the railroad subject to the provisions of the Railroad Retirement Act of 1937. All Belt Line freight-switching employees would now fall under federal regulations governing the railroad industry's retirement and unemployment policies. It also meant the Belt Line owed back payments supporting those benefits—amounting to about $27,500.

End of an era. The end of electrically powered cars—such as this service car—came when the Belt Line upgraded its rolling stock in 1944.

Switching cars in 1945. The charge for new Belt Line Superintendent Neil Kime—get the line on solid financial ground. Kime steered it toward shaky stability.

Now the Belt Line truly had a split personality. Though still a municipal entity, it was also an ICC common carrier. This dual role has been troublesome at times, particularly in the delicate field of labor relations. Service industry or self-sufficient business operation? Public or private? The Belt Line has struggled with its identity ever since.

How to run a railroad

In 1945 Neil H. Kime became the new Municipal Belt Line superintendent. A fugitive from the State Tax Commission, Kime didn't know how to run a railroad, but he did know how to manage. His charge: get the Belt Line on solid financial ground.

Free of the money-siphoning bus line, the Belt Line began to handle more traffic and make money with Kime steering it toward shaky stability. Net income jumped from $29,000 in 1947 to well

A pair to draw to. Neil Kime and Clif Erdahl admiring one of the two new 65-ton, 590-horsepower Whitcomb diesel-electric locomotives purchased in 1947.

over $55,000 in 1952—nearly all the surplus going to pay off the war-time bus debts.

After a brief lull, post-war traffic began to grow, reaching 82,000 cars switched by 1952. To handle the load, Neil Kime bought a pair of war surplus diesel locomotives in 1947. The two 65-ton, 590-horsepower Whitcomb diesel-electrics cost $50,000 to repair and replaced the old steam engine. The Belt Line now had a fleet of four locomotives.

The Belt Line was growing up. The new locomotives, track extensions and an addition to the classification yard had all been paid for with Belt Line revenues. "For the first time in 32 years," said a 1948 City Council resolution, the Belt Line "is a modern first class railway equipped to adequately take care of the industrial area it serves without financial loss to the City of Tacoma . . ."

The same resolution also christened one of the new diesel locomotives "The Jay W. McCune," honoring one of the Belt Line's early champions and pioneers.

Kime and crew. Engine 904 was christened "The Jay W. McCune" for one of the Belt Line's Founding Fathers.

Chips and cracks

Kime gets credit for pulling the Belt Line up by its bootstraps. On closer inspection, however, the rosy facade reveals chips and cracks. The Belt Line didn't shake off 30 years of debt quickly or easily.

Yes, the Belt Line was making money in the post-war period, but most of it was going to pay off past debts. Little was left for track maintenance and repair. The line's 50- and 65-ton locomotives were still operating on 1918 streetcar rail. By 1952 it had outgrown its eight-year-old classification yard. The Belt Line administrative office at Taylor Way, home of the superintendent and staff, was a decrepit old structure heated by a pot-belly stove.

And there was more bad news—the roundhouse and shop building built in 1928 were so out of date and in need of repair they were called "worthless" in a 1958 city report.

Nor was the rolling stock in very good shape. The frames of both locomotives No. 903 and 904 were cracked and required constant welding and maintenance. Five crankshafts had broken on "The Jay W. McCune" alone between 1947 and 1957. No. 903 had outlived its useful lifespan.

The track also required attention—some 15,000 untreated railroad ties needed immediate replacement.

In short, the Belt Line was limping along. It was operating, but not operating efficiently. And it would take a substantial investment to turn things around. A formal survey by a railroad consultant called for an improvement program of well over $400,000. The city's own five-year plan would cost $87,400.

Haggling with the railroads

The problem was the railroad's fee structure—the switching rates charged the trunk lines. Though it had been successful in negotiating increases of 20, 5 and 15 percent between 1947 and 1952, the rate boosts were time-consuming—one took three years of negotiation—and never enough.

The Belt Line, said a city report in 1958, was staying afloat only by spending depreciation allowances and deferring maintenance. In 1957, the line wouldn't have been able to meet its payroll if it hadn't received a retroactive $33,000 lump payment from the trunk lines.

The trunk lines, on the other hand, tended to balk, believing that—as a municipally owned utility—the Belt Line wasn't entitled to a profit. The Belt Line answered by saying, "Funds for maintenance, replacement of equipment, depreciation, normal expansion, improvements and necessary additions are not profit and in no way do the meager switching fees paid to the Belt Line reflect a profit."

It was a problem that wouldn't go away, with both sides agreeing to disagree. Through the 1950s and the following three decades, the municipal railroad was a captive of its poor finances and caught in a Catch-22.

Unable to win substantial rate increases from the trunk lines, the Belt Line deferred maintenance and took on debt. Saddled with debt, the Belt Line couldn't attract new loans to improve

No. 905 on the job. In the early 1950s the Belt Line was saddled with debt and the railroad simply floundered.

facilities and replace equipment. The stock deteriorated further, driving up operating costs and forcing the Belt Line to dip into its annual revenues to keep the operation running. The city's railroad simply floundered.

Neil Kime saw the Belt Line through 13 trying years, retiring in April 1958. Described as an "aggressive manager" by former Utilities Director Paul Nolan, Kime presided over many of the railroad's most profitable years before 1960 and some of its major improvements.

The Belt Line gets a break

In 1953 Tacoma changed to a city manager form of government, a move that benefitted the Belt Line in two ways. First, the superintendent job was no longer a political appointment. The days of

The city's revised 1953 charter wiped the Belt Line's age-old debt to City Light off the books in one fell swoop. Now, the Belt Line would sink or swim on its own financial merits.

using the Belt Line as a dumping ground for political allies and campaign favorites were over.

Second, and more important, the city's revised 1953 charter wiped the Belt Line's age-old debt to City Light off the books in one fell swoop. If the Belt Line had been financially solvent in 1953, the gesture certainly would have had greater meaning.

Still nursing debts from the bus service and from the purchase of a brand-new 1950 Alco diesel locomotive and classification yard extension—totalling $264,000—Kime had little reason to celebrate. Still, the debt cancellation cleaned an aggravating 35-year red stain from Belt Line ledgers.

Now, after 1953, the Belt Line would sink or swim on its own financial merits.

1945 - 1962

12

Post-War Growth And the Battle For the Cowlitz

"Official Tacoma can't afford to wait much longer to make one of the most important decisions in its 51-year history," reported *The Tacoma Times* in August 1944. The question posed by a special blue-ribbon planning commission was how to meet the spiraling demand for power—continue building and operating its own hydroelectric plants or "accept domination" from the federal government and the Bonneville Power Administration.

Power shortages were on the way following World War II, even though the second Nisqually Project had just gone on line.

(Facing page) Corralling the Cowlitz. In a photo that became nationally famous, some of the 400 workers at Mayfield Dam site prepare the dam's foundation—1956.

Called "Tacoma, The City We Build," the report predicted the end of the war would not end the demand for more power. "If anybody thinks that the highest point of electrical use has been reached, he'd better just sit down and revise his figures. . . . If half the dreams of the scientists come true in the next 20 years, the average home will demand far and away more electricity than it ever has before."

Keeping well ahead of demand was critical, the report concluded, and gave municipal ownership a ringing endorsement. "Tacoma MUST produce its own power and the only way to do that is to own and operate its own plants."

Nisqually on line

In September 1945, a month after the Japanese surrender and the end of World War II, Tacoma City Light took another step in that direction, flipping the switch on its second Nisqually Project. The celebration was muted, however, by the plagued history of the project and the realization that, even with the new generators on line, it was not the final answer to looming power shortages.

"The second Nisqually's history is one of trouble piled upon trouble," explained the *Times.* "Undiscovered faults in the rock developed in both dam sites. That called for more excavation than was expected. The war was on and it became increasingly difficult to get efficient men. Costs rose. Finally, the worst luck of all occurred last spring when the 6,500-foot tunnel from LaGrande Dam to its powerhouse sprung a leak, caused a big slide and held up the project for about five months."

Editorializing on the project, the *Tacoma News Tribune* said, "About the only positive thing about the whole affair is that Tacoma did need the additional power, for it has had to purchase about

The battle for the Cowlitz became one of Tacoma's top news stories for years, stopped construction in mid-stride and delayed Cowlitz power until 1963.

$1 million annually from the Bonneville and Seattle systems in the past few years." The project's ballooning cost—from a proposed $11 million to $23.6 million—"makes frugal minded Tacomans shudder."

But the difficulties with this project were small potatoes compared to the challenges awaiting City Light and its next hydroelectric venture—two dams and power plants on the Cowlitz River in eastern Lewis County.

With load doubling every seven or eight years, City Light had acquired water rights and construction permits in 1946 for a project that would double hydroelectric capacity. Completion was expected "three or four years after the date of authorization," according to the 1947 City Light annual report.

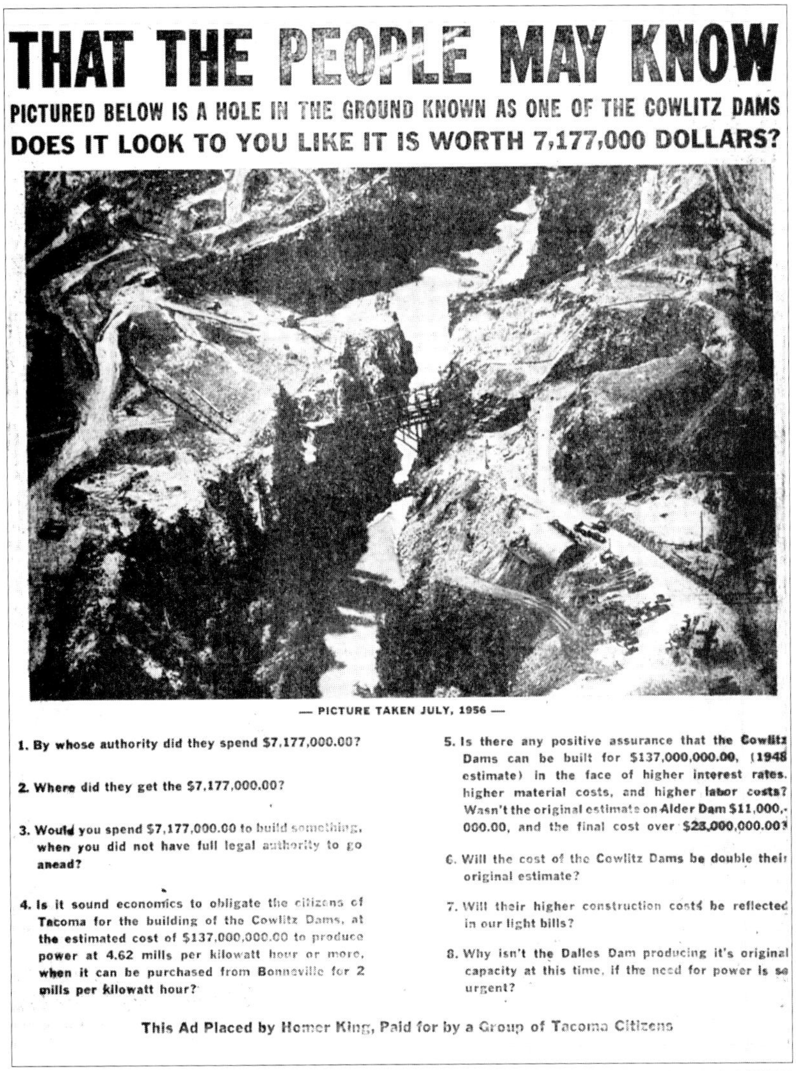

THAT THE PEOPLE MAY KNOW

PICTURED BELOW IS A HOLE IN THE GROUND KNOWN AS ONE OF THE COWLITZ DAMS
DOES IT LOOK TO YOU LIKE IT IS WORTH 7,177,000 DOLLARS?

— PICTURE TAKEN JULY, 1956 —

1. By whose authority did they spend $7,177,000.00?

2. Where did they get the $7,177,000.00?

3. Would you spend $7,177,000.00 to build something, when you did not have full legal authority to go ahead?

4. Is it sound economics to obligate the citizens of Tacoma for the building of the Cowlitz Dams, at the estimated cost of $137,000,000.00 to produce power at 4.62 mills per kilowatt hour or more, when it can be purchased from Bonneville for 2 mills per kilowatt hour?

5. Is there any positive assurance that the Cowlitz Dams can be built for $137,000,000.00, (1948 estimate) in the face of higher interest rates, higher material costs, and higher labor costs? Wasn't the original estimate on Alder Dam $11,000,000.00, and the final cost over $23,000,000.00?

6. Will the cost of the Cowlitz Dams be double their original estimate?

7. Will their higher construction costs be reflected in our light bills?

8. Why isn't the Dalles Dam producing it's original capacity at this time, if the need for power is so urgent?

This Ad Placed by Homer King, Paid for by a Group of Tacoma Citizens

PHOTO COURTESY OF THE MORNING NEWS TRIBUNE

Battle for the Cowlitz. City Light's plans to build two dams on the state's top steelhead river inflamed sportsmen, touching off a bitter fight that lasted for years.

Bitter battles ahead

The key word is "authorization"—the project touched off a bitter fight between City Light, sportsmen and the State Game Department that led all the way to the U.S. Supreme Court—three times. The battle for the Cowlitz became one of Tacoma's top news stories for years, stopped construction in mid-stride and delayed Cowlitz power until 1963. City Light didn't know it back in 1946, but the "good old days" of unquestioned public support for its decisions were numbered.

Full head of steam. Even with all generating sources going full blast, including Steam Plant No. 2 pictured here, Tacoma faced a severe power shortage and blackout.

Meanwhile, Tacoma and the entire Pacific Northwest were face-to-face with a critical power shortage—one that would not go away quickly. In 1949 *The Tacoma Times* said, "Continued below-freezing weather . . . had power generators wobbling on their shafts Monday as the week's industrial loads came on lines already squirming under heavy domestic and heating demands." So serious was the power crunch, the Northwest's entire interconnected power system was in danger of collapse and the possibility of a blackout loomed.

The shortage reduced generator frequency from 60 to 59.5 cycles, making all Tacoma clocks run about six minutes slow during the day. Don't re-set them, advised City Light Superintendent Frank Ward—they'll catch up at night when the load drops and generators pick up speed.

By 1952, with the nation at war in Korea, the situation became even more acute, requiring load curtailment throughout the Northwest. All major industries were placed on a quota of 90 percent of their previous year's weekly use. Smaller businesses were asked to cut their use also.

Tacoma City Light was also doing what it could to squeeze extra power out of existing facilities. In 1952, Cushman No. 1 generator units were boosted from 20,000 kilowatts to 24,000 kilowatts each. At Cushman No. 2, a third penstock and a 30,000-kilowatt generator were added. And a major addition at Steam Plant No. 2 put a second 25,000-kilowatt turbine-generator in service.

Growth and maturity

And, in spite of its power supply difficulties, the utility was growing and maturing, beginning construction of a new central facility at South 35th Street and Union Avenue that would consolidate

Let there be light. Recognizing the need for better streetlighting, Tacoma went to the polls twice in the 1950s and approved $2.5 million for more streetlights.

Emphasis on safety. Employee safety began receiving increasing attention in the 1950s. By 1952, some 730 employees worked for City Light.

Safety at work. Two City Light employees practice rescue techniques—credited with saving four lives in the late 1940s and early 1950s.

City Light forces and streamline operations. The facility would share the 25-acre campus with the Department of Public Utilities' $1.2 million administration building, also under construction.

Pent-up demand and post-war growth also brought power distribution problems and City Light designed and began implementing a new, efficient "checkerboard" pattern of distribution substations. Installing the new, compact units brought customers good voltage regulation, better service through control of outages and ample capacity for the future. Completed in 1953, the program tripled substation capacity in 10 years.

By 1952, some 730 employees worked for City Light. The annual payroll climbed to $3.2 million—an average of $4,403 per employee. Employee safety was receiving increasing attention, with the safety program credited with producing savings of $225,000 since its inception in 1941 and, more important, saving four lives in the previous five years.

The power shortage continued—made even worse by one of the century's driest years. Just 16.95 inches of rain fell in 1952, compared to 40.5 in a normal year. Where was the Cowlitz hydroelectric project when Tacoma needed it? Hung up in court.

The troubled project's history dated back to 1946 when City Light purchased the development rights from a Minneapolis paper firm. Two years later the utility announced its plans to build Mayfield and Mossyrock dams.

Opposition erupts

"Practically overnight," said a City Light annual report, "small interest groups, specialized leagues of sportsmen and others challenged Tacoma's right to build the dams." Erupted, was more accurate. Attending a sportsmen's club meeting, *The Tacoma Times* described ". . . uncontrolled anger, vitriolic verbal assault. They quivered visibly. They whirled on their feet, arms sweeping wildly, they shouted. Parliamentary law lay dead on the floor."

Onward and upward. After three trips to the U.S. Supreme Court, the Mayfield Dam was back on track. Here construction workers build spillway forms.

State Senator Barney Jackson of Tacoma even introduced a bill in the legislature that would authorize the State Department of Fisheries to blow up the Cushman hydro project because it had no fish ladders. Though that tongue-in-cheek bill failed, the legislature did create a "fish sanctuary" on the Cowlitz, blocking construction of the dams. "We took a hell of a beating," said Commissioner Clif Erdahl when asked for his reaction.

Finding little luck at home, City Light turned to the federal government for help. In 1951, following extensive hearings, the Federal Power Commission ruled that the dams were in the best interests of all the people and the United States Supreme Court issued the first of its three decisions upholding Tacoma's right of construction.

"The City Council presided last night over the official death of the Cowlitz contract," said the* Tacoma News Tribune. *But reports of the project's death were greatly exaggerated.

Emotional arguments and court cases continued, but in August 1954 Tacoma's Public Utility Board once again underscored its commitment to municipal ownership, approving construction of the $146 million, two-dam Cowlitz River installation.

Over the 27-year period necessary to pay off the project, the cost per kilowatt-hour might be slightly higher than that paid for Bonneville power, said Utilities Director Dean Barline, but federal power "will be just like paying rent. We won't have anything to show for it."

Cowlitz gets nod

The two-dam hydro project is located on the Cowlitz River, the state's top steelhead fishing river, 65 miles south of Tacoma. Mossyrock Dam was to be a concrete arch dam 1,300 feet long and 325 feet high, with a reservoir extending 21 miles up the river.

Mayfield Dam, some 13 miles downstream, would be 850 feet long and 185 feet high. The dams' two powerhouses and generators would have an installed capacity of 460,000 kilowatts.

Construction began at the Mayfield site on July 7, 1955. Within a year, heavy machinery and more than 400 men from general contractor Arundel-Dixon Corporation dug their way to bedrock to pour the foundations.

It was a sweet but fleeting victory. In 1957, the Washington State Supreme Court ruled that City Light couldn't condemn a State Game Department fish hatchery without legislative permission. So, as the spring brought fresh green leaves to the trees and a spectrum of flowers to the fields, the Cowlitz Project stopped dead in its tracks—mothballed!

"The City Council presided last night over the official death of the Cowlitz contract," said the *Tacoma News Tribune* in November 1957. At the end of the year, the dams were voted the top local news story of 1957, along with the indictment of Seattle Teamster leader Dave Beck.

Tacoma wins

But, to paraphrase Mark Twain, reports of the project's death were greatly exaggerated. In a unanimous decision, the U.S. Supreme Court overturned the lower court decision. "Tacoma Wins," shouted the headlines. Mayor Ben Hanson said, "This decision should at long last firmly establish Tacoma's right to continue with this valuable project. We hope it will help prevent further opposition."

Washington Attorney General John O'Connell also hoped the ordeal was over, saying, "We want no more of the ridiculous sight of departments of the government fighting themselves in the courts and making our state look ridiculous in the U.S. Supreme Court."

The sportsmen, however, vowed to continue the fight and immediately began gathering signatures for an initiative that would limit the height of the dams. But it was the end of the road for the opposition, with the State Supreme Court eventually ruling that the measure couldn't block construction.

Meanwhile, engineers and draftsmen dusted off blueprints, new bids were drawn and appraisers turned to the task of purchasing some 2,500 acres along the Cowlitz.

Shortly before Independence Day 1959, men and machines returned to complete the giant 860-foot power tunnel that would carry some 13,000 cubic feet of water per second to the Mayfield powerhouse turbines.

City Light also reached an accommodation with the State Game and Fisheries departments, working with them to design a unique downstream louver system to carry fish safely past Mayfield Dam, and committing some $4.5 million to protect the river's fisheries.

Shining example of what outdoor lighting could do for baseball—Cheney Stadium, dedicated June 1960. For trivia buffs, Tacoma played Vancouver, and Rosy Ryan was the Tacoma Giants' general manager.

The sizzling sixties

Entering what the *News Tribune* called the "sizzling sixties," the paper forecast a decade of record growth for City Light and sketched the following picture of the utility's position: After a recession that cut load growth in the late 1950s, ahead was a "more normal growth pattern of about eight percent annually . . . more than 2 billion kilowatt hours were consumed in 1959.

"Nearly 60 percent of all power is now bought from other sources, at a cost approximating $3 million. . . . Ten years ago the average Tacoma home used less than 6,000 kilowatt hours; last year it was 9,200—one of the highest amounts in the nation. . . . Television sets, alone, have required City Light to supply about 25 million kilowatts more electricity each year."

The report underscored the urgency of the work on the Cowlitz. Four weeks later, the Public Utility Board awarded a $9.9 million contract for Mayfield Dam to the Perini Corporation and in May 1960 the first concrete was poured.

On July 11, 1961, the contractor ignited 5.5 tons of dynamite to divert the river and gave the green light to the upstream fish passage system. The project began to grow dramatically. Land was being cleared in all directions and brush and debris burned. The powerhouse began to rise and the spillway took form. Workmen labored around the clock.

In October, a huge concrete bucket dumped the first pour for the dam, raising it a modest 2.5 feet, one percent of the total height. In all, 19,000 cubic yards of concrete would be used to form the thin arch dam.

On April 14, 1962, two heavy gates slammed shut over the diversion tunnel and Mayfield Lake was born. In just four days water began sliding over the spillway. A trickle at first, the water rushed downward forming a spectacular "roostertail" as it catapulted out of the "ski jump" type bucket at the base of the spillway.

Big picture—sort of. A model of the Mayfield Project, showing powerhouse at left, fish ladder to its right and the dam itself—850 feet long and 185 feet high. Mossyrock would be almost twice as large.

Storm rips Tacoma

As Tacoma was getting ready to celebrate the completion of Mayfield Dam, it was to find out that not all elements of nature could be harnessed. In October, the infamous Columbus Day Storm, the tail-end of a vicious Pacific Ocean typhoon, slammed into the Pacific Northwest with 85-mile-an-hour winds, causing more than a million dollars in damage and knocking down power lines throughout Tacoma.

More than 200 Tacoma trees were toppled, power was out all over the city and major highways were blocked. Wright Park and Allenmore Golf Course were a shambles, Fircrest was littered with fallen firs and the Lakewood area appeared as if "its trees had moved bodily onto the streets," according to the *Tacoma News Tribune.* Two lions escaped from their cage in Spanaway, one biting a boy. A Yelm couple was killed—two of 36 deaths on the West Coast attributed to the storm.

City Light was hit hard, answering thousands of requests for service the day after the storm. Every available lineman, helper and more than 100 other qualified employees were pressed into service.

"The crews, which worked throughout the storm Friday and all day yesterday, were continuing to work throughout last night and this morning without a rest," reported the *News Tribune.* Working beside his crews and sharing the long hours, Utilities Director Clif Erdahl called his workers heroes and said, "As far as it is humanly possible, we will keep working."

Erdahl estimated it would take a month to completely repair all damage to the facilities and sympathized with the customers affected. "We know that everyone depends on electric power for daily living. We do not wish to mislead anyone. Our lines have been damaged extensively. We are doing everything humanly possible. We urge all those still without electricity to take whatever steps they can to be comfortable."

As 1962 drew to a close, President Kennedy and the nation were breathing easier after the Cuban missile crisis and City Light was fighting a two-front war—working long hours to repair storm damage while working full speed ahead on what it hoped would be the long-term answer to the city's power needs.

After years of frustration, bitter argument and interminable court battles, the Cowlitz Hydroelectric Project was about to start paying dividends.

Penstocks—the giant pipes that would feed the Mayfield powerhouse, carrying 13,000 cubic feet of water per second.

1958 - 1969

13

City Water: "Lester Gate" and the Watershed Battle

When W. A. Kunigk hung up his spurs, City Water needed a strong leader for the years ahead—some of the most challenging in its history.

It found him in Aldo Benedetti, a young civil engineer, Naval Academy graduate and Korean War veteran. Affable, handsome and hardworking, Benedetti was only 25 years old when he began working his way up through City Water's ranks in 1947. Groomed for the superintendency, Benedetti was unanimously chosen to become City Water's sixth superintendent after the retirement of Julius Kuehl in 1958. He was just 35 years old.

Benedetti brought with him firsthand experience with Tacoma's outdated distribution system. During Benedetti's 14 years as superintendent, City Water invested millions of dollars in improving water distribution. The renewed assault on the wood mains—most were 50 to 60 years old—and substandard galvanized iron pipe continued, ending in 1975.

(Facing page) On the way out—a logging company in the Green River watershed. Protecting the watershed meant moving people out—an important goal for City Water in the 1950s and 1960s.

Digging out the wood

It took City Water 30 years to root out all the wood pipe and forgotten pieces still turned up from time to time, recalled Benedetti:

"When we got down to the last five miles [of wood pipe] they never seemed to disappear. We'd say we had replaced the last five and then somebody would find another two or three [miles] some place else because the records weren't all that great."

Rooting out the wood. Aldo Benedetti made replacing wood water mains a top priority—a job that never seemed to end.

Putting a lid on it. The North End Standpipe got a cover in 1963 to protect water purity.

Dozens of miles of cast iron and asbestos cement pipes were laid and hundreds of hydrants and new services added (748 services in 1970 alone) during the intensive LID replacement programs of the 1960s and 1970s.

Benedetti spearheaded many other programs, including improvements to comply with federal water sanitation standards. Reservoirs were fenced 100 feet from the edge of the basins and the open-topped standpipes were covered. Hood Street Reservoir, entering its eighth decade of service in 1955, was outfitted with a partial cover in 1959–1960.

Not all of City Water's maintenance was preventive, however. In January 1965, a massive mud slide at the Green River intake completely wiped out part of City Water's access roadway and pushed a field office down the embankment into the settling basin—requiring major repairs.

Rate increases on the way

Rates and relations with neighbors were also major focuses between 1957 and 1975 for the City Council, Public Utility Board and City Water. They tussled with the sticky issues of water rate increases, acquisition of and service to small mutual water companies in rural Pierce County and the city's obligation to pay for fire protection service rendered by City Water.

With City Water threading its way through rocky financial times, a rate increase was a top priority. By 1956, net annual revenues had slipped below $130,000. One year later they plunged to $36,000, a pitifully low sum that wouldn't sustain growth or expansion.

Independent consulting firm Ford, Bacon & Davis, hired in 1957 to assess City Water's financial status, recommended a 25 percent rate

What a mess! A massive mud slide in 1965 pushed a City Water office into the headworks settling basin.

hike for all residential customers. Public rate meetings were poorly attended, but Utility Board member John D. Rue raised an issue echoed by many ratepayers: Should City Water's primary obligation be to give present customers "a fair shake"? Or should it look after its own growth, funding expansion and services that can be offered at reasonable rates to future customers—a tricky question still debated today.

Board member Rue came down on the side of the consuming public while Utilities Director Dean Barline argued in favor of an increase, demonstrating that City Water stood to gain $386,000 per year with a 25 percent rate boost and would pass those earnings on to consumers through improved and expanded service.

In the end, public apathy ruled the day and in the absence of any public clamor, the increase went into effect on October 19, 1957. City Water would go 14 years before the next increase—a 23 percent rate hike in 1971.

Rates for number one

Meanwhile, separate contracts were negotiated with the city's largest customer, the St. Regis Paper Company, a practice dating back to the late 1930s. The St. Regis pulp mill consumed vast and ever-rising quantities of water; use skyrocketed from 18.7 million gallons daily in 1958 to 31.1 million in 1971.

Negotiations with St. Regis proceeded smoothly enough, even when City Water asked for a 55 percent rate boost in 1959. St. Regis absorbed a steady stream of rate hikes, from $21.50 per million gallons in 1956 to $37.57 per million gallons in 1966.

At the same time, City Water also was attempting to define its responsibilities to outlying, rural communities. Tacoma, after all, claimed the most abundant water source within a 35-mile radius. City Water had long served towns and settlements adjacent to the Green River pipeline—the towns of Cumberland and Enumclaw among the first.

A year's supply. The amount of water consumed by the average Tacoma household in a year, a stunt dreamed up by Tacoma Public Utilities public relations legend, Bill Dugovich. Peggy Ervin is the employee pictured.

In February 1957, Mayor John Anderson decided to change all that—and Fife was the first victim. Anderson presented the City Council with a resolution effectively barring the city from supplying any municipal service (especially sewage disposal and water) to incorporated communities outside city limits, such as Fife. Stating

Portland Avenue Reservoir and Tacoma in 1961.

unequivocally that Tacoma's resources were reserved for use by Tacomans, the resolution passed.

But Aldo Benedetti and Dean Barline believed City Water had the resources to serve Fife—and the utility needed the revenue. Carrying their fight to serve Fife back to the Council, they succeeded in amending Mayor Anderson's resolution two years later—breaking the Council of its isolationist bent toward outside communities.

County residents who used Tacoma water—about 9,100 people in 1960—paid anywhere from one-fifth to two-thirds more for their water, on average, than city dwellers. They represented a substantial source of revenue for City Water. From late December 1966 through the early 1970s, Tacoma City Water acquired a half-dozen small mutuals, extended water service to Fife and improved service to Northeast Tacoma and communities along the Green River pipeline.

Fighting for the watershed

Then came one of City Water's greatest and most important campaigns since the Green River gravity line's construction—the fight to gain complete control of the Green River watershed.

Going up—The Eagle Gorge Dam (later renamed Howard Hanson) under construction in 1961 was in the heart of City Water's watershed, an area it fought to protect in the 1960s.

Keep out.

While Eagle Gorge Dam was going up, City Water was defending its policy of denying the public access in the 1960s.

The watershed management program begun under W. A. Kunigk and carried on by Julius Kuehl and Chief Sanitary Engineer John Roller was still in place in the late 1950s, proceeding as planned. Aldo Benedetti, entering office in 1958, would become its strongest and most vocal advocate.

The first skirmish came in the winter of 1957 with the Eagle Gorge Dam under construction (later renamed the Howard Hanson Dam in memory of project engineer Col. Howard A. Hanson) when Tacoma was first forced to defend its policy of prohibiting public access to the Green River watershed.

John Roller was called to Olympia to testify against two bills, both backed by sportsmen's interests, which demanded access to municipal watersheds (specifically the Green River watershed and Seattle's Cedar River watershed) for fishermen, hunters, campers and hikers.

Roller and Washington State Health Director Dr. Bernard Bucove spoke in favor of keeping the watersheds closed, Roller testifying that Tacoma would be forced to construct a $5 million water filtration and treatment plant if the public were allowed access. Their testimony prevailed, but it was only the opening shot in the first of annual

All aboard for a good, old-fashioned, bare-knuckled fight between City Water and the residents of Lester over access to the watershed.

battles that went on for years between Tacoma, sportsmen's clubs, King County, watershed residents and the United States Forest Service (a branch of the Department of Agriculture).

Tacoma's strategy was to continue purchasing and trading for land in the watershed whenever the opportunity presented itself. Beginning in 1957 and continuing through 1962, City Water set aside $100,000 a year for land acquisition in the watershed, especially around the Howard Hanson Dam reservoir.

Bits and pieces

The victories came in bits and pieces. City Water bartered with the Corps in November 1957 and in one exchange purchased 3,000 acres for $125,000, then sold the Corps water storage and flood control rights to the land for $50,000.

City Water also negotiated with the St. Regis Paper Company, Scott Paper and Weyerhaeuser for watershed lands. A May 1959 swap with Weyerhaeuser garnered 766 acres for Tacoma, including portions of a vital access road, and acquired another 1,000 acres from private owners in December 1958. In addition, City Water had arranged with these companies and the Northern Pacific Railroad to patrol and indirectly regulate 90 percent of the watershed.

Watching suspiciously were the 125 residents of the old railroad town of Lester, the one populated town in the watershed. The railroad provided one of only two means of access to Lester—the other was U.S. Forest Service Road 212, which crossed the watershed from City Water's headworks to Stampede Pass.

In October 1960, City Water signed an agreement with King County to limit access to the watershed by erecting a locked gate across its road. Keys were handed to Weyerhaeuser, the Bonneville Power Administration, the Forest Service and the townspeople of Lester.

Lester's isolation

Lester residents didn't like it—their only year-round access to the town had been cut off and access restricted. Though derisive of their treatment, Lester residents could do little but accept City Water's action. City Water, meanwhile, purchased the remaining

Lester in 1959—125 residents linked to the outside world by rail and Forest Service Road 212.

Howard Hanson in 1961. The $40 million dam was dedicated in 1962—the first and last time it was opened to visitors.

land belonging to St. Regis that lay in the Howard Hanson Dam reservoir basin.

In the early '60s the utilities got new leadership. J. Dean Barline, utilities director since May 1954, died suddenly of a heart attack on February 12, 1961. The "quiet administrator" was eulogized by friends and co-workers for his admirable work and dedication. Political speculation about Barline's successor began hours after his death. Aldo Benedetti, though hesitant, was named acting director four days later. Benedetti kept his job as superintendent, performing both tasks for eight months.

This means you. Just a friendly greeting from City Water to remind travelers that it was serious about protecting its watershed.

The Public Utility Board tossed about many candidate names in the ensuing months, eventually narrowing the field to two: Benedetti and another familiar name and face—Clif Erdahl. The job was Benedetti's for the asking, but he eventually turned it down. The Board then unanimously chose Erdahl to succeed Barline and Erdahl promptly appointed Benedetti assistant director—and he retained his position as City Water superintendent, as well.

Looking back, Benedetti regards this transition period and the following decade as a crucial time in City Water's history.

"I think a lot of the things we were able to do during that time—and we made a lot of major policy changes—were helped by the dual role I had," Benedetti recalls. "I had direct access to the Utility Board, I had direct access to the director, I controlled the agenda for the meetings, so City Water didn't come up second on things that had to be done."

Howard Hanson Dam was dedicated May 12, 1962. An estimated 3,000 people visited the dam and attended the ceremonies—the first and last time the $40 million dam was opened to visitors. And the long-simmering dispute between City Water and opponents of the Green River watershed's closure broke into open warfare.

The infamous Lester Gate incident. After first agreeing to a locked gate to limit access to the watershed, King County changed its mind, blew the gate off its hinges and dragged it away.

The Lester Gate incident

In June 1962, Ed Munro, Chairman of the King County Board of Commissioners, fired a shot—an ultimatum to Tacoma City Water. Either open the Forest Service road gate near Lester by July 3 or King County would "have to take some means" to remove it. Benedetti suggested a conference to iron out legal differences and claims, but insisted that until that time King County would have to abide by its 1960 permit granting Tacoma control of access into and out of the watershed and the town of Lester.

In answer, a raiding party led by King County Engineer Walter Winters blew the four locks from the Lester Gate, cut the gate off its

City Water fights back with Sanitary Engineer John Roller (right) and watershed inspector Vern Meyer (center) supervising the installation of a chain across the road.

hinges and dragged it away behind a pick-up truck. Tensions ran high. John Roller and watershed inspector Vern Meyer welded a thick chain between the two bare poles and City Water staked two sentries at the gate to watch the road.

The press loved it, the first of the so-called "Lester Gate War" incidents. Editorials split along county lines with one sensational *News Tribune* editorial trumpeting Tacoma's rights and the county's misdeeds in the "rape of the Lester Gate."

Both sides assembled their attorneys and went to court, with Tacoma winning the first round. Meanwhile, the residents of Lester were irrevocably drawn into the issue a few months later when City Water sought to condemn 1,450 acres of watershed land, most privately owned.

The judge accused City Water of "attempting to exercise police powers under the guise of condemnation."

The land was needed to retain a protective "filter blanket" of natural vegetation that would act as a half-mile-deep "buffer zone" on either side of the river and form the linchpin of City Water's watershed management and control plan.

Lester residents rallied against the condemnation, holding bake sales and barbecues to help pay attorneys' fees. The 84 property owners named in the court action were represented by Lewis Bell, an Everett attorney. The case lasted several days and was heard by Superior Court Judge James W. Hodson, also presiding judge of the Lester Gate case.

Hodson ruled in favor of the watershed property owners, stating that before the city could condemn private lands for public use, it would have to prove the residents represented an existing or foreseeable threat to Tacoma's water. Hodson also accused Tacoma City Water of "attempting to exercise police powers under guise of condemnation."

City of Tacoma Attorney Marshall McCormick promised an appeal to the Supreme Court.

The feds try to back out

Mere days before the condemnation suit action, City Water was hit on another front—a U.S. Forest Service report to Tacoma Mayor Harold Tollefson, which proposed opening the Green River watershed.

Essentially, the Forest Service was asking for the overturn or modification of the 1914 agreement signed by Tacoma Mayor William W. Seymour and Acting U.S. Secretary of Agriculture B. T. Galloway—Tacoma's primary defense against multiple use of watershed lands. City Water answered with a resounding "no."

The utility also accused the Forest Service of attempting to open the watershed's 148,000 acres of woodlands while it was preparing to close 346,000 acres of land nearby in order to establish a protected wilderness area.

On yet another battlefront in 1963,City Water's attempt to purchase 279 acres of state-owned land in September was thwarted

Eagle Gorge Depot served logging operations in the watershed, a source of frustration for Lester residents. In 1985, an agreement with the logging companies forbade them to hire Lester residents.

Doomed.

After years of festering battle, City Water purchased the Lester townsite for $37,000. It was the beginning of the end. The school was the last battleground.

by a group of "anonymous sportsmen"—actually watershed landowners—led by Walter Fransen. The "sportsmen" (a misnomer played up by the press and the utility) filed an injunction against City Water in Thurston County Superior Court, which tied up the transaction for nearly three years.

The 279 acres were the last parcel of land not yet owned by Tacoma in the Howard Hanson Dam reservoir basin. City Water attorneys refused to give in and, after months of planning and negotiations, City Water managed to sidestep the injunction and legal hoops by swapping land with the State Department of Natural Resources for the watershed acreage.

More opposition

The city–state land swap angered City Water's opponents, including outdoors enthusiasts and the hunting and fishing lobby, who blasted City Water's stance and lobbied for the opening of Washington's municipally owned watersheds. Informally allied with the U.S. Forest Service, the sportsmen clubs were formidable and tenacious adversaries.

Then came opposition from an unexpected quarter—the U.S. Army Corps of Engineers. In November 1963, it notified City Water that it intended to appeal a federal court ruling that restricted access to Howard Hanson Dam. The Corps wanted to open the Howard Hanson Dam road to the public. After some initial court skirmishes,

Going, going . . .

By 1973, only 18 Lester homes were occupied.

Benedetti, Mayor Harold Tollefson and Public Utilities attorney Paul Nolan flew to Washington, D.C., to meet with Justice Department, Corps of Engineers and Forest Service attorneys and officials.

After two and a half days of talks, the Tacoma delegation returned home with a tentative agreement to maintain the status quo in the watershed. Tacoma's other opponents refused to settle for the status quo, however.

King County renewed its struggle with City Water in June 1964. On June 9, City Water attorneys argued before the Washington State Supreme Court for the reversal of the 1963 Superior Court decision that prevented the city from condemning 1,450 acres of private land in the watershed. After an eight-month battle, the State Supreme Court overturned a lower court ruling, giving the city the right to condemn the property. The city's attorneys quickly applied for a trial date to begin the condemnation process.

But Lewis Bell, the Everett attorney representing Lester residents, fought a rear-guard action. With a series of delays and continuances,

Bell blocked the condemnation hearings for a year. In the interim, many Lester residents had grown tired of the hassle. City Water settled privately with individual owners for 14 of the 42 parcels in the original lawsuit. And, in spite of Bell's stalling, the State Supreme Court verdict in Tacoma's favor opened the door for the city to complete its watershed land acquisition program without opposition.

Beginning of the end for Lester

The Public Utility Board and City Council passed resolutions in April and May 1965 authorizing City Water to acquire land in and around Lester. Rather than condemn the town property outright, City Water set out to take over the land as it became available through the death or departure of the owners. When Lester residents moved, died or put their property up for sale, City Water was there to purchase the land.

Not all Lester residents moved out peacefully. Some rented out their property so they would not have to sell it. City Water cars were targeted by stone-throwers, and in one instance, a wall of flame greeted two utility vehicles as they tried to drive through the town.

The hard feelings and tempers didn't cool. Lesterites distrusted Tacoma (a feeling perhaps returned by the city) and confrontations

Worth protecting. Rather than condemning Lester property, City Water took it over on the death or departure of owners.

with the watershed inspection crews were not uncommon. The worst for Lester residents was yet to come when City Water purchased the townsite itself from the Northern Pacific Railroad in March 1967 for a mere $37,000.

City Water honored Northern Pacific tenancy agreements until they expired, issuing rental permits to Lesterites who wished to remain in town. But the number of year-round inhabitants in Lester dwindled steadily until only 18 homes were occupied in 1973.

Concerns about sanitation in Lester lingered, even if most of its residents did not. Two cases of hepatitis discovered in 1975 prompted the county and state health departments to shut down Acey's Friday Creek tavern and a restaurant. Other businesses followed at varying intervals.

The town of Lester limped on until 1985, a shell of its former bustling self. Prevented from leasing, selling or deeding their property to others, the handful of remaining town residents knew there was no future for them. An agreement with the logging companies in the watershed forbidding them from hiring Lester residents—ruled illegal in 1981 by King County Superior Court—forced Lesterites to search for work outside the watershed.

The few that remained scorned Tacoma. How, they wondered, could City Water tolerate a herd of elk defecating in the Green River and heavy logging operations around the watershed, yet still seek to remove a town of 75 residents? In the end, Tacoma simply outlasted Lester.

1914 agreement in the news—again

But King County and the United States Forest Service remained adamantly opposed to closing the watershed to public access. The Forest Service posed the greatest threat to Tacoma's "no multiple use" policy. In November 1964, City Water received a letter from U.S. Secretary of Agriculture Orville Freeman saying his department was

Mission accomplished. By 1968, the battle to protect the watershed from civilization and pollution was over.

"reviewing" its 1914 agreement with the city restricting access to the watershed. Less than three weeks later it canceled the agreement.

Mayor Tollefson fired off a series of angry letters and telegrams to Freeman, President Lyndon B. Johnson and Washington State

Mayor Tollefson fired off a series of angry letters and telegrams to Freeman, President Johnson and Washington Senators Magnuson and Jackson.

Senators Warren Magnuson and Henry Jackson. Tollefson saved his harshest words for Freeman, refusing to "to cooperate [with the Secretary of Agriculture] in the rape of our watershed."

The Mayor urged Senators Magnuson and Jackson to come to Tacoma's aid and pleaded with President Johnson to recognize the city's claims.

Then, it was back to Washington, D.C., to meet with the Secretary of Agriculture and his assistant, John Baker. Tacoma's delegation consisted of Utility Board Chairman Leo McGavick, Clif Erdahl, Benedetti, Tollefson, State Representative Floyd Hicks and Senators Magnuson and Jackson.

Concessions from the feds

After three days of rocky meetings, in which the Tacomans nearly stormed out, city officials wrung two concessions out of Assistant Agriculture Secretary John Baker. He agreed there would be no activity by the Forest Service in the watershed until the U.S. Public Health Service had completed a survey to determine whether the proposed recreational facilities would be "injurious" to Tacoma's water. He also agreed that the Department of Agriculture would abide by the Public Health Service findings.

The four-year, $250,000 U.S. Public Health Service survey produced no conclusive results—but it was a great delaying tactic for City Water. By the time the utility learned of the findings in 1969, it had successfully concluded the bulk of its watershed acquisition program. In January 1968, Aldo Benedetti announced the decade-old watershed protection program a success. Tacoma owned more than 10,000 acres of land in the watershed—9,000 more than it owned in 1951—and over the next several years City Water purchased another 1,000. The fight to protect the watershed from pollution and the encroachment of civilization was over.

TACOMA
PUBLIC
UTILITIES
901

1958 - 1976

14 The Belt Line Up For Adoption

Neil Kime retired from his 13-year stint as Belt Line superintendent in April 1958, having done much to help the railroad shed its image as the Tacoma Public Utilities' "orphan and stepchild." He liked to boast that the Belt Line "was not as long as other railroads, but just as wide," and the old superintendent could point to record-setting—though volatile—financial results as proof that the "muni line" had achieved some measure of stability.

Neil Kime, Belt Line superintendent for 13 years, retired in 1958.

Kime retired without securing a regular switching agreement with the trunk lines, however; that task fell to his successor, Carroll Burks. Unlike Charles McEachron, Amos Booth or Kime, Burks was a professional railroader, with considerable experience with the Pennsylvania Railroad and with U.S. Army rail operations (the Transportation Corps) during World War II. Before joining the Belt Line, he supervised the building of a railroad in Liberia, Africa.

Burks began his new job May 1, 1958, and was recognized by his employees as efficient and well-organized, someone who liked to "get his desk clean." His immediate challenge—boost the line's switching rates enough to put the railroad on solid financial ground.

(Facing page) Money was always tight, but the Belt Line managed to upgrade its rolling stock in the '60s and '70s. Its track, however, remained in terrible shape.

With the Belt Line running in red ink, Burks proposed a 22 percent rate increase, which was rejected by the trunk lines. Turning to the Public Utility Board for support, he got a mixed reaction. Board member E. K. Murray saw the railroad as a monumental 35-year headache and wanted to sell it to the Port of Tacoma. But, after intense lobbying by Burks, the Board authorized Utilities Director J. Dean Barline, City Attorney Marshall McCormick and

Burks to "get tough" with the national carriers and bring them to the bargaining table.

The first offer

Burks got more than he bargained for—the trunk lines offered to buy the railroad. But with Burks lobbying against the sale, city officials eventually decided the carriers would not take the necessary steps to promote Tacoma's industrial growth on the tideflats. Meanwhile, the trunk lines' interest in the deal waned and they proposed a compromise five percent increase.

The Public Utility Board reluctantly agreed, but Burks was decidedly unhappy with the increase—after originally asking for 22 percent. But the ink was hardly dry on the rate hike, when Barline and Burks came right back—almost within the year—asking for another increase. When the trunk lines wavered, E. K. Murray threatened to force the issue by filing a tariff with the Interstate Commerce Commission. The railroads responded in February 1960 with another 10 percent increase—and another offer to buy the railroad.

Carroll Burks, the new "super," was a professional railroader—efficient and well-organized.

A cat-and-mouse-game ensued. The Public Utility Board "declined to consider" the trunk lines' $300,000 offer—official appraisals valued the line at up to $1.1 million—and countered with a demand for a 15 percent increase.

The national lines dug in their heels. Three rate hikes in rapid succession were more than they could stomach. But, after a year of intense haggling, the Board and railroads reached a compromise 8.36 percent retroactive rate hike.

The rate increases gave the Belt Line's revenue picture a rosy glow and the Belt Line turned a net profit of more than $58,000 in 1960, one of its best years ever. But steadily climbing operating, maintenance and labor costs drove net income down.

Still, Burks scraped together $44,650 in April 1961 to pay for a 1950-vintage, 660-horsepower, 100-ton diesel locomotive, using one

New fleet member. A $44,650 purchase by Burks in 1961—a secondhand 660-horsepower, 100-ton diesel.

of the small, diesel-electric engines as a trade-in. The switching fleet remained at five engines.

Up for sale?

Then, following a successful regional convention of the American Short Line Railroad Association, a crisis suddenly loomed. With the city caught in a financial crunch in 1962 and looking for ways to raise revenue, the Public Utility Board floated a proposal to sell the Belt Line to the Port of Tacoma.

It was not a new idea, with the Port and Belt Line talking of combining operations as early as 1956 to facilitate the Port's long-range plan to extend the Port Industrial (Wapato) Waterway south across Lincoln Avenue. Dredging the Port Industrial Waterway meant detouring municipal tracks—a huge expense for the Belt Line.

The Port made its move after talks broke off with the national carriers, making an offer roughly $100,000 less than the trunk lines'. Why would the city even consider such a low-ball offer? The Belt Line was a troublesome "dark horse" operation and selling it seemed a convenient, acceptable way to generate revenue for Tacoma's stricken government. The sale would also streamline the Port's switching operations, save industrial customers money and ensure that the line would be operated with the city's welfare in mind.

By August 1962, it appeared the Belt Line would be the city's sacrificial lamb. A sale price of $317,000 was set—a one-time shot in the arm for Tacoma—and the deal endorsed by the Public Utility Board, a majority of the City Council and the Tacoma Chamber of Commerce. Everybody hoped to get the sale on the November election ballot.

Off the track

Their plans were derailed, however, by Councilman Richard G. Haley, who opposed the sale after discovering that not all the legal

Talk turned again to selling the railroad to the Port for $500,000. After three meetings, the Council said no—it was close, but no deal.

hoops had been jumped through. The proposed sale did not make the ballot. After further dickering with the Port, the City Council on December 12, 1962 declared the Belt Line no longer for sale.

But the issue popped up again when the Port was getting serious about building its planned Port Industrial Waterway extension in early 1964. By February, the Port Commission had agreed to pay all the Belt Line's moving costs except construction of a new headquarters building to replace the ancient office on Taylor Way. The new headquarters and classification yard would be built on East-West Road, about a mile south of the Milwaukee Way yard.

The most significant aspect of the waterway extension from the Belt Line's point of view was the Port's proposed construction of a new circular route around the end of the waterway. The extended Port Industrial Waterway would divide the Belt Line's service area in two, while opening up acres of barren tideflats land for industrial development. This meant more customers—a larger client base—for the municipal railroad.

As the Public Utility Board and Port Commissioners debated how the new Belt Line facilities would be financed—it would cost $1.1 million to relocate its tracks and build a new classification yard—talk turned again to selling the railroad to the Port. In April 1964 the Port made its offer—eventually amounting to $500,000. But, after three meetings, the City Council said no—it was close, but no deal.

Limping along

Meanwhile, Burks kept the Belt Line limping along. Net income climbed to more than $67,000 in 1963, but plummeted to just $6,392 in 1964. What money was left over at the end of the year went to pay off a long-term debt owed City Light for its help in financing construction of the Milwaukee Way classification yard in 1944. As always, the Belt Line could not afford large-scale renovation of track or buildings.

Burks did upgrade the fleet, purchasing a 1950 100-ton diesel locomotive (No. 907) in June 1964 from the Milwaukee Railroad

Struggling. **The Belt Line desperately needed new track and buildings in the mid-1960s, but couldn't afford either.**

for $15,000—"an exceedingly good buy." To help pay for it, he sold the last of the 50-ton diesel-electrics bought by Amos Booth to the Portland Union Stockyards for $15,000, gaining a "new engine" and breaking even on the deal.

Carroll Burks resigned his Belt Line job in early October 1964 to accept the presidency of the American Short Line Railroad Association, headquartered in Washington, D.C. During his six and a half years with the railroad, he was unable to improve anemic Belt Line revenues, though he did manage to keep the railroad from slipping back into annual deficits. He was well organized and a decent manager, but he couldn't get around the Belt Line's inherent shortcomings.

In October 1964, Clif Erdahl announced that the new Belt Line superintendent would be Donald E. Carlson, a lifelong railroader "who cut his baby teeth on a railroad spike." With previous experience as assistant superintendent for Northern Pacific, Carlson settled into his job after the Public Utility Board and Port had discontinued sale negotiations. The city's attention now shifted to the Port's waterway extension program and accompanying municipal track relocation.

Construction got underway in 1964 and by May 1965, the Belt Line detour route around the southern end of the Port Industrial Waterway was completed. The Port absorbed all costs and paid the Belt Line an annual sum to cover higher operating costs it incurred by using the new bypass route.

Overdue improvements

Construction of the Belt Line's new classification yard and office headquarters followed in fairly short order. The $909,000 yard job, including turnouts and track connections for handling 440 cars—with possible expansion to 1,000—was put into use in July 1969. Work also began on a $226,000 project to build the Belt Line's new office building, roundhouse and storage garage.

The new facilities were long overdue. The administrative offices were located in a modest, one-story rectangular building and behind it were the roundhouse and classification yard. The garage stood off to the right. The nucleus of Belt Line operations was for the first time in one place, under one roof.

The fleet had also improved and, though old, was larger and more powerful than ever. In 1967 Carlson bought two additional locomotives to replace engines No. 903 and 904. The 1950-vintage 100-ton, 660-horsepower Alco engines cost the Belt Line $9,000 each. All five engines were then repainted gold and maroon.

The two new engines were christened in July 1968 with a formal ribbon-cutting ceremony at the Belt Line's new classification yard by several civic dignitaries. But despite the celebration, the Belt Line still had a long way to go—the "new" locomotives were rolling on rails that were in terrible shape.

Derailments were common over the 70- and 72-pound rail. Retired switch foreman Joe Peterson recalled that the old rail "was small . . . and would break [easily]. You didn't move as fast . . . because of the ties and small rail." According to Peterson, even the Belt Line's East-West Road classification yard had its problems:

"The turnouts coming from the yard were too sharp and the trains would derail so they had to rebuild the whole yard. [They] put in more ballast and better rail . . . but at first it was quite a problem."

Such a deal. In 1964 Burks bought this used locomotive for $15,000 and sold the last of the line's 50-ton diesel-electrics—for $15,000.

Heavy traffic

Heavier cars transporting a bigger volume of goods rolled over the aging rails. Logs and grain remained the Belt Line's "bread and butter," making up 41 percent of all loads handled in 1974. The line hauled a record 19,450 carloads of logs in 1973. Ores and chemicals were also a mainstay and the Belt Line began hauling automobiles (Toyotas beginning in 1971) in greater numbers.

In fact, business picked up considerably in the early 1970s, with net income rising in modest increments to record levels in 1972 and 1973. And, in 1973, the Belt Line broke the "million dollar barrier" in gross operating revenues. But in just four years, expenses jumped almost 70 percent—fueled by a higher city gross earnings tax and the skyrocketing price of diesel fuel.

In December 1971 Superintendent Carlson launched a track rehabilitation program, hiring Jack W. Kanan—a Northern Pacific roadmaster and old Army buddy—to oversee the job. Kanan was a "hands on," hard-edged manager with quite a temper, as his employees remember him.

He was also resourceful, according to current Belt Line Superintendent Dennis Dean: "Jack had a railroad sense about him that I think few railroad men have. He was able to see things a civil or mechanical engineer couldn't. . . . When there was no money to build materials, they could be procured. So his management style was to, literally, do the job. Period."

A Herculean task

Working their industry connections, Carlson and Kanan began the Herculean task of rebuilding the railroad's 33 miles of track. Old rail was sold for scrap to purchase heavier 90-, 100- and 112-pound rail. Switches were relocated, grade crossings improved and turnouts replaced to lessen track curvature.

With money short, the program proceeded piecemeal through the 1970s and into the 1980s and when things got really tight, maintenance was deferred—a longstanding Belt Line custom.

The situation improved, but only a little, recalls Dennis Dean. "When I first came to the Belt Line in 1977, it wasn't unusual to have 10 derailments in a week, sometimes five in a day."

Don Carlson guided the Belt Line through 12 fairly stable years until his retirement in 1976 at age 59. With revenues a continuing problem, keeping pace with tideflats car load growth was always a challenge, but Carlson did manage to buy four 1,000-horsepower, 115-ton diesel locomotives between 1971 and 1976. They replaced the smaller 660-horsepower locomotives acquired during the 1950s and 1960s.

"It wasn't unusual to have 10 derailments in a week."

Financially, it was a bleak picture. With inflation rampant in the 1970s, net income peaked at $194,196 in 1973 and ranged from $16,459 to $94,750 during the next four years.

Carlson retires

Personal and personnel problems drove Carlson into early retirement. After four months as acting superintendent, Jack Kanan was appointed the Belt Line's 10th superintendent in January 1973.

The 1960s and 1970s were periods of both change and stability, redefinition and status quo for the Belt Line, with the Public Utility Board almost selling the Belt Line at least four times. The line moved into new quarters, saw its client base expanded and its locomotive fleet revamped. But a secure place in Tacoma industry was far from guaranteed. Financial solvency was as hard to grasp as quicksilver.

The Belt Line turned 60 years old in 1979—still struggling with some of the same problems it had started with.

1963 - 1975

15

Atoms, Inflation and Protest

After years of shortage and enforced conservation, completion of Mayfield Dam couldn't come soon enough to suit Public Utilities Director Clif Erdahl. Dedicating the dam in April 1963 Erdahl said, "We've waited a long time for this day . . . we've been anxious to get this first generator on line and make some money off it."

After years of opposition, many of the 500 spectators jammed into the high-ceilinged powerhouse had thought the day would never come. Utility Board Chairman E. K. Murray moved to bind up the wounds, paying tribute to the dam's opponents as "men of determination supporting those things they believed in."

Then his 10-year-old granddaughter pushed a button to start the dam's turbine and generator. Klaxons sounded, the dam's 40,000-kilowatt generator began to hum and power from the Cowlitz River surged onto Bonneville Power Administration transmission lines. The chilled, overflow crowd gave the dam a standing ovation.

The *Tacoma News Tribune* called the $44.5 million hydro project "a monument to the progress of this area, to industry, to the work of men and to the ideal that the people's water shall be used for the good of all at the lowest rate."

Clif Erdahl called it a good start. Mayfield Dam represented only a third of the total generating capacity of the Cowlitz Project. He was anxious to get on with Mossyrock Dam, which would be built 13 miles upstream, be twice as big—and twice as expensive.

Meanwhile, Tacoma City Light was gathering power resources wherever it could find them. In 1964, it purchased 12.5 percent of

(Facing page) Mayfield Dam dedication. The 500 spectators jamming the powerhouse in April 1963 thought the day would never come.

Canada's entitlement to the Columbia River Treaty. Under the treaty, Canada would build three storage dams on the upper Columbia that would add generating capacity to all downstream dams. Canada was entitled to half the power, but wouldn't need it immediately—thus the sale to City Light.

The utility also announced participation in the Pacific Northwest–Southwest intertie. Improving the region's ability to share surplus power with California and other southwest states, the intertie was the nation's biggest single electrical transmission program ever attempted.

The power of fun. By the mid-1960s, recreational areas around City Light hydro projects were attracting thousands of visitors.

The recreation resource

By this time, another resource was becoming increasingly important at City Light facilities—recreation. With the sparkling water, beautiful natural settings and good fishing, the hydro projects began to attract thousands of visitors. Resorts, campgrounds, picnic areas, boat launch facilities—built or funded by City Light—sprung up at all of the hydro reservoirs. City Light donated hundreds of acres of land for nearby parks, increasing the recreational value of the facilities even more.

City Light also committed itself to protecting and enhancing the fisheries affected by its dams. In 1958, after years of negotiations with the State Fisheries Department, the utility helped build and operate the George Adams Fish Hatchery on the Skokomish River to compensate for any losses caused by the Cushman Project.

Concerned about the long-term protection of the Cowlitz fishery, City Light also began investing thousands of dollars in research with state and federal fisheries agencies to find ways of allowing fish and hydroelectric projects to co-exist.

One of the results of the research was a pioneering "skimmer" method of transferring fingerlings from a reservoir to the river below a dam. The skimmer was designed to attract the tiny fish by creating a water current near the dam to guide them into a collection trap.

Cowlitz Trout Hatchery, a $3.4 million facility that would produce 3.5 million eggs a year and help keep the Cowlitz the state's top steelhead river.

A $4.5 million "cable car for fish" was installed at Mayfield Dam where adult fish, after following instructions to "swim to the rear," were taxied up and over the dam.

In 1965, the *News Tribune* was pointing out that there was a "fishy deal ahead for City Light. Tacoma City Light will enter the fish business on a large scale," the paper reported, "to build and maintain two large hatcheries along the river to compensate for fish losses, which may result from the Mossyrock Dam."

The hatcheries, according to City Light fisheries biologist Quentin Edson, would be capable of replacing the river's entire average fish run, though natural spawning was expected to continue up-river from the reservoir. By 1967, the utility had refined its plans and nailed down the cost of the hatcheries—$20 million, or 15 percent of the total cost of the hydro project.

City Light workers replace insulators on the Tacoma Narrows crossing transmission line. In the mid-'60s City Light announced participation in the nation's biggest single electrical transmission program—the Northwest-Southwest intertie.

Splashing into a holding pond, adult salmon will soon contribute their eggs to the $8 million Cowlitz Salmon Hatchery.

Home for 28.5 million eggs, the salmon hatchery near City Light's Mossyrock Dam showing holding tanks and fish separation facilities.

No business like fish business

City Light was going into the "fish business" in a big way. Near the dam an $8 million salmon hatchery, one of the world's largest, would have the capacity to produce 28.5 million eggs. Six miles further downstream, a $3.4 million trout hatchery would produce 3.5 million eggs.

Though the utility didn't know it at the time, the hatcheries—the world's largest and most modern—would not only protect the fish, but keep the Cowlitz the state's top steelhead fishing river.

The battle over the Cowlitz may have been a turning point in City Light's relationship with the public. The messages from the public were clear—City Light was expected to be a wise steward of the resources it used (not owned), the public wanted to be involved in key decisions regarding those resources and it wanted more information about City Light operations and plans.

Daffodils on parade. Growing aware of the need for good relations with the public, City Light provided the queen's float for the Puyallup Daffodil Festival Parade for years.

Bill Dugovich was a man right for the times. A former *News Tribune* staffer, Dugovich joined City Light in 1955 and went on to build a reputation as a public relations legend.

Dugovich, according to the *News Tribune*, publicized City Light with attention-getting devices "which other PR men still speak of with reverence:

"It was Dugovich who had a sign reading PLEASE SWIM TO THE REAR posted in the cable car which carries fish over City Light's Mayfield Dam.

". . . who put a million pennies on display in the utilities building lobby in connection with one of City Light's Penny Power awards.

". . . who urged City Light employees in the utilities magazine to 'Drive Safely—the pole you hit may be your own.'

". . . who conceived the idea of transforming the J Street standpipe into a giant candle for the Christmas season (but was never able to talk Utilities Director C. A. Erdahl into it).

". . . who almost got thrown out of Erdahl's office when he suggested that City Light pick a queen to dedicate Mayfield Dam and call her the 'flower of power.'"

In the years ahead, with mounting public concern over environmental issues, inflation, rate increases and the utility's controversial

Up with Mossyrock. Workers set steel for the spillway in 1967.

involvement in nuclear power, City Light would need all the public relations and communications expertise it could muster.

In 1966, with construction continuing on Mossyrock Dam, City Light was growing and maturing in other ways. The utility took the first steps toward automatic control of its generating facilities using microwave transmission. And City Light entered the computer age, installing an IBM No. 1130 "digital computer" to be used for engineering operation studies.

Meanwhile, Tacoma was using more electricity and paying less for it than any city in the nation. Tacoma needed more power and the answer—at least temporarily—was Mossyrock Dam, formally dedicated on May 16, 1969.

Mossyrock dedicated

Clif Erdahl praised just about everyone connected with the dam—even the once unfriendly "fish people" and private power people—for helping build the dam.

Senator Henry M. Jackson told the 1,250 spectators he didn't expect to attend many more dam dedications—"the state is running out of good hydroelectric sites."

Casting a bit of a pall over the celebration, Jackson predicted the state's power needs would triple in the next 20 years and that the

First pour for Mossyrock in February 1966. The dam was formally dedicated three years later.

(Facing page) Up, up and away. Mossyrock Dam and powerhouse take shape.

PHOTO COURTESY OF THE MORNING NEWS TRIBUNE

Majestic. Mossyrock Dam rises 605 feet from bedrock. Behind it, Davisson Lake—named for the legendary Ira Davisson—backs up 23 miles toward Mt. Rainier. The lake was later renamed Riffe.

region would have to invest $2 million per day for 20 years in new generating facilities—many of them nuclear.

But the day belonged to Mossyrock, the largest single project in the history of Southwest Washington. Following the oratory, according to the *News Tribune*, "the Cowlitz River dam showed what it could do.

"The two huge generators, each capable of producing 150,000 kilowatts of power began spinning with a quiet hum—which gradually became a deep-throated roar. And the four massive spillway gates opened to release the waters of Davisson Lake—named to honor Public Utilities legend Ira Davisson—which cascaded more than 300 feet to the plunge pool at the base of the dam as photographers snapped away.

"The dam which rises 605 feet from bedrock is the highest in the Pacific Northwest."

As the sixties rolled to a close, it was hard to find much good news. Yes, Neil Armstrong had become the first human to set foot on the moon, but President Nixon and the nation had also seen a massive anti-Vietnam War demonstration—some 250,000 peace marchers descended on Washington, D.C. Inflation was driving prices out of sight. Dissatisfaction with the quality of America's products had spawned the consumer movement. And the nation's newfound concern for pollution and environmental issues was white-hot.

The promise of nuclear power

In retrospect, the timing could not have been worse for the introduction of nuclear power. Yet, at the time, there seemed to be few alternatives. In 1970, City Light agreed to buy eight percent of the proposed coal-fired steam plant near Centralia and it was continually looking for ways to wring more power from existing hydro facilities. But Tacoma was still growing rapidly and nuclear power, at the time, seemed to hold the most promise.

Senator Warren G. Magnuson agreed. An early nuclear power advocate, he called for immediate action on nuclear plant construction to "keep the lights on in the Pacific Northwest." Noting the eight years needed to bring a nuclear plant on-line, Magnuson told the American Public Power Association, "there is no time to waste."

In a 1969 study conducted for the Bonneville Power Administration, Battelle-Northwest said that nuclear power offered the Northwest "the optimum method of meeting our long-term power needs and conserving our natural resources."

Asked in a 1968 Tacoma City Council meeting whether nuclear power figured in City Light's future, Clif Erdahl said Tacoma, Seattle and other Northwest utilities were discussing joint financing of a large nuclear plant. "You need a million kilowatt plant to make nuclear generation feasible," he pointed out, "and that's too big for one utility to undertake alone."

In 1972, Tacoma made the fateful decision to join the Washington Public Power Supply System, later called "Whoops."

In 1972, Tacoma made the fateful decision to join the Washington Public Power Supply System, later called "Whoops."

By April 1973, the *News Tribune*, covering a protest at the site of a nuclear plant near Aberdeen, said the Supply System was "getting caught in a cross-fire of conflicting public and private goals that some experts in the field say could cost the agency millions of dollars and, more importantly, affect the course of nuclear plant development in Washington State." It was a prophetic reading of the future.

Public protest aimed at delaying construction became a standard tactic of nuclear protestors, driving up costs while gathering large amounts of anti-nuclear publicity.

Nader joins the battle

Consumer activist Ralph Nader and the environmental group Friends of the Earth joined the battle, suing for closure of 20 large nuclear plants in 12 states, claiming they threatened the lives of millions of Americans.

The *News Tribune* called Nader's move an "Inquisition of Fear. Will the nation's consumers . . . lose the new source of power they so critically need?" an editorial asked. "They will unless they let him know he is wrong."

In March 1974 the paper ran another editorial, quoting pro-nuclear experts who said the protests of radical environmentalists must be ignored so that more nuclear plants could be built.

"While the environmental movement has been very helpful in calling attention to certain abuses," said one expert, "we just can't shut this country down because of some possible harm to the environment." The way to lick the growing energy problem, said the paper, was more nuclear plants—"We have to build, build fast, and build now."

Later that year, City Light took the advice to heart, agreeing to help finance studies for construction of two new nuclear plants at Hanford in Eastern Washington and Satsop, near Aberdeen. It was a gamble, but said new Utilities Director Aldo J. Benedetti, it's "the only alternative we've got."

Fresh in his memory, no doubt, was the "energy crunch" of 1973. Few Americans who lived through the period will forget it. It was the year the Arab oil-producing countries turned off the oil spigot with an embargo, causing a worldwide shortage, massive inflation—and two-hour waits in long lines at gasoline stations. Overnight, automobile gas mileage became a hot topic of conversation.

To make matters worse, Mother Nature also hit the region with a precipitation embargo—another record dry year. In April, City Light Superintendent Joseph D. Cockrell said, "If the situation doesn't ease by July, all bets are off." Mountain snowpacks, he said, were the lowest in 30 years.

City Light turned to conservation with an innovative "Watt-Watcher" program to reduce load and store more water in its hydro reservoirs. "Conservation is simple enough," Cockrell said. "People should just not use what they don't have to use." The campaign worked, reducing use by 10 percent, well above the regional average.

The end of an era

When precipitation picked up later in the year, a worse energy crisis was averted. Still, it was clear to the *News Tribune* that it had witnessed the end of an era:

"1973. Mark this year well. It will be remembered as the year in which we Americans changed our entire philosophy on energy—electricity, gasoline and heating oil.

"It is the time when we had to make up our minds to live with shortages and therefore energy conservation from now on . . . All of us received earlier warnings complacently. Many have not yet begun to conserve gasoline or electricity.

"But we must or have our energy curtailed.

"This is the year of decision . . . we will remember this year for a long time."

The next year also brought lasting and sometimes painful memories for City Light. It was the first time the utility faced organized, highly vocal and disruptive protest over a proposed rate increase.

Caught in the vise-like grip of spiraling inflation and faced with a 36 percent rate increase for the power it bought from Bonneville, City Light had no choice but to ask for a rate increase of "up to 25 percent."

In response, an angry group of 30 persons formed the People's Committee Against the Rate Hike, planning a petition drive against the increase and confrontations at City Council and Utility Board meetings.

PHOTO COURTESY OF THE MORNING NEWS TRIBUNE

Protest! **Angry voices ring out, protesting a proposed City Light rate increase. On November 14, 1974, demonstrators disrupted a Public Utility Board meeting, shouting insults and heckling speakers. It was a taste of things to come.**

On November 14, about 50 sign-waving demonstrators disrupted a Public Utility Board meeting, marching into the Tacoma Public Utilities auditorium, shouting insults and heckling speakers.

Rate hike protestors waving signs and chanting again disrupted a City Council meeting in December, with one of the protestors arrested and removed.

The villain inflation

Though the protests were understandable, the villain was inflation, not City Light, said the *News Tribune.* ". . . What we are facing in City Light's present proposal is 'Inflation Up Close.'"

City Light was granted a 20 percent increase, just the second since 1959. It also gained a following of protestors who would challenge future rate increases and become so effective it would gain the respect of City Light and even be considered for representation on the Utility Board.

And as 1974 drew to a close, Nature also did its part to keep City Light humble, hitting the utility with one of the worst blizzards in decades. City Light crews worked around the clock for almost four days to repair damage and handle 63,000 outages.

"Every man, every piece of equipment was in use," said the *News Tribune*, "trying to restore heat and light to Tacoma power users from Point Defiance to Loveland on the Mountain Highway, from McMillin in the upper Puyallup Valley to Lakewood and University Place—900 square miles."

As 1974 rolled to a close, City Light could look back on some of the most challenging years in its history—years of shortages, crippling inflation and now, for the first time, public protest.

It would not be the last.

1970 - 1987

16

Pipeline 5 and Environmental Issues Take Center Stage

Though Tacoma had won control of its watershed, it still wasn't in complete command of its destiny. The longest, most costly and time-consuming City Water endeavor in the past 30 years has been its monumental effort to construct a second pipeline—Pipeline 5—from the Green River to Tacoma, a battle still going on today.

Pipeline 5 was first proposed by City Water in 1963 as a two-phase, 11-year construction project scheduled to begin in 1970. The complete project would be a 30-mile gravity pipeline, a well field in the Green River watershed, a water quality and flow control station and 10-million-gallon storage tank at the headworks and a 50-million-gallon reservoir in the Federal Way area.

The city needed the new source to meet projected growth in Tacoma and Pierce County and to control turbidity in the water during the winter and spring. City Water could provide Tacoma with turbidity-free water from its wells for only 21 days and feared an unseasonably warm spring, coupled with a turbid Green River, would push consumption beyond the well system's capacity.

The Pipeline 5 project got off the ground in 1967 when City Water purchased a 22-acre tract for the new Federal Way reservoir and began purchasing land along the future pipeline right-of-way.

(Facing page) Pipe dream? A section of 96-inch pipe for Pipeline 5 is laid near the Green River headworks, under the close supervision of Superintendent John Roller and Project Engineer Ken Olson (later City Water superintendent).

Well field gets under way

In 1970 Aldo Benedetti reported to the Public Utility Board that geohydrologic tests of the North Fork Valley in the Green River watershed had discovered a substantial groundwater supply—an aquifer five

The plan for Pipeline 5. The dotted line (top) shows the proposed path of the 30-mile pipeline, the North Fork well development and the Green River headworks.

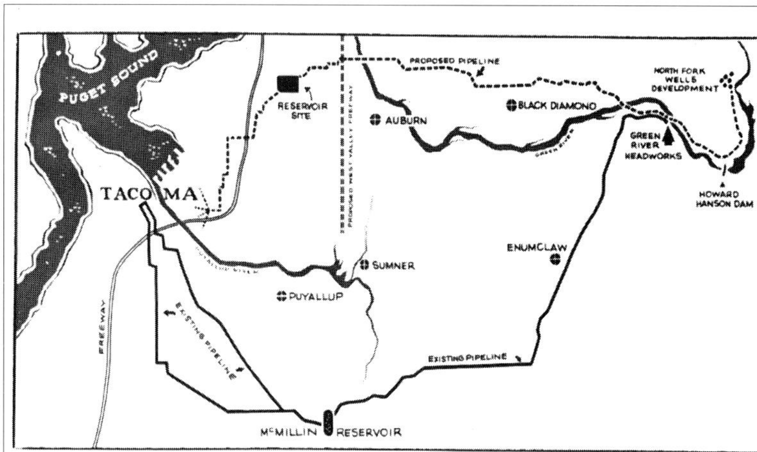

PIPELINE NO. 5 AND NORTH FORK WELLS

miles long, 80 feet deep and a 520 feet wide, capable of supplying at least 72 million gallons a day.

Wells to tap the water would be the solution to the turbidity problem during the spring thaw. Blending North Fork well water with Green River water could reduce turbidity significantly.

The North Fork well development, land condemnation and a pipeline to the headworks became Phase I of the Pipeline 5 project. Obtaining the land was the first challenge. Altogether, City Water had to acquire some 200 separate parcels of land—a process accelerated by the hiring of a consultant who settled most claims within eight months and largely wrapped up the entire process by 1975.

North Fork wells—tapping an aquifer five miles long, 80 feet deep and 520 feet wide, capable of supplying at least 72 million gallons a day.

City Water managed to secure most of the land it needed—either by outright purchase, condemnation or land swaps—to lay Pipeline 5. A number of road crossings in King County remained in contention, but the land acquisition program was a success. City Water was able to lay some of its pipeline before major highway crossings were built. Sections of the pipeline were also laid in Auburn and Federal Way before ground was broken for local building projects.

Meanwhile, work was scheduled to begin on modifications to the Green River headworks and construction of the Lake Dolloff receiving reservoir near Federal Way. At the headworks, City Water planned to raise the height of the diversion dam about 5.5 feet, enlarge the pipeline intake and build a water quality control station.

Inflation boosted pipeline costs $8 million above estimates in just three years.

City Water also prepared an environmental impact statement for the pipeline and a similar, but far less extensive, "negative impact declaration" for the North Fork well site.

Roller gets rolling

Overseeing the first five years of the pipeline project were superintendents Aldo Benedetti, Hank S. Baarslag, Jr. and John Roller. When Roller, the city's former chief sanitary engineer and its "point man" in the watershed battles of the 1950s and 1960s, took the top water job in 1974, Phase I of the pipeline was nearly under way.

John Roller, City Water superintendent and point man for the battle over the Green River watershed.

Things weren't going quite as they were planned. Higher than expected inflation boosted costs $8 million above estimates in just three years. Clearing the pipeline right-of-way and drilling the North Fork wells had been held up for further review of the city's environmental impact statement, but drilling of the wells was about to begin.

Hendrik S. (Hank) Baarslag, City Water superintendent from 1972 to 1974, focused much of his energy on developing additional well capacity.

As hoped, the wells tapped a 72-million-gallon supply. Remote-controlled Byron-Jackson submersible pumps were ordered for the wells in December 1975. The Public Utility Board issued the contracts for a 10-million-gallon headworks reservoir the same day.

When the North Fork well development and its 6.5 miles of 48- and 60-inch pipe, water control building and reservoir were formally dedicated in June 1978, Superintendent John Roller hailed it as "a major milestone for the city." Phase I of Pipeline 5 cost City Water about $14.5 million, two-thirds of it paid for with a 1975 bond issue. State funding supplied some $2.6 million.

Head start. City Water was able to lay some pipeline before major highways and other structures were built.

The North Fork well system technology was state-of-the-art, with the pumps remotely controlled by a solar-powered microwave communication system. When a button was pushed in Tacoma, the signal was transmitted from a microwave dish atop the Public Utilities Administration Building to another on McDonald Ridge above the North Fork well field, 43 miles away, and the pumps began working instantaneously.

Turning on. North Fork wells are remotely controlled using a solar-powered microwave system.

A bureaucratic tangle

While Phase I was completed almost on time, the transmission pipeline to Tacoma was mired in a bureaucratic mess. City Water had

The easy part. John Roller and Ken Olson watch another section of Pipeline 5 go into place. Construction was easy, compared to the bureaucratic tangle ahead.

finished clearing the right-of-way and the land condemnation process, with the exception of 29 contested King County road crossings. Plan drawings of the pipeline were complete.

But, with 20 stream crossings and three major wetlands to be considered along the route, City Water was forced to rewrite its 1974 environmental impact statement—a $500,000 task assigned to a consulting firm. So, the groundwork for Pipeline 5 was laid and virtually complete by 1979. But the modern realities of building a pipeline across 21 miles of territory in a neighboring county vexed and slowed City Water.

Finishing touches. Control equipment is lowered into North Fork Well No. 1.

And it got worse in the early '80s with the combined impact of politics, rising interest rates, inflation and tough new environmental laws delaying construction. By 1981, the projected cost of completing the pipeline had soared to $55 million—more than twice the original estimates.

In September 1980, Superintendent Roller, updating the Public Utility Board on the pipeline's progress (or lack of it), warned that if the pipeline wasn't finished by 1985, City Water would find it difficult to meet the demand for water during hot, dry summers. And without a compromise with King County on the disputed road crossings, Pipeline 5 was in danger of becoming permanently waylaid.

Aggressive water sales

Another concern of Roller's during his nine-year administration was City Water's increasing involvement in supplying water service to small water districts, cooperatives and mutual water companies in Pierce and South King counties. Though small and scattered, these water utilities provided City Water with a reliable source of income—about 20 percent of its net revenues.

As rural Pierce and King counties grew, City Water aggressively tried to sell water to outside users in the early 1970s. Tacoma generally supplied water to neighboring communities in Pierce County on request. City Water would also supply water to new housing developments outside city limits at the contractor's request.

Things would get sticky, however, when a new development was already served by another water company. Then, the other company would strenuously object to City Water's "invasion" of its service area, even though City Water simply may have been responding to a request by the county, a municipality or a developer.

City Water butted heads with a number of these small water companies in the 1970s and early 1980s, with the most celebrated case occurring in June 1978 when the Pierce County Council asked the city to take over the ailing University Place Water Company.

Overloaded. One of the two wells serving University Place, soon to be taken over by City Water.

Bad taste and foul odor

The University Place district, located several miles west of downtown Tacoma overlooking the Narrows, had been served by the University Place Water Company, owned by Robert Bourgaize, since 1935. Growth in the area coupled with a summer heat wave in 1961 led to water shortages—overloading the company's two wells—and the first requests from area residents for City Water service.

City Water to the rescue. Laying pipe to hook up University Place residents to City Water mains—1978.

City Water and the rival water company tangled on several occasions over service to areas within reach of Bourgaize's company. But rising complaints and pressure from the state to improve his facilities signalled the beginning of the end for the University Place Water Company.

In 1978, after bitter complaints by vocal University Place residents about poor water quality—bad taste and foul "skunk cabbage odors"—the Pierce County Council ordered Bourgaize to open talks with City Water about buying his system.

Though Bourgaize was in a tough spot, he tried to sell the company for millions more than the city was willing to spend—City Water had determined that only two of the company's seven wells and three storage tanks would be of any use. After several weeks of intense haggling, City Water agreed to buy the system for $590,000 and the Public Utility Board voted its approval on September 27, 1978.

City Water immediately began a program to connect its nearby mains with the University Place pipes. By Christmas 1978, Tacoma water was flowing into the community and, despite periodic complaints, water service to University Place has steadily improved.

Mounting environmental concerns

The 1970s ushered in a new era of mounting public awareness of environmental issues ranging from groundwater pollution to wetlands preservation. Changing attitudes toward land use and water conservation have prompted City Water to seek compromises on issues considered almost insignificant 30 years earlier. Under the guidance of John Roller from 1974 to 1983 and Ken Olson from 1983 to 1993, City Water has attempted to navigate these rocky and uncharted waters.

Groundwater pollution reared its ugly head in 1981 when City Water faced the possibility that its South Tacoma aquifer, which supplies the "A" series wells, might be polluted. Environmental Protection Agency tests of the industrial corridor adjacent to the well field revealed that pollutants had somehow seeped into the groundwater table. Traces of the contaminants had shown up in Wells 9-A and 12-A—serious enough to close them down.

The EPA drilled 11 test wells over a two-year period and eventually determined the pollution was coming from property owned by the Time Oil Company at South Fife Street. Ground excavation removed the contaminated soil, but the pollutants had already fouled the water. In March 1983 the EPA funded the $1.2 million construction of five 30-foot "stripping towers" to remove the impurities.

Purifying.

Giant "stripping towers," erected in 1983 to remove pollutants from South Tacoma well water.

The incident was a hard lesson for everyone. Sued by the city, the State Department of Ecology and the EPA, Time Oil paid $8 million in a negotiated settlement. And the incident illustrated the vulnerability of the South Tacoma aquifer to pollution.

At the state legislative session in January 1984, Tacoma representative Brian Ebersole introduced a bill requiring Washington to adopt the 1974 Federal Safe Drinking Water Act, which sets acceptable levels for organic chemicals in residential water. Two years later, Tacoma adopted the South Tacoma Groundwater Protection District, one of the first programs of its type in the state.

A softening stance in the watershed

Along with the dangers of pollution, there were continuing threats to the integrity of the Green River watershed. City Water had to ward off a proposed oil pipeline crossing the watershed, along with federal and state attempts to sell watershed land to private agencies.

But Tacoma's hard-line stance of "no public access" has been tempered somewhat in recent years in favor of compromise with other watershed landowners, particularly the state.

Today, in cooperation with other watershed landowners, a yearly "permit only" elk and deer hunt is allowed in the watershed with 50 elk permits and 75 deer permits issued by the State Wildlife Department. The annual hunts are closely monitored by the city and state. City Water pays the cost of supplying and maintaining portable toilets.

The permit hunting program is a success—limiting but not denying hunting and human intrusion in the Green River watershed. It was a fairly easy compromise, compared to City Water's fight to keep trout and salmon runs from being reintroduced into the Green River. The State Fisheries Department's push to reintroduce native fish runs in the Green River, City Water's request for additional water diversion rights and the construction of Pipeline 5 have become increasingly interwoven.

Negotiating for more water

When the city built its water headworks and diversion dam across the river in 1910 to 1911, existing law required City Water to build a fish ladder or trap. Perhaps because the law was vaguely worded and unenforceable, fish runs in the early 1900s simply didn't get the attention they do today. Though City Water built a trap to catch migrating salmon and transport them to hatcheries, it was later abandoned.

In 1933, City Water filed a request with the state for the right to divert an additional 100 cubic feet per second (cfs) of water from the river. Since the water was not immediately needed, the state held City Water's request "in abeyance" indefinitely.

The fisheries question began to heat up considerably when Aldo Benedetti filed for a diversion of 400 cfs in January 1971 in anticipation of the Pipeline 5 project. His request was also placed on indefinite hold. The situation remained unchanged until July 1979 when City Water asked the Department of Ecology to reconsider the utility's original 1933 filing for a second diversion.

The move brought protests from the King County Executive's office and the South King County Chapter of the Northwest Steelhead and Salmon Council. King County worried about adverse effects on downstream water users. The fish people, the Muckleshoot Indian Tribe and State Department of Game were concerned about the potential impact of a second water diversion on fish runs.

The fish planting controversy

Then, in the mid-1970s, the State Department of Fisheries began pressuring City Water to plant salmon fry above Howard Hanson

Dam. Superintendent John Roller resisted, fearing the possibility of thousands of four- to six-inch fish swimming into Tacoma's intake. And he worried about the potential health risks from decaying salmon carcasses settling to the bottom of McMillin Reservoir and the impact of anglers tromping through the watershed.

City Water hired a consultant to investigate the situation, but the results were inconclusive. However, the risks were clear enough to Roller—he filed a federal court injunction blocking the Department of Fisheries from planting the fish.

Roller feared City Water would be unable to meet state water standards with the reintroduction of fish runs. A $142 million filtration plant would be required at the headworks, he believed.

With neither City Water nor the state able to prove its point, the court could do little but lift the injunction. The first 92,000

Roller believed a $142 million filtration plant would be required to meet state water standards.

salmon fingerlings were planted—under close supervision—by City Water on October 14, 1982. No adult salmon were planted above the dam.

Win some, lose some—the Ecology Department approved City Water's second diversion request, but said it could withdraw no more water than was required to keep minimum river flow levels at 150 cfs in the summer and 300 cfs in the winter.

The Steelhead and Salmon Council (later Trout Unlimited) demanded a hearing with the Washington State Pollution Control Board. The meetings lasted one month and were often heated, according to Ken Olson, but the Board found in favor of Tacoma. Trout Unlimited appealed the decision, but it was ultimately denied in August 1983.

John Roller was retired by then after nine busy and often troubling years and a long career of tireless work to protect Tacoma's watershed. Ken Olson picked up where Roller left off.

Compromise and collaboration

Olson joined City Water during the early construction of McMillin Reservoir No. 2 and had overseen development of the North Fork well field and pipeline. He was appointed by Utilities Director Paul Nolan, Aldo Benedetti's successor. Nolan, a former Public Utilities attorney with firsthand experience with the watershed battles of the 1960s and 1970s, was intimately familiar with City Water's concerns about the Green River.

If Olson and Nolan entertained any thoughts about a quick resolution of the Pipeline 5 debate, their hopes were soon dashed. Though Trout Unlimited was unsuccessful with the Pollution Control Hearings Board, it backed up for another try—filing suit in Thurston County Superior Court.

The case lasted until 1985, when City Water proposed an out-of-court settlement with Trout Unlimited and the State Departments of Wildlife and Fisheries. The settlement included a list of conditions governing when City Water could withdraw extra water from the river. City Water also paid, at Trout Unlimited's request, $50,000 to Thurston County Superior Court for use in fish enhancement projects.

City Water also agreed to allow the planting of adult steelhead above Howard Hanson Dam, a concession that pleased Trout Unlimited. One year later, in June 1986, Tacoma was finally awarded its long-sought second diversion on the Green River.

A skirmish had been won, but the battle for Pipeline 5 was far from over.

1977 - 1993

The Belt Line Builds for a Brighter Future

17

The 1970s had been a tough decade for the railroads and tough years for the Belt Line, even though Superintendent Jack Kanan had some success pulling the line up by its bootstraps. Taking office in 1973, Kanan put the railroad on a 24-hour operating schedule and the short-term financial prospects, at least, looked good.

With improved earnings, Kanan was able to make some modest improvements—adding an elevated yardmaster's office to the administration building and buying a 1,200-horsepower diesel locomotive (No. 1200) in July 1978. Now, all the 660-horsepower engines—too lightweight for the Belt Line's purposes—were gone. And the entire five-engine fleet sparkled in a fresh coat of red and white paint designed to increase visibility and safety—the same color scheme used today.

Pride of the fleet. Number 1200, added in 1978, replaced the last of the smaller, 660-horsepower engines.

It doesn't get any easier

Revenues improved with increased freight-switching volume—up to 128,000 cars in 1980. But hard times were catching up with the Belt Line's customers—the major railroads. The number of log hauls dropped off dramatically in 1980 with the bankruptcy of the Milwaukee Railroad. The Northern Pacific also had disappeared—swallowed by competitor Burlington Northern in the 1970s—leaving only the Union Pacific and Burlington Northern serving the Port of Tacoma.

(Facing page) Bleak. Entering the 1980s, the Belt Line faced an uncertain future with declining revenues, an archaic rate structure and deteriorating physical plant. The Belt Line was at a crossroads—again.

Help!

The sad state of Belt Line track made it an accident waiting to happen. With a history of insufficient revenues, the line had been forced to defer maintenance for years.

The Belt Line signed a contract to switch cars for the Chehalis Western Railroad (owned by Weyerhaeuser Company) in 1980, but only two of the four major trunk lines now remained.

Meanwhile, Jack Kanan had retired in September 1979. He had kept the Belt Line in the black, but with a string of problems that never seemed to end, employee morale sagged. The Belt Line's physical infrastructure, upgraded piecemeal in the 1970s, continued to deteriorate. And rumblings of a possible takeover by the Port of Tacoma surfaced again.

In short, almost every problem that had bedeviled the Belt Line since World War II came to a head in the mid-1980s. Deferred maintenance, Port–Belt Line relations, contracts with the national railroads—all key issues in the post-war years—would not go away. It was a pivotal period for the Belt Line. Would it confront its past and change—or limp into the future?

The task of raising the Belt Line above its history fell to Dennis Dean. A former Burlington Northern assistant yardmaster and then Kanan's assistant superintendent, Dean was appointed superintendent a week before Kanan retired.

Fending off the Port

There was no honeymoon period. First problem out of the chute—the Port of Tacoma wanted to take over the Belt Line.

Consultant's report: "... switching in the port represents an inefficient and time consuming practice."

In 1980, the Port of Tacoma was planning a 20-year program to streamline and refurbish its facilities to remain competitive into the 21st century. As part of that effort, the Port was interested in combining its small switching operation with the Belt Line.

A merger would eliminate some overlap and duplication of the two services, the Port reasoned, and increase the efficiency and cost-effectiveness of switching freight on the tideflats. In 1981, the Port hired a Seattle engineering and planning firm to analyze shipping trends and the Port's ability to meet the future needs of its customers.

Among the findings was the conclusion that "switching in the port represents an inefficient and time consuming practice" and the consultant recommended the Port take over Belt Line operations. Port Executive Director Richard Dale Smith agreed, saying, "The Belt

Line is an extra service between us and the trunk lines. I don't think it's needed . . ."

Much ado about nothing

Superintendent Dean and the Public Utility Board wasted no time finding a consultant and conducting their own "feasibility study" on consolidating the Port and Belt Line railroads.

After interviewing more than 35 organizations and industries, the consultant concluded that the Belt Line rated higher in five of the six study categories. Yes, there should be a merger, the report said, but Tacoma's industrial switching operation should be consolidated under Belt Line management.

Then, two events made the question moot. First, the Union Pacific threw a monkey wrench into the works, threatening to bypass the Belt Line entirely by connecting its tracks directly to the Port's. This would have been a blow to the Belt Line, the Burlington Northern and the Chehalis Western, which would have had to absorb higher switching costs to make up for revenue lost to the Union Pacific.

Next, a major tideflats customer—United Grain—severely cut back operations in 1982. That scuttled Union Pacific's plans and dealt Belt Line revenues a devastating blow. Switched cars dropped to 84,322 in 1985, down from 122,620 in 1977.

Two nagging problems

The early 1980s were some of the line's most difficult years in the past three decades. Something simply had to be done about two serious problems plaguing it since birth—an archaic rate structure and deteriorating physical plant. Dean tackled the rate issue first, contacting the Burlington Northern and Union Pacific about a switching fee increase. In return, the Union Pacific studied Belt Line operations and offered a number of recommendations for cutting expenses—offering a band-aid for a gaping wound.

Then, the Public Utility Board took decisive action, instructing Dean to hire a consultant to examine Belt Line rate structures, physical plant, track maintenance and capital facilities. In April 1984, Dean asked the Federal Railroad Administration (FRA) to assess the state of the line's physical health. The Utility Board also asked another consultant, Stoery Transportation Services (STS), to address the Belt Line's financial well-being.

Airing dirty laundry

Between them, the two investigating agencies inspected nearly every facet of Belt Line operations—from switching agreements to safety procedures. The FRA report, reaching Dean in July 1984, catalogued a long list of deficiencies—in safety, accident reporting, radio use procedures and employee training in handling hazardous materials.

Getting on track. A federal study of track conditions was a catalyst for improvement. It found 400 defects in 24 miles of track, ranging from missing bolts to cracked rails.

The Belt Line's three working locomotives (two had been idled with mechanical problems and used for spare parts) fared somewhat better, but the FRA pointed out the sad condition of track. In 24 miles of track, the FRA found more than 400 defects—ranging from missing bolts to cracked rails. Some 58 percent of the turnouts had deficiencies. Ballast and roadbed were also in poor condition.

With years of deferred maintenance behind it, the Belt Line wasn't surprised with the FRA findings. Dean took immediate steps to correct the violations, launching safety workshops and employee training. New rules and regulations were posted. Train speeds were lowered to 10 miles per hour to compensate for the poor track. In a letter to the FRA, Dean promised full compliance by the end of 1984.

The FRA report gave the Belt Line an objective bargaining tool, backing its claim that revenues were insufficient to keep up its facilities. Meanwhile, STS announced similar findings and put a price tag of $1.6 million on the line's deferred maintenance. And it recommended scrapping the Belt Line's old 1950 contract with the national railroads that called for periodic negotiations to set fees.

In addition, STS recommended an independent tariff switching rate of $159 per car. Belt Line management took the recommendations to heart and launched an ambitious program to revamp the switching rate structure—trying conventional bargaining methods one more time. After months of fruitless bargaining, however, it got nowhere with the national railroads.

The shoe goes on the other foot

The result: The Public Utility Board and City Council agreed that the Belt Line should cancel its contract and file a tariff with the Interstate Commerce Commission. Dean gave the trunk lines three months' notice and filed the tariff.

Now, as a tariffed carrier, the shoe was on the other foot. The Belt Line could now dictate terms. The tariff—$77.45 per car—went into effect on October 1, 1985, 61 years after Mayor Angelo V. Fawcett and Ernest Dolge signed the first contract with the trunk line railroads.

In addition, the Belt Line developed a new "cost of service" methodology to govern future rate increases. By determining in advance the revenue required for a two- or three-year period, the Belt Line was now able to suggest rate increases according to a projected schedule and provide its customers stable rates. For the first time since World War I, the Belt Line was able to take on extended debt—and still meet its payments.

As for the national carriers, they had two choices—absorb the rate hikes or have the Belt Line bill their customers for switching. To date, the national lines have absorbed all increases.

Port and city, railroad rivals for decades, sat down in the late summer of 1984 and forged a compromise.

Merger talks—again

Another significant event—a merger with the Port—took place almost simultaneously in 1985. With a new port executive director and new members on both the Utility Board and Port Commission, the time seemed ripe for ending the Port–Belt Line turf war.

Catalyst for the deal was the move of Sea-Land Service Inc., a large steamship and container transport company, from Seattle to Tacoma. As part of the deal, the Port promised land for an intermodal rail yard next to the company's terminal site.

First choice was a parcel of land owned by the Union Pacific Railroad, which the Port intended to lease. That possibility was scuttled, however, when the Puyallup Indian Tribe filed a lawsuit, claiming it owned the land through long-standing treaty rights.

Still needing a site, Port Executive Director Larry Killeen turned to the Belt Line, whose old yard at Milwaukee Way lay within a stone's throw of the disputed Union Pacific site. Port and city, railroad rivals for decades, sat down in the late summer of 1984 and forged a compromise. In late August, the Port Commission and Utility Board laid out a "memorandum of understanding" dictating the terms of a two-year trial merger.

Under the terms, the Belt Line agreed to lease its old classification yard to the Port at an initial rate of $200,000 per year in return for Port expenditures of $1.6 million for track improvements and four new tracks to the Belt Line's East-West Road classification yard.

An economic asset

The Belt Line took over Port rail operations and began service on a 24-hour basis, promising a 30-minute response time to Port customers—allaying Port concerns that the Belt Line might favor its own customers at the expense of the Port's. The trial merger was to be administered by a six-member board composed of Port and Public Utilities members and was approved by the City Council on June 18, 1985.

Dean was pleased with the agreement, saying that it clearly established the Belt Line as an asset to economic development in the tideflats.

With the tariff in place and the merger behind it, the Belt Line took on another nagging problem—the repair and replacement of its sagging trackage. Money, in spite of the new cost-of-service rate structure, was still a problem—the Belt Line still didn't have the capital to upgrade its physical plant.

Dean and Utilities Director Ted Coates met the problem head-on. After an exhaustive, piece-by-piece inventory of the line's existing track, they applied to the city's Capital Improvement Program for a $500,000 loan. The money was to be used for three immediate tasks: upgrade the East-West Road classification yard, replace 2,000 feet of "critical access" track along with the crossing at Milwaukee Way and install new floodlighting in the classification yard.

A plea for help

The Belt Line's arguments were compelling: The poor track had caused 17 derailments in two years, costing the Belt Line $165,000. And with eight of 10 cars hauling chemicals of some kind, the potential for a spill—as yet avoided—was high. Major customers supported the petition.

The Belt Line made a good case, but with 83 applicants competing for only $3 million in city funds, it got only half its request—$250,000.

The Belt Line, however, also got a $750,000 three-year loan from the City General Fund—giving it a $1 million fund for a 10-year track and upgrade program. In addition, the Belt Line received another $500,000 loan, allowing it to buy a pair of 2,000-horsepower locomotives.

Expensive. Belt Line track caused 17 derailments in two years, costing $165,000. With loans from the city, the Belt Line began a 10-year track and upgrade program.

On its way.

With an improved rate structure and upgraded physical plant, the 1980s were good to the Belt Line. Annual revenues climbed as high as $6 million.

The Belt Line built a brighter future for itself in the 1980s by dramatically improving its rate structure and launching the track replacement program. Financially, the line is strong, though earnings in the early '90s were affected by the national recession. Hauling more cars that carry more freight, the line saw its annual operating revenues climb as high as $6 million in recent years.

But the Belt Line remains at the mercy of economic and political forces beyond its control. Losing a major customer can cut deeply into earnings. A national recession or weak local markets can impact rail traffic in and out of Tacoma.

Labor disputes have been a constant threat. A walkout of city clerical staff and subsequent picketing by the International Brotherhood of Electrical Workers (Local 483) in October 1992 held up business at the Belt Line for nearly two weeks. Belt Line crews honored the picket lines for 11 days before returning to work. While they were on strike, switching at reduced levels was done by Burlington Northern and Union Pacific crews.

An 85-year search for identity

On January 1, 1994, the City of Tacoma Municipal Belt Line will celebrate its 85th birthday. The Belt Line's history has not been glamorous or romantic—it has been a search for identity. Passenger or freight service? Industrial magnet or self-sustaining operation? Railroad, business or city utility?

The modern Belt Line is a little bit of each. It is a railroad—"not as long, but just as wide"—operated as a budget-balancing, service-based business and taxpaying member of Tacoma Public Utilities.

The Belt Line's roots run deep into Tacoma's history. When the joint city–Tacoma Railway & Power Company street railway to the tideflats began operation in January 1915, 1,000 curious citizens boarded the trolleys for a quick, 2.5-mile round trip over the tideflats.

In August 1991, history repeated itself when 4,000 people attended a Belt Line open house and climbed aboard a special passenger car for quick tours of the tideflats. In 1915 and 1991, most riders were seeing an unfamiliar part of Tacoma—an area where industry, railroads and international shipping have converged, operated and prospered for almost a century.

From electric streetcar to 2,000-horsepower locomotive, the Belt Line has been a part of that growth. Modern engines retrace the steps of the first tideflats trolleys, day after day, following much-used rails round and round—while the Belt Line forges straight ahead to what it hopes will be an even brighter and more productive future.

The Belt Line Railway. Not as long as other railroads, but just as wide—a key part of Tacoma's growth and an important building block for its future.

1975 - 1980

The Search For Alternate Power Sources

18

The mid-'70s—a time when our world seemed upside down. Institutions were attacked, long-held beliefs challenged and protested. In Vietnam, the unthinkable was about to happen—the United States would lose a war for the first time in its history. And in 1975, not even the U.S. presidency was safe, with the Watergate affair leading to the resignation of Richard M. Nixon.

Our beliefs about the traditional roles for men and women were also under attack. One of the results—greater opportunity for women and minorities in the work place.

In 1971 a report issued by the Washington State Advisory Committee to the U.S. Commission on Civil Rights found that among the City of Tacoma's 2,525 employees—including those in Tacoma Public Utilities—only two percent were minorities, compared to 14 percent in the general population.

Change was on the way. In 1972 Shirley J. Durgan became the first woman and the youngest member ever appointed to the Public Utility Board. And by 1975, Eric Herrmann, assistant personnel manager for Tacoma Public Utilities, could say that "more and more women are interested in male-oriented jobs as a part of the city's Affirmative Action program." The annual report for that year shows steady hiring progress, with more than 15 percent women and almost six percent minorities in the work force.

Meanwhile, the weather was keeping City Light in an uproar. Following a drought and an energy crunch came a year of too much

(Facing page) Not enough—by the mid-'70s, City Light realized that hydro power alone would not meet Tacoma's demand. Finding other resources was critical.

PHOTO COURTESY OF THE MORNING NEWS TRIBUNE

water in 1975, with record rains causing $2 million in damage to City Light and City Water facilities that took two years to repair.

Too wet was followed by too dry—and another serious shortage loomed over the city. In 1976, the U.S. Bicentennial, City Light saw a three-year-old consumption record shattered and exceeded by 30,000 kilowatts during a November cold snap.

Conservation and surcharge

By 1977 the regional power situation was close to a crisis, with compulsory statewide energy rationing a distinct possibility. City Light was in a bind, short of power and forced to buy some $12 million worth from other sources to keep the lights on. Two things were needed quickly—conservation and a surcharge on customers' bills to pay for purchased power.

Buying power at 1.6 cents a kilowatt-hour and selling it for 1.2 cents, City Light needed "more conservation now," said Utility

Close watch. City Light power dispatcher Fritz Hymer monitors the utility's transmission system as the utility faced a severe power shortage.

PHOTO COURTESY OF THE MORNING NEWS TRIBUNE

Board Chairman Ted Cross, "because we're losing money on every kilowatt-hour we sell. We've used up most of our capital reserves . . . we have to raise money with a surcharge. We just can't run with this kind of deficit."

With the drought and surcharge City Light's phones were ringing off the hook, so many calls flooding in that League of Women Voters volunteers helped answer phones and customer questions on a special surcharge "hotline."

City Light also launched a large-scale "Tight Watt" advertising campaign urging conservation. The city did its bit, turning off 25 percent of its streetlights and saving three million kilowatt-hours. In a taste of things to come, the campaign proved that conservation works, reducing the load almost seven percent below forecasts.

Clearly, finding new sources of energy was critical and City Light was investigating several possibilities.

Ironically, the drought ended in a rush—more record rains that damaged City Light's hydro facilities on the Nisqually and Cowlitz rivers.

In 1976, City Light got a severe jolt when the Bonneville Power Administration announced that it, too, was facing a power crunch and would not be able to meet new power demands after 1983. At the time, City Light was buying some 30 percent of its power from Bonneville.

Clearly, finding new sources of energy was critical and City Light was investigating a number of possibilities: solar, wind and "weather modification"—seeding clouds to cause rain. Judged moderately successful, a $74,100 seeding experiment boosted stream flows enough to bring benefits of up to $1.5 million.

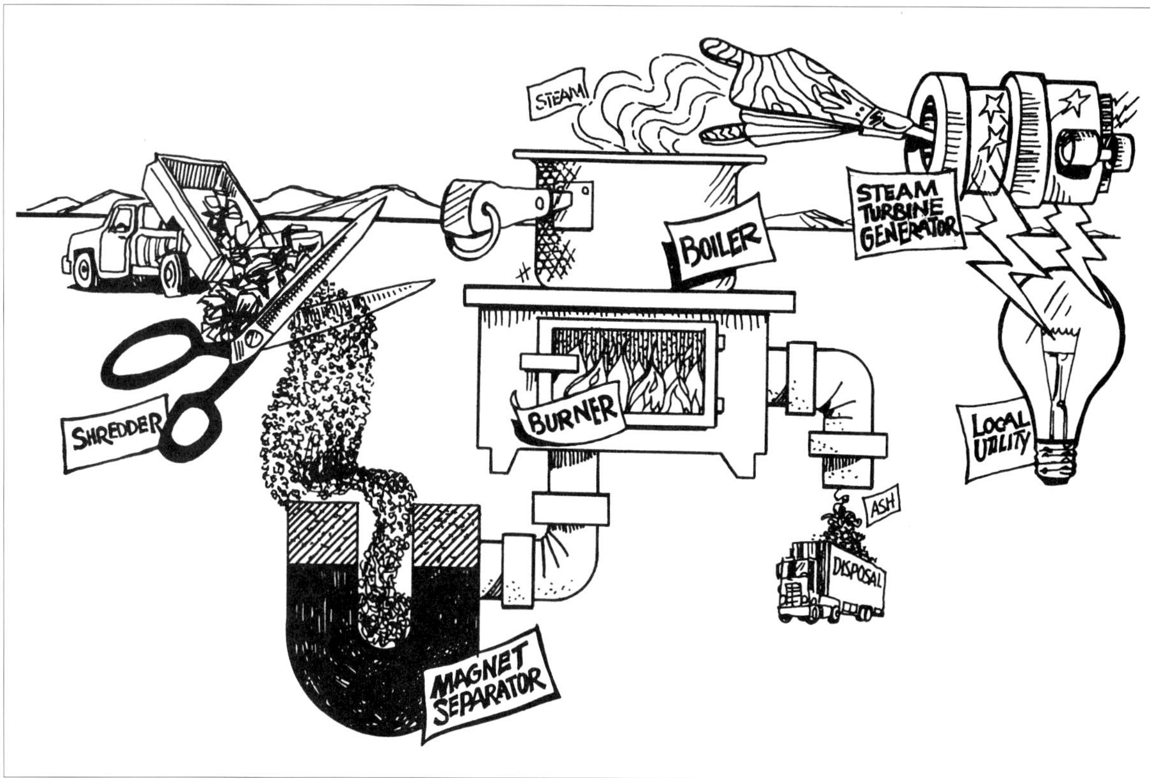

COURTESY OF THE MORNING NEWS TRIBUNE

Garbage power? City Light was exploring the idea of using wood and municipal wastes to help fire a turbine-generator at its tideflats steam plant.

"Garbage power"

The utility was even looking at "garbage power," using wood and municipal wastes to help fire a turbine-generator at its tideflats steam plant. Though somewhat amusing at the time, it was an idea that would bloom and bear fruit in the next decade.

City Light also found power in Eastern Washington irrigation canals, joining Seattle City Light in funding a series of six "mini" hydroelectric plants. In all, the plants would generate as much power as City Light's Alder Dam on the Nisqually.

The Cowlitz was also tapped for more power, with the Public Utility Board in 1975 approving a fourth 40,500-kilowatt generating unit at Mayfield Dam. It ran into a now-familiar problem—opposition from state fisheries officials who feared the impact of fluctuating river flows on spawning.

"Tacoma City Light is no neophyte on the Cowlitz River," snapped Utilities Director Aldo Benedetti, according to the *News*

Tribune. "To be treated like a foreign aggressor is not the way it should be."

The state saw it differently: "I'm not simply going to roll over and play dead for those who want more energy at the expense of some other major resources," said Governor Dan Evans.

The controversy took two years to resolve, with the Federal Energy Regulatory Commission finally approving the Mayfield unit in 1978.

But it was clear that hydroelectric power couldn't be counted on to meet all new power needs. All the best sites had been used and the '70s had proven conclusively that the weather—despite Washington's rainy reputation—couldn't be counted on.

PHOTO COURTESY OF THE MORNING NEWS TRIBUNE

How to meet the demand, Aldo Benedetti seems to be asking himself in this 1977 photo.

Nuclear the answer?

Meanwhile, City Light customers were setting new peak load records every couple of years—there was a building boom going on and all new apartment complexes and 93 percent of new homes in 1977 were installing electric heat.

Where would the city get the new power it needed? Nuclear power seemed the only answer and in 1975 nuclear power boosters

PHOTO COURTESY OF THE MORNING NEWS TRIBUNE

Nuclear? In the mid-'70s, nuclear power seemed the only answer. The local media were urging full speed ahead on these "proven power producers." Photo shows nuclear plant cooling pipes.

had a strong advocate in the governor's mansion—Dr. Dixy Lee Ray, former head of the Atomic Energy Commission.

Nuclear power, she said, is the best and cheapest method devised for the production of energy since the discovery of fire.

Safety? The *News Tribune* quoted Governor Ray as saying, "The possibility of a catastrophic accident from a nuclear power plant is as great as a jet transport falling out of the sky. And landing on two trainloads of explosives. Which have just collided. On a bridge over a supertanker. Next to an oil refinery."

A nuclear plant called Three Mile Island would soon make most Americans much less complacent about the dangers of nuclear power. But in 1975 the *News Tribune* was editorializing against the "practically non-existent" dangers and urging full speed ahead on these "proven power producers."

It was to be a rare victory for the pro-nuclear forces. . . protest was growing.

But opposition was mounting. In 1976 an initiative to ban nuclear plants sparked some of the hottest debate in recent Washington history. The *News Tribune* urged a "no" vote, saying it would be "sad to see a whole new field of energy thwarted by fears based mostly on old wives' tales."

A pre-election poll of voters showed that almost 63 percent would vote against the Initiative 325 and, true to their word, they went to the polls and soundly thrashed it.

It was to be a rare victory for the pro-nuclear forces. In 1976, City Light received permission to participate in two more Washington Public Power Supply System plants, bringing total participation to four plants. But the obstacles were getting tougher to hurdle.

Protest was growing. At the Satsop plant under construction near Aberdeen, a thousand protestors paraded through the streets of Elma, Washington, and 157 were arrested at the plant site.

A spokesperson for the Crabshell Alliance, an anti-nuclear protest group, said, "It won't be long before 3,000 go on the site and Gray's Harbor County can't arrest 3,000 people. I really feel we're going to shut it down."

Delays and unanticipated construction costs were pushing up the price tag of the plants—from $4 billion when first announced to a projected $10.4 billion by the end of 1979. Costs were going up $5.8 million per month. And the plants were from 18 months to four years behind schedule.

"Ukelele-playing activists"

Voicing his frustration, the Supply System managing director attacked the environmentalists and their delaying tactics: "No longer can we afford the luxury of writing a blank check to every environmental activist who can strum a ukelele, lobby in the back rooms of Congress or stop a billion-dollar project with a $20 lawsuit."

But, with the near-meltdown of a nuclear reactor at Three Mile Island, Pennsylvania, and the release of a movie called *The China Syndrome,* a fictitious account of a reactor accident and cover-up, the advance of nuclear power was about to come to a screeching halt.

At the same time, another power source was gaining momentum—conservation. In 1977, U. S. Representative Norm Dicks told a Tacoma audience that conservation was America's newest energy resource. "We have to take stringent steps to protect our power," he said. "And of all the options, conservation seems to be the most efficient."

City Light was increasingly emphasizing conservation. In 1976 its "Peak Eater" campaign urged customers to shift their power use from the peak consumption period and a program called "Stop the Great Escape" encouraged weatherization to prevent heat loss.

In 1978 City Light's Energy Efficient Home program, aimed at homebuilders, established a conservation standard for all new homes—less than 5.5 watts of heat loss per square foot of floor space.

And in 1979, the utility distributed some 500 water heater blankets and 33,000 shower flow restrictors.

But conservation groups claimed City Light was dragging its feet on conservation and living in the 1950s with a rate structure designed, in some cases, to actually encourage consumption. City Light agreed that it should look at an inverted rate structure—in the future.

Conservation got a tremendous boost in 1980 when President Carter signed the Pacific Northwest Power Planning and Conservation Act, a bill City Light had pushed hard. The legislation put Bonneville squarely into the conservation business, requiring the agency to provide financial incentives for conservation and the development of renewable resources.

Aggressive conservation

Almost immediately, City Light began an aggressive conservation program—destined to be one of the nation's most effective—conducting almost 1,500 free home energy evaluations and providing some $121,000 in low-interest loans for the installation of energy conservation measures.

Fierce.

The worst windstorm since the infamous Columbus Day Storm raked Tacoma in 1979, destroying the Hood Canal Bridge and knocking 20,000 City Light customers out of power.

PHOTO COURTESY OF THE MORNING NEWS TRIBUNE

As City Light closed out one decade and entered the next, it was a good news/bad news story.

The good news: Construction began on the fourth generating unit at Mayfield. Mossyrock Dam marked a decade of operation with the Cowlitz River ranking as the state's top steelhead river for the seventh year in a row. The Bonneville Power Administration had hiked its rates a total of 112 percent, but because Tacoma was generating half its own power, Tacoma customers saw an increase of just 15 percent.

The bad news: More natural disasters. In February 1979 the fiercest windstorm since the 1962 Columbus Day Storm hit the area, destroying the Hood Canal Floating Bridge and knocking some 20,000 Tacoma City Light customers out of power.

And in May 1980 Mount St. Helens erupted, requiring an extensive cleanup effort to remove tons of ash from City Light's outlying facilities. Considering that the blast was 500 times more powerful than the Hiroshima atomic bomb, killed at least 25 persons and caused an estimated $3 billion in damages, City Light got off easy.

With the challenges facing City Light in the 1980s, starting off the decade with a bang was probably most appropriate.

1987 - 1992

19

City Water Prepares for a Second Century

The second Green River pipeline wasn't the only challenge in City Water's future. Mother Nature had a few tricks up her sleeve, severely testing City Water with droughts in 1987 and 1992.

City Water was also busy improving its system. Its pioneering cross-connection control program in 1970 was a major effort to protect and improve water quality. By installing back-flow prevention devices, contaminated water from a customer site—during a water-main break, for example—could be prevented from flowing back into the water network. City Water's work in this program set the state standard.

Tacoma's water reservoirs were also completely rebuilt with covers during the late '80s to prevent evaporation and contamination. With the aid of some $3.1 million in state grants, the Hood Street, Alaska Street and North End reservoirs—large, uncovered turn-of-the-century structures—were completely rebuilt.

City Water also mounted a comprehensive leak detection program in 1990, pinpointing and stopping some 216 leaks—at a time when water losses totaled 3.5 million gallons daily. After the 1987 drought, Tacoma knew it needed to preserve every drop of water it could.

With the Pacific Northwest's rainy weather—it sometimes seems like the rain will never stop—it's hard to believe the region could suffer a drought. But it has had two in the last five years. And there may be more challenges in the years ahead as growth, coupled with seasonal fluctuations, push the region to the limits of its resources.

(Facing page)
Soon to be covered. The Alaska Street and other City Water reservoirs were completely rebuilt and covered in the late 1980s.

The two droughts were similar, with their roots in low mountain snowpacks, unseasonably warm temperatures and light rainfall. And, though different in length and impact, the results were the same—Tacoma water consumption had to be radically curtailed.

Drought strategies

City Water's response to the drought brought it face-to-face with a whole new series of challenges, cast a new light on the long-delayed Pipeline 5 project (now referred to as the second supply pipeline) and raised questions about City Water's role as a regional water supplier.

City Water didn't actively pursue water conservation before 1987. Lawn watering restrictions were implemented during prolonged hot weather or when construction of the gravity line was in progress, but there was no formal policy for dealing with a long drought.

The paradox for City Water has always been that encouraging conservation deprives the utility of revenue—especially during the hot months. In earlier years, City Water had encouraged summer water use through such advertising mottos as "water any time" and "pure and plenty." John Roller warned in the early 1980s, however, that water shortages would loom in Tacoma by the end of the decade unless additional water could be obtained from the Green River. Still, City Water could not have predicted the impact—physical, financial and psychological—of the 1987 drought.

It simply caught the utility unaware and unprepared. Because City Water was committed to maintaining stream flows from the Howard Hanson Dam to protect spring steelhead runs, water storage was only 80 percent of full at the start of the summer.

As the water crisis developed, the biggest problem was the lack of coordination between affected agencies. Tacoma, the Army Corps of Engineers, the State Fisheries and Wildlife departments and the Muckleshoot Tribe had no experience coordinating their efforts during a drought. Initially, they put more energy into finger-pointing than finding a workable solution. But everyone learned the lesson well—in the 1992 drought, cooperation improved dramatically and much of the ill-will and backbiting of the 1987 drought was eliminated.

Tacoma faces a crisis

On September 1, 1987, the Army Corps of Engineers asked City Water to reduce its use of Green River water to "natural flow of the river," a condition of the city's water right. For the first time since the construction of Howard Hanson Dam, Tacoma had been asked to cut its use of the Green River.

Three weeks passed without rain. On September 25, Olson asked water users to "cut back immediately." Without rain and with releases to assist fish runs, water flows in the Green River dropped to their lowest levels in recent memory, risking the salmon runs.

By the second week of October, the drought was a crisis. The Corps of Engineers predicted the Howard Hanson Dam reservoir had only enough water to maintain minimum river flows through October 15.

City Water scrambled to impose a complete watering ban and drafted a "Water Curtailment Plan." City Water asked its largest customer, Simpson Tacoma Kraft Company, to cut water use at its pulp mill, but it was too little too late. Tacoma, for the first time since the early 1900s, was forced to look to nearby communities for additional water.

City Water also obtained permission from the Department of Ecology to pump Eagle Lake, a mountain lake on utility property north of the Howard Hanson reservoir. To protect fish runs, 20 million gallons a day for 30 days were pumped into the North Fork of the Green River.

As the days ticked by, there was still no rain. The crisis worsened. City Water's use of the Green River dropped to a low of 45 cubic feet per second in late October. City Water explored the possibility of pumping seven wells still at risk of contamination from the Time Oil

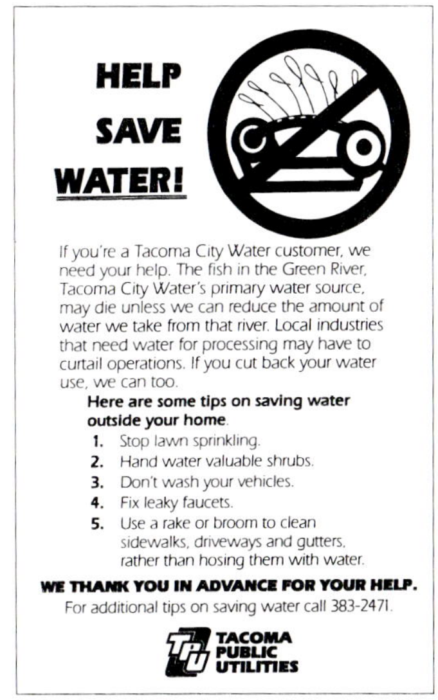

Help!

An ad encouraging water conservation during the 1987 drought.

Stopgap. Looking for more water during the drought, City Water pumped from Eagle Lake, a mountain lake north of the Howard Hanson reservoir.

site. When the Simpson Tacoma Kraft mill shut down for its yearly maintenance, the company laid off more than 100 workers and kept its doors shut for several additional weeks to reduce consumption.

Rain again

Finally, in early November, the rains came. River flows and reservoir levels slowly returned to normal. Left in the wake of the drought—a bevy of new problems. City Water was criticized for its management of the drought, raising concerns about its ability to manage its greatest resource. Negotiations for the new pipeline suffered.

Much of the criticism was justified. Coordination among city, state and federal agencies was sadly lacking and the absence of a City Water conservation program became painfully obvious. Tacomans followed City's Water restrictions fairly well, but residents and the Simpson mill were caught off guard by the drought's severity.

In response came the leak detection program and, in 1991, a detailed water conservation plan drafted with the help of a 20-member panel of community leaders and the Public Utility Board. Conservation was encouraged and City Water introduced a conservation-based water rate schedule in the spring of 1992.

Tacoma had a chance to apply its hard-learned drought education in 1992. This time there was an early warning. A mild winter, thin snowpack and light rainfall prompted the Army Corps of Engineers and City Water to store an additional five feet of water behind Howard Hanson Dam. The drought arrived, as predicted, in early May.

May rainfall in Western Washington was only 0.07 inches, a record low. Communities from Ashland, Oregon, to Seattle imposed water-use restrictions in early June as the river flows decreased.

Planning pays off

By June 17, the first elements of a two-phase "Water Shortage Response Plan," a modified version of the 1987 program, were in place. Lawn watering was limited to once a week. Ornamental fountains were turned off. Simpson Tacoma Kraft Company and

Management and coordination were far superior to the drought of 1987.

other water-using industries were urged to reduce consumption. The Simpson mill had already reduced its daily consumption from 30 million to 25 million gallons since 1987.

City Water and the Public Utility Board set a consumption goal of less than 81 million gallons daily, a 20 percent reduction. If consumers could meet it, further restrictions wouldn't be necessary. City Water proposed a surcharge to offset lost revenue during the drought, but it initially was rejected by the City Council.

A heat wave struck one week after the lawn watering restrictions went into effect, pushing consumption well above the goal. The Public Utility Board grappled with the idea of fining water wasters, but opted for an educational campaign instead. Though it appeared to work, City Water and the Public Utility Board completely banned lawn watering on July 1.

The weather also improved. The watershed received enough rain in July to maintain a full reservoir behind Howard Hanson Dam.

And Tacomans used well under 81 million gallons a day in July and August, though many did so grudgingly. Lawn watering restrictions were eased in mid-August and lifted completely in September. A surcharge finally was approved to offset revenue losses and cover drought expenses.

With a conservative approach to the 1992 drought and by encouraging conservation (which included a water-efficient shower head exchange program), City Water weathered the drought. Overall management and communication were far superior to that of 1987.

A new pipeline

Both droughts underscored the importance of gaining approval from King County and others for the second water supply pipeline. There have been significant advances in the last five years. The final environmental impact statement was approved by the City of Tacoma Hearings Examiner and the South King County Regional Water Association agreed to participate in the project, adding clout and $15 million to help build and maintain the pipeline.

Then, City Water started its second century with a landmark achievement—agreement on a mitigation package with King County. The King County Council consented to the second pipeline plan in October 1989, but the two sides had been unable to agree on mitigation guidelines.

The plan answers the King County Council's concerns about the impact of the pipeline and Tacoma's increasing water use on stream flows and streamside habitats, the loss of recreation on the Green River and potential damages to wetlands.

The Comprehensive Mitigation Plan outlines protection of the region's environment from the pipeline and streamlines the permit and authorization process for construction. The 33-mile, $100 million pipeline could be in operation as soon as 1996, carrying 65 million gallons of water a day to thousands of residents in Tacoma, Pierce County, South King County and Federal Way.

With a proposed Tacoma–Seattle intertie, the pipeline will provide the means to control, transfer and redirect water resources regionally.

All parties have had to consider the fears and concerns of the Muckleshoot Indian Tribe. City Water agreed to support tribe members' requests for limited deer and elk hunting in the watershed and has considered building a new fish rearing facility on the river.

So, the pipeline project moves forward. The clock is ticking—City Water's second diversion claim on the Green River will expire in 1996 if construction of the pipeline is not in progress.

Defining a future

Tacoma City Water is at a crossroads, with several important issues facing it in the near future. At the top of the list is the second supply pipeline. Its completion is certain to be a defining moment in City Water history.

It's also clear that with the second supply pipeline City Water will continue to develop and define its role as a regional water purveyor in the next several years. Tacoma could very easily retreat behind its boundaries and satisfy demand within the city limits only. But as the region grows and water needs escalate, where will the water come from?

Tacoma City Water—with its 100 years of experience and its major water resources—is clearly destined to play a leading role in answering that question and defining the future of this region.

ROXY
SEE HOW THE WEST WAS
BURT LANCASTER LEE
THE HALLELUJAH TRA
SEE THE CLAY PATTERSON

20 Accommodation, Conservation, Negotiation

The 1980s opened with good news for Tacoma Public Utilities. After a six-month review of its operations, Theodore Barry & Associates—a nationally respected utility consultant—described Public Utilities as "a soundly managed municipal utility making impressive progress toward meeting the challenges of a rapidly changing operating environment."

One of the recommended changes brought the end of a City Light institution—its appliance repair service. A money loser for years, the service had been retained for its public relations—and public service—value. But, in an age of increasing public scrutiny and cost-consciousness, the service was a luxury that had to go. After months of debate, the Public Utility Board administered the *coup de grace* and abolished the service.

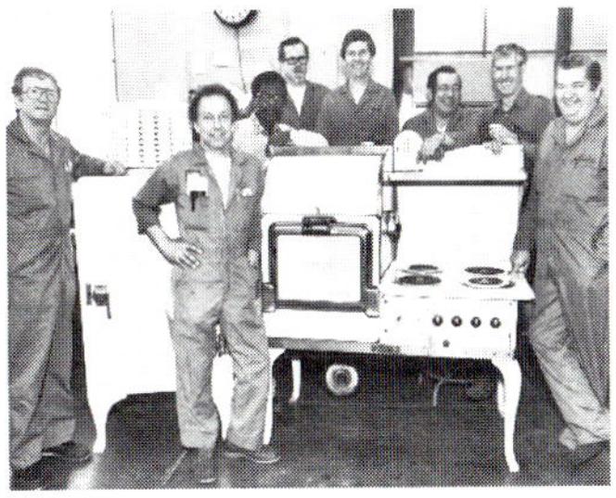

Another victim—losing money for years, City Light's popular appliance repair service had to go.

Two other long City Light traditions also vanished during this period—involvement in the downtown Christmas tree celebration and the Daffodil Parade.

For decades, City Light crews had cut a giant tree at Fort Lewis, erected it on the Broadway Plaza, strung it with lights, organized the lighting ceremony and then removed the tree at the end of the season. But now, state auditors questioned City Light's donation of the $8,000 in services required. And, times had changed—the retail heart of the community was now Tacoma Mall and after the ceremony the Christmas tree was left glowing alone.

(Facing page) End of a tradition. With increasing public scrutiny, City Light could no longer donate the $8,000 in labor and services required to erect the downtown Christmas tree.

City Light involvement in the Puyallup Daffodil Festival Parade came to a similar end, with the utility no longer able to donate the

COURTESY OF THE MORNING NEWS TRIBUNE

An unhappy end. **By 1982, Supply System Plants No. 4 and 5 were in deep trouble. "WPPSS agony has to be faced," said the *Tacoma News Tribune*.**

thousands of dollars in employee labor and materials needed to build the queen's float in the traditional parade.

Nuclear plants 4 and 5—painful

Another—more painful—end was in sight as the '80s opened: City Light's involvement in the Washington Public Power Supply System. By 1981, Supply System Plants No. 4 (at Hanford) and 5 (at Satsop), in which City Light had a 10 percent share, were clearly in trouble. Costs were escalating, questions about management of the projects were surfacing and public confidence in the two plants was plummeting.

"WPPSS agony has to be faced," said the *News Tribune* in June 1981. The agony was twofold: What to do about the plants and how to pay for the solution.

Discussion moved from mothballing the plants for two years to—

eventually—abandonment. All the answers were expensive. Termination costs and interest for the two plants would cost the 88 utility owners some *$7 billion.* As Tacoma City Councilman Jack Hyde said at the time, "It's a hell of a mess."

It was a mess that would touch each ratepayer. Paying for termination required a 46 percent rate increase in April 1983, though it was later reduced to 15 percent when the State Supreme Court ruled that City Light and the other participants were not liable for the costs of Plants No. 4 and 5, a decision upheld by the U.S. Supreme Court in 1985.

City Light was still not off the hook, however. To protect its financial integrity with Wall Street and its ability to finance future construction, the Supply System realized that the bondholders must be paid.

"Default is not an option," said the *News Tribune.* "Governor Spellman, government and business leaders . . . are involved in a Herculean effort to secure this region's credibility as well as its energy future. . . . Sometimes we have to swallow bitter medicines when the alternative is a greater illness. This is one of those times."

COURTESY OF THE MORNING NEWS TRIBUNE

Rescued at the last second. Defaulting on the Supply System plants was not an option. City Light eventually paid $40.3 million to put the matter to rest.

The matter dragged on in the courts until 1988 when City Light agreed to pay $40.3 million as its part in an overall settlement that included Bonneville, the State of Washington and several other Washington utilities. It was a matter City Light was very happy to put behind it.

Charge of the Light Brigade

Public opposition to the Supply System and the associated rate increases were key reasons behind the abandonment of Plants No. 4 and 5 and no one was more vocal—or more effective—than the Tacoma Light Brigade. Begun in the late '70s in Seattle with a handful of members, the group would grow to over 1,000 members with an annual budget of more than $100,000 by 1982.

The Light Brigade became a fixture at Public Utility Board and City Council meetings, often disrupting the proceedings with noisy demonstrations. In 1981, to urge that City Light abandon the Supply System, three dozen demonstrators invaded a City Council meeting and ate a symbolic meal of bread and water while Supply System and city officials dined on steak. In May, 250 protestors turned out for a

PHOTO COURTESY OF THE MORNING NEWS TRIBUNE

Not much was funny, except the gorilla who appeared at a public protest meeting called by the Tacoma Light Brigade in 1982. From left, Public Utility Board Chairman David Dye, Mayor Doug Sutherland and Public Utilities Director Paul Nolan.

combined City Council–Public Utility Board meeting to testify against a rate increase.

In February 1982 the Light Brigade fanned "the hot wind of electric ratepayer protest" by interrupting a Public Utility Board meeting and inviting the Board and Utilities Director Paul Nolan to a citywide public protest meeting. Held at Mt. Tahoma High School in March, the meeting attracted a crowd of 1,000.

By April, the group had become a force to be reckoned with, said the *News Tribune*. "As recently as two years ago, the Brigade was regarded by many . . . as a horsefly on City Light's rump." But, now, when asked if the City Council was going to appoint a Light Brigade member to the Utility Board, a councilman's answer was a tentative "probably not." Though the Brigade wasn't interested, the incident underscored the group's growing maturity and clout.

It also signaled the beginning of a growing City Light effort to involve the public in its decision-making processes. By the late '80s, citizen committees were helping set policy on issues ranging from rates to environmental matters.

Earlier, Utility Board Chairman Dr. David Dye acknowledged the Brigade's influence on the decision to abandon Plants No. 4 and 5: "I tip my hat—my black one—to the members of the Light Brigade. They studied, worked, attended the critical meetings, if not the informative ones, and undoubtedly made some personal sacrifices. They won a smashing victory and in the process showed me political reality . . ."

PHOTO COURTESY OF THE MORNING NEWS TRIBUNE

Some of the customers testifying against supply system involvement at Mt. Tahoma High School in 1982.

Lowest rates in the nation

Though public concern over rising rates was understandable, Tacoma rates were still among the nation's lowest. In 1981, the average City Light customer paid $27.78 for power, compared to the national average of $74.55 and as much as $150.43 in San Diego.

Meanwhile, the power outlook for the 1980s seemed brighter than it had for some time. Annual energy growth was down to about

3.4 percent annually and City Light was predicting plentiful power through 1991.

Among the sources:

- 40,500 kilowatts from the fourth generating unit at Mayfield Dam, which went on line in December 1982 after two years of construction and a decade of planning.
- Eight percent of the power from the Centralia coal-fired plant, available in 1983.
- 50,000 kilowatts from the "mini-hydro" projects on Eastern Washington irrigation canals.
- 50,000 kilowatts from the renovated steam plant.

One of the major accomplishments of the 1980s was the conversion of City Light's tideflats steam plant to burn processed waste from

Environmentalists feared air pollution and toxic residue in airborne ash.

the city's landfill, wood waste and coal. On-line in 1990, the state-of-the-art plant was controversial.

On the one hand, it could extend the life of the city's landfill—a serious problem. "We're on the verge of a crisis with our landfill," said Phil Ringrose, chief of the city refuse utility in 1987. "If this incinerator isn't the answer, then we're in real trouble."

On the other hand, environmentalists feared air pollution and toxic residue in airborne ash. At one point, Greenpeace activists locked themselves on the roof of the steam plant and hung banners reading, "Don't Use Our Lungs for a Landfill."

City Light took extra steps to satisfy public concerns, filing an environmental impact statement even though none was required. Studies of actual plant operations indicated the health risks from the plant were 100 times lower than originally estimated.

Power in a pipe

Other new generation projects during the 1980s and early '90s included a unique hydro generating unit—inside a city water pipe. Moving water between two reservoirs generates so much energy, City Light and City Water installed a turbine to capture it. The unit generates enough power for 300 homes.

And in 1991 the utility announced a $25 million project to install a power generator at an existing flood control dam on the Wynoochee River near Aberdeen. In a unique partnership with Aberdeen, City Light is building the power plant and will own 100 percent of the output—enough to power 2,600 homes.

Hydro power from municipally owned plants would continue to be a major source of power for the future, said a long-range power planning study completed in 1989 with the help of regional power experts, environmentalists and citizens. Another major source—conservation.

With Bonneville providing financial incentives to encourage conservation, City Light's conservation program began to gather momentum. By 1982, the utility was participating in five Bonneville programs—with dramatic results. Shower flow restrictors produced annual savings of 5.2 million kilowatt-hours, water heater wraps saved 9.4 million kilowatt-hours, water heater wraps for commercial customers saved 1.1 million and home weatherizing saved 2.5 million.

As City Light improved and refined its conservation program over the years, the potential became clear: Conservation was the most attractive resource—the easiest and cheapest, with no environmental impact. By 1987 conservation was "big business" at City Light and by 1989, the utility's Least Cost Resource Plan forecast 85 average megawatts available from conservation in the next 20 years. Just as important—annual load growth would drop to just 1.1 percent, compared to five to seven percent in the '70s and '80s.

Working harder, smarter

Meanwhile, City Light was going about its business of meeting the needs of its customers, improving and streamlining operations while taking a number of steps to protect and enhance its resources.

In 1984 City Light opened its new $2 million Energy Control Center at the headquarters complex. With the help of $1 million worth of computer equipment, City Light could now begin to remotely regulate the output of its dams and route power through various substations and transmission lines and detect trouble on the system. With the complete automation of all City Light hydro facilities, technicians at the Energy Control Center will have control of the entire City Light network at their fingertips.

The state ran the hatchery and City Light funded in blind faith whatever the state said it needed.

Ted Coates, director until 1993. Conservation and the protection of the environment were key concerns during his tenure.

The mid-'80s also saw a new Public Utilities Director—Ted Coates in 1986—and major City Light investments to protect and improve fisheries, wildlife and recreation resources. In 1986, 1988 and 1989 City Light reached milestone agreements with the State Department of Wildlife on comprehensive game fish and wildlife issues for the Cowlitz River project.

In 1986, nearly 18 years after City Light built the state's largest steelhead hatchery on the Cowlitz River, the State Wildlife Department finally agreed to establish mitigation levels for game fish, operations and maintenance protocols and assign responsibility for hatchery improvements to City Light.

Until this time, the state ran the hatchery and City Light funded in blind faith whatever the state said it needed—with no specific limit on the numbers or kinds of fish produced. With no limit on operations, it's not surprising that the state had moved slowly—or that the Cowlitz had become the state's top winter steelhead river.

By contrast, the state Department of Fisheries, which operated the salmon hatchery built by City Light—the world's largest and most modern—inked a similar agreement before the concrete had dried.

Other elements of the important 1986 accord called for further studies to reduce the impact on fisheries of the fourth Mayfield generating unit—a decade-old debate—and study the impact of the Cowlitz Project on wildlife.

PHOTO COURTESY OF THE MORNING NEWS TRIBUNE

An osprey nest at the edge of Mayfield Lake.

Protecting the furry and feathered

In 1988, following the studies, City Light built artificial nesting structures for eagle, osprey and other birds. Quail and wild turkeys were introduced near some facilities, grain and corn planted for elk and deer and marsh and wetlands created for waterfowl.

Monitoring programs were established to ensure the efforts were successful. In addition, City Light installed a $2.8 million state-of-the-art ozone water treatment facility at the Cowlitz Trout Hatchery to help eradicate a parasite that kills young fish, an improvement that will help keep the Cowlitz the state's premier steelhead river.

More milestone agreements

Protecting fisheries was the centerpiece of a historic agreement with the Nisqually Tribe in 1989. Under the settlement, City Light

PHOTO COURTESY OF THE MORNING NEWS TRIBUNE

Home sweet nest. City Light wildlife biologist Jim Murphy checks a City Light-built nesting structure in Mayfield Lake, one of the results of a historic 1986 wildlife mitigation agreement.

and the Tribe agreed on optimum river flows released from the Nisqually hydro project and are working together to enhance the fishery through operation of a new hatchery programmed to be compatible with native fish stocks. City Light will fund the Tribe's operation of the facility. In return, the Tribe dropped damage claims associated with City Light's Alder and LaGrande dams and agreed to support hydro plant relicensing efforts.

Later that year, Tacoma Public Utilities was involved in the Puyallup Tribe land claim settlement, which involved the transfer of certain land parcels to the City of Tacoma. The settlement cleared the way for greater development in the city's industrial area.

Then, in January 1993—in its centennial year—City Light announced an innovative settlement with the Washington Department

"We were fortunate to have an opportunity now to acquire and preserve an important, large area for wildlife habitat," said Mark Crisson.

of Wildlife that created the largest state wildlife area in Western Washington. Also involving the federal government and a private timber company, the agreement almost triples the size of the Cowlitz wildlife area near the town of Morton, helping to restore wildlife populations and habitat lost when City Light's two Cowlitz hydro projects flooded the valley in the 1960s.

Under the terms of the agreement, City Light:

- Bought from John Hancock Mutual Life Insurance Company 6,900 acres of timberland for $6 million near Morton and Riffe Lake for wildlife habitat. For 34 years, the company will be allowed to log portions of the land, which will be reforested by City Light.
- Will fund the state purchase of $3 million worth of wetlands.
- Will pay at least $250,000 a year to the State Wildlife Department to manage the area.

City Light Superintendent Mark Crisson was satisfied with the agreement, saying, "We know we will have significant obligations to meet when we renew our federal license for the Cowlitz Project.

"We were fortunate to have an opportunity now to acquire and preserve an important, large area for wildlife habitat, and to reach an agreement with the timber company and state and federal agencies that meets all our needs for both our current and future license period."

Bill Wilkerson, former state Fisheries director and professional negotiator representing City Light, said, "This is the first agreement of its kind in the state's history. By working together, the parties found a way to enhance wildlife, maintain jobs and keep electricity affordable for ratepayers."

Similar programs are in the works for City Light hydro facilities at Lake Cushman and on the Nisqually River.

As the '80s rolled to a close, City Light was also putting the finishing touches on a $2.5 million Alder Lake Park on the Nisqually River featuring a boat launch, floating dock, restroom and parking facilities as well as picnic and overnight camping areas for tenters and recreational vehicles.

PHOTO COURTESY OF THE MORNING NEWS TRIBUNE

Mark Crisson, appointed City Light superintendent in 1987 and director of utilities in 1993.

The traditional storm

Throughout City Light's history, the end of the decade always seemed to bring a natural disaster of some sort, and 1990 was no exception. City Light was hit hard by two winter storms, with 10,000 customers out of service at one time. Crews worked around the clock in bitter weather to get the lights back on and helped neighboring utilities that had been hit even harder.

Meanwhile, City Light was beginning a program to relicense its three major hydro facilities during the '90s and was mounting a major program of modernization. Older plants were getting almost complete overhauls, and new plants were getting improvements to reduce maintenance, improve reliability and increase power output.

City Light was getting ready for a second century.

21

All the Past Is Prologue

Tacoma Public Utilities enters its second century with a vision of itself as a dynamic, innovative organization second to none in the delivery of quality service to our customers.

The roadmap for making that vision a reality and getting Public Utilities off to a fast start in our second century is a strategic planning effort charting a 10-year course toward excellence. Called "TPU 2000," it identifies critical areas for success and establishes measurable goals.

Perhaps more important, TPU 2000 asks all employees to set their personal objectives to support utility goals and live the values expressed in the plan.

Year in, year out for 100 years our employees have been our strength, in some cases literally laying down their lives to provide service to their customers. There are not many problems in the utility business they haven't seen—and conquered. Droughts, record rains, windstorms and snowstorms, volcanic eruptions, wars, power shortages, water shortages, the demands of growth, the impact of depression and recession, public praise and public criticism. It goes with the territory.

Going with the flow

History flows like a river—equal parts rocks, rapids and smooth sailing. So, we take a moment to congratulate ourselves on navigating successfully through our first 100 years.

(Facing page) Preparing for a strong future. At Tacoma Public Utilities, we believe we have the resources, people and determination to make our second century even more successful than our first.

But there is no resting on our oars. More rapids are ahead. Our customers must be served—no matter what natural or man-made challenges come our way. But we also know we have the resources, the people and the determination to make our second century even more successful than our first.

Index